RURAL SETTLEMENT IN AN URBAN WORLD

Rural Settlement in an Urban World

MICHAEL BUNCE

ST. MARTIN'S PRESS NEW YORK

Library of Congress Cataloging in Publication Data

Bunce, M. F.
    Rural settlement in an urban world.

    Includes index.
    1. Villages. 2. Social change. I. Title.
HT431.B86   1982   307.7'2   81-52986
ISBN 0-312-69605-1   AACR2

CONTENTS

FOR BARBARA, SUSANNAH AND JONATHAN

ACKNOWLEDGEMENTS

Acknowledgements are due to the following for photographs and diagrams: Bill Cowie for Figures 2.5(a) and 6.1; David Harford for Figure 5.4; the United States Department of Agriculture for Figures 6.3 and 6.5; Mary-Lynn Tapscott for Figure 6.4; the Ontario Ministry of Natural Resources for Figures 7.2 and 7.5; and Karen Vibert for Figure 3.4.

PREFACE

We live in an urban world; a world dominated by the urban-industrial complex into which people continue to crowd in ever greater numbers, and from which emanates most of the world's power, wealth, innovation and change. Yet the history of human society has been a predominantly rural one. Our very urbanism is built on a rural base. Much of our culture and most of our regional landscapes have been shaped by rural life. And, even today, rural areas still house more than half the world's population and contain the lion's share of all settlement units.

In writing this book I have been conscious therefore of the need to promote the idea of the continued significance and distinctiveness of rural settlement, while at the same time recognizing the great changes of recent decades. These are changes, however, that have occurred within a settlement framework which exhibits great historical continuity. The book is therefore divided into two parts. The first four chapters review the field of rural settlement study and trace the evolution of man-land relationships in the establishment of the basic and traditional elements of rural settlements. In the second half of the book, the changes wrought by urbanization, industrialization, commercialization and the growth of government intervention are discussed.

Throughout the book the emphasis is upon the processes which underlie rural settlement structure, and, consistent with its geographical bias, upon the functional and cultural foundations of settled landscapes. I have attempted to recognize the diversity of expression of these by drawing upon examples from different regions. Yet this is not a general survey, for, as one geographer's view of the world beyond the city, it is inevitably selective rather than comprehensive.

My interest in rural geography has been sustained by the experience of many memorable landscapes. For my youth in the rolling country-side of Hampshire and the Isle of Wight, and for the opportunity to savour the richness and variety of rural North America I am especially grateful. I am indebted to many people, who, directly or indirectly, have assisted in the completion of this book. First and foremost, I wish to thank my wife, Barbara, for her patience, encouragement and interest. I am grateful, too, to David Grigg who first kindled my academic interest in matters rural, to my colleagues in geography at Scarborough College for a stimulating intellectual environment, and to

Preface

fellow rural geographers in Ontario who have done so much to keep
alive interest in a minority field of study. My thanks go also to the
members of the Scarborough College Graphics and Photography
Department who reproduced illustrations, and to Joan Barnes and
Barbara Holst who did the bulk of the typing. Finally, I am grateful to
Bill Cowie for our conversations about rural society and his knowledge
of rural Africa, and to Richard Lonsdale for his valuable comments on
an earlier draft of this book.

Scarborough College,
University of Toronto.

1 THE STUDY OF RURAL SETTLEMENT

Despite the continuing increase in urban population and the proliferation of towns and cities, rural settlement still dominates much of the
world's occupied land. The majority of the world's population lives
in rural areas, the great bulk of the world's land is used for rural
activities, and most settlement units are rural. In addition, the reality
and importance of rural life and land continues to be significant in the
culture of most societies. Rural settlements, too, are the subject of
considerable academic investigation and the object of much political
and economic activity.

Doxiadis has estimated that, if rural settlements are defined as those
with populations of less than 2,000, there are 14 million such settlements
in the world.[1] This includes single dispersed settlement units as well as
nucleated or composite settlements, and represents 99 per cent of the
total number of settlements in the world. Clearly this figure obscures
the considerable range of regional variations in the frequency of rural
settlement. It also disguises the fact that those areas which are dominated
by dispersed settlement units will inevitably have a greater proportion
of rural settlements than those in which nucleated villages are more
common. Yet it does indicate that rural settlements are far more
numerous than urban ones. Even in a highly urbanized country such
as Britain, areas of predominantly rural settlement can occupy large
regions. In urbanized Britain, too, it is possible to identify as many as
17,000 small settlements (villages and hamlets).[2]

However, simply because of their size it is logical to expect rural
settlements to be more numerous than urban ones. A more realistic
measure of the significance of rural settlements is that of the proportion
of population that lives in them. Again we must be satisfied with rough
estimates. Doxiadis calculates that in 1960, 53 per cent of the world
population lived in rural settlements (under 2,500) and nearly 6 per
cent in semi-urban settlements (up to 5,000).[3] In 1970, the United
Nations still put the figure for rural population at 60 per cent of the
world's total.[4] This was derived from the definitions used by each
country, and was therefore based upon widely different categories of
rural population.

A global figure obscures large regional variations, in particular the
difference between 'more developed' and 'less developed' areas. Despite

13

recent and often dramatic changes, the population of rural settlements in much of the less developed world remains more numerous than the urban population.[5] In contrast, decades of decline of rural population in advanced, industrial regions, has resulted in an increasingly sub-servient demographic position for rural settlements.

The Distinctiveness of Rural Settlement

Statistical measures of the importance of rural settlement are difficult to interpret. Furthermore they tell us little about the economic and cultural significance of rural settlement in a rapidly changing and increasingly urbanized world. A central question therefore must be what constitutes a rural settlement. In the use of the adjective 'rural' to identify a particular area of human settlement there is the assumption of the distinctiveness of rural settlement; that it is different from other types of settlement, that rural areas have their own settle-ment forms, and therefore should constitute a separate field of academic enquiry. Before accepting this assumption, however, it is important to have a clearer idea as to what is rural and what contributes to its distinctiveness.

Belief in the reality and importance of rural life has been central to the philosophies of many societies since the earliest recorded civilizations. Rurality has been the subject of mythology, religion, literature, painting, music, political and social ideology, and of academic study. Much of this has occurred in the context of the dichotomy of urban and rural society. The sharp contrast between the country and the city is a theme which runs through art and literature from classical times onwards.[6]

Much of what has been written about rural life and landscape is romantic and at times utopian. Yet the sheer volume of literature and the passion with which it has been written and read reveals the great importance of ruralism and pastoralism in many societies. If we add to literature the large number of paintings and musical works which portray rural scenes and emotions, we are left in little doubt that, however defined, the rural area has been and remains a fundamental and distinct element in our view of the world.

In order to pursue our study of rural settlement we must, however, search for a more positive interpretation of rurality than that presented by art and by our emotions. Lewis Jones has written, 'The concept "rural" is one of those whose usefulness would be enhanced by some refinement.'[7] In doing so he was echoing the concern of social science for more precision in the meaning and use of terms. Rural is indeed a concept, and within a largely positivist framework the various branches of social science have sought to define and systemize it. It is the sociologists who have been most preoccupied with the search for rigorous definition. Some of this has been directed towards a discussion of the nature of the rural-urban dichotomy.[8] However, much has aimed to broaden the criteria by which rurality can be defined.[9]

The problems of defining rurality are succinctly explained in the United Nations *Demographic Yearbook*. Urban and rural designations are inseparable from cultural, historical, political and administrative considerations, and this slows down the process of developing uniform definitions.[10] Yet official definitions of urban-rural differences are made by most national censuses and in these we can identify the whole range of criteria that are used to define rurality. Broadly speaking four main criteria can be identified: demographic, political, economic and socio-cultural. Generally these are employed only to distinguish urban areas and population from the rest. Thus rural is simply what remains.

The simplest and most commonly employed criteria are those of population size and density. The Census of Canada classifies as urban, 'cities, towns and villages of 1000 or more inhabitants whether incorporated or unincorporated including the urbanized fringes of cities classed as metropolitan areas or other urban areas.' Variations on this approach abound in the world official statistics bureaux. Some censuses emphasize the political or administrative status of an area in their definitions. Thus, in the Census of England and Wales an urban area may be a county borough, a municipal borough or urban district. Rural areas are those which are not governed by such administrations. Such political definitions emphasize the low position of rural settlements in the administrative hierarchy. The use of economic criteria to define rural areas tends to concentrate upon the proportion of the population engaged in agriculture. So the Indian census defines rural settlements in part according to the proportion of people engaged in agricultural occupations Socio-cultural variables are rarely used in official definitions of rurality, although Czechoslovakia is one country which employs a wide range of such criteria to distinguish between urban and rural communities.[11]

The criticism levelled at most official definitions of rural areas and populations is that mere size and administrative status cannot be satisfactory measures of rurality, for in the drawing of the boundary between rural and urban they are based upon other, more sophisticated, criteria. So a number of scholars have introduced a range of socio-economic criteria for defining what is rural. The most widely accepted

and discussed are the various economic criteria by which the functional
and occupational characteristics of urban and rural areas are distinguished.
Traditionally the predominant economic activity of rural areas has been
considered to be agriculture and other primary resource industries such
as forestry and fishing.

Yet the dominance of agriculture in rural economy and society has
recently been questioned. In the United States, official definitions of
rural population have recognized rural non-farm as well as rural farm
people, a distinction stressed by Berry in his study of rural Ontario.[12]
Indeed the trend of recent research has been to emphasize the increasing
complexity of the occupational structure of rural areas. While a
functional definition of rurality may be acceptable, the functions today
may include a lot more than just agriculture or other primary economic
activities.

So other criteria have been considered in definitions of rurality; what
have been termed 'socio-cultural' variables.[13] In its most behavioural
form this approach attempts to tap the psychology and sociology of
the rural inhabitant in an attempt to identify differences in behaviour
and attitudes between urban and rural society. Another approach has
been to use various level-of-living criteria such as service provision,
housing standards, employment levels and income.[14] A number of
sociologists have employed community characteristics, such as visiting
relationships, social contacts and organizational structures, to describe
the essence of rural life.

However there is no agreement as to the cultural and economic
qualities which comprise rurality. A major reason for this is that the
analysis of the characteristics of rural society must, by reference to
some other criteria, delineate the rural area and population *a priori*.
The main problem is that the assignment of various socio-economic
characteristics makes the unrealistic assumption that such things as
mobility, class differences, fertility levels and social participation vary
according to degrees of urbanity and rurality. In fact, there is little
reason to believe that any satisfactory generalizations could be made
about many of the social and economic characteristics of rural society,
for regional and temporal variations are of great importance. Even in
the dualistic societies of many so-called developing nations, the
division between urban and rural is not as clear-cut in societal terms as
one would suppose. This is largely because many of the cities are
populated by recent and even temporary immigrants from rural areas
who bring with them values and lifestyles which become part of the
urban fabric. Through a reverse process the values of urbanism and

industrialization find their way to the remotest villages.

A Geographical View of Rurality

The main limitation to many of the attempts to define rurality has been the failure to concentrate upon the criteria which are common to all regions. Dewey has suggested that 'the only definition that seems to be agreed upon generally by writers on rural or urban topics is that in some vague way the terms rural and urban are related to city and country, to community variations in size and density of population.'[15] But just what is signified by 'city' and 'country' and the question of size? The most satisfactory answer to this is to be found in the three variables which influence the geographical nature of rural settlement: land use, landscape and scale.

Regardless of which part of the world we consider, cities and their suburbs use land intensively with a more or less continuous occupance by buildings and associated structures. In contrast, beyond the urban area, open space dominates and natural elements emerge more clearly, for most of the land is used by activities which do not require the construction of large numbers of buildings and other fabricated structures. The drawing of a boundary between these two different landscapes is difficult, for in most, although not all, areas there is the urban-rural fringe zone beyond the city in which built-up and open areas exist coterminously.

The landscape of open space is, then, an important distinguishing feature of the settlement of rural areas. It has evolved primarily because of the types of use to which the land has been put. In nearly all the world's rural areas, the most important of these uses has been that of agriculture. Despite recent changes in some regions in the status of agriculture as the basis of the rural economy, the distinctiveness of rural settlement is principally a function of the allocation of large areas of land to farming in its various forms. This is a point which is made by the French geographers, George and Bonnamour, who, with the German school of rural settlement, emphasize the importance of agricultural land use as the basis for rural settlement and landscape.[16] To a lesser extent other types of economic activity use land extensively and ensure the maintenance of open-space domination. Forestry, certain types of mining and quarrying, and in recent times, recreation have competed for and added to the wide tracts of agricultural land.

In this situation there is a low ratio of producers to land production

units and so the built environment, in contrast to that of the city, tends
to be subservient to open space. The most persistent characteristics of
settlements which have evolved as part of an agrarian landscape is that
they are small in both areal extent and population size. It is not possible
to establish with any degree of satisfaction the statistical measure of
this smallness, nor can we draw a definite boundary between rural and
urban which is based on size. The many official censuses which use
population size as a criteria for distinguishing between urban and rural
areas have, however, recognized the significant difference between the
scales of urban and rural settlement.

The distinctiveness of rural settlements, then, is dependent primarily
upon the scale of settlement and the land use of the regions in which
they are situated. Whether agriculture still forms the basis of the
economy or not, most rural settlements have evolved in an agrarian
landscape, and this continues to influence their form and extent. Their
size is an inherent feature which restricts the diversification of the
economy, limits the amount of service provision and diminishes
political and administrative status. Many such settlements, whether
nucleated villages or dispersed farmsteads, are farming settlements,
others are fishing communities or even mining settlements. All are
functionally, spatially and demographically small in scale.

The Place of Rural Settlement Studies

It is these distinctive features of rural settlements and their global
significance which has strongly influenced the scope and status of
rural settlement studies. Within academic research in general the
concern has been with small communities set in agrarian or other
primary resource environments. In the social sciences in particular, this
has led to the dominance of interest in the structure of agricultural
society, village communities and rural economies. Attempts have
been made to define a field of rural settlement geography but most of
these merely state that it involves the study of settlement in a rural
environment.

For many years rural settlement study was dominated by a
concern with historical development, and to some extent this remains
true. Thus for the classic studies of rural settlement we must look to
Meitzen's cultural interpretation of European settlement, to Roger
Dion's examination of the relationship of evolving field systems to rural
settlement in France, and to Lefévre's study of rural Belgium.[17] We

should look too at the studies of cultural impact upon rural settlement form and pattern such as the work of Jones on Celtic settlement, of Wooldridge on the Anglo-Saxon influence, or, more recently to that of Harris on the seigneurial system in Quebec.[18] Nor should we ignore the contribution of historians such as Seebohm and Marc Bloch who saw the rural community as an integral part of an evolving agrarian system.[19]

Much of the work on rural settlement, too, has been subsumed under the study of the historical geography of particular regions and periods. This is largely because the study of other than the immediate past has been of landscapes which were predominantly rural. Thus European historical geographers have dealt with field systems, settlement patterns and village society. They have, as in the Domesday Geographies, compiled detailed accounts of rural settlement structure, or have illustrated, as in Roberts' admirable study of Britain, the evolution of man-land relationships in rural settlements.[20] The spread of rural settlement across new lands has also been traced as, for example, in Lemon's work on Pennsylvania.[21]

The powerful influence of the historical geography of settlement has meant that the study of rural settlement is frequently seen as an historical topic. Yet rural settlement has also been studied from other than an historical perspective. At the micro level the description of the physical structure of settlements has been an important theme. As Stone has shown, an essential part of rural settlement studies is the examination of individual buildings and rural house types.[22] The study of village morphology ranges from Thorpe's largely empirical interest in settlement layout to Demangeon's concern with the classification of village types.[23] This is a concern that has led to successive attempts to achieve an empirically-based rural settlement taxonomy.

On a broader scale, a large section of rural settlement study has dealt with the description of settlement patterns. Aurousseau's 1920 paper on 'The Arrangement of Rural Population' is the classic example of a strongly empirical approach to the interpretation of rural settlement that is such an important feature of the field.[24] Regional descriptions of rural settlement abound and must follow the rules of regional synthesis in which settlement characteristics are explained in terms of the observed influences of the physical, cultural and economic environment.

To a large extent, the historical and empirical study of the spatial characteristics of rural settlement has been the traditional niche of the field. However, recently rural settlement studies have begun to achieve more breadth. Essentially this has involved increasingly sophisticated analyses of rural settlement patterns and the examination of the contemporary processes which affect the structure of modern rural settlement.

The development of spatial analysis with its important emphasis upon settlement patterns inevitably meant that rural settlement would be subject to the development of spatial theory. Thus Hudson and Bylund have proposed theories of rural settlement, while a number of empirical studies have been set within spatial theoretic frameworks.[25] Central place theory, and various diffusion theories have been particularly important in recent analyses of rural settlement patterns. The statistical measurement of these patterns has also experienced some development in recent years. Over 50 years ago Demangeon proposed a simple formula to measure degrees of dispersal and nucleation,[26] but more recently, a number of studies have used techniques such as network analysis, nearest neighbour analysis and Monte Carlo models to provide a quantitative description of rural settlement distribution.

The other great expansion in the range of rural settlement studies has been in the consideration of contemporary processes. To some extent we must look at the work of rural sociologists and anthropologists who have examined the structure of rural communities in modern society. Yet geographers, too, are paying more attention to these questions. Thus we can identify an increasing interest in changes in rural-urban relationships and can look for the study of rural settlement in research on such topics as rural depopulation, problems of remoteness, the question of rural services, residential land use and the impact of recreation. Of increasing importance, too, is the study of the planning and development of rural settlements in both agricultural and urban societies.

These recent developments in the field are symptomatic of the recognition of the increasing complexity of rural settlement structures. Certain elements of rural settlement exhibit permanence and continuity. Others are undergoing rapid changes. As we shall see in the chapters which follow, the place of rural settlement studies today is to examine both of these aspects: the continuity and foundation of traditional rural settlement and the structures that are emerging from the processes of recent change.

The Elements of Rural Settlement

Rural settlement is composed of a complex set of structural elements.
In their place on the scale of human settlement, these range from the
intimate level of personal space to the agglomeration of these spaces into
nucleated units. The fundamental ingredient, however, is the individual
building, for it is the variation in the spatial arrangement of buildings
that results in different elements of settlement. Thus the units which
are the subject of rural settlement study are identified largely in terms
of relative degrees of nucleation and dispersal. This approach divides
the basic elements of settlement into the clustered forms of the hamlet,
village and small town, and spatially discrete forms such as the individual
farmstead.

The single criteria which distinguish these units from each other are
the number and relative proximity of buildings. But the elements of
rural settlement are considerably more complex than this. In the
predominantly agrarian setting in which they have evolved, they are
associated with an important set of related elements. Thus where
agriculture persists as the dominant economic activity, the basic units
of rural settlement cannot be considered separately from the layout of
fields, of fences and boundaries, and of roads and tracks. These
elements are integral parts of the fabric of rural settlement, for the
arrangement of farmsteads, hamlets and villages is, in various ways,
dependent upon the systems of fields, boundaries and routeways.

In addition the nature of the basic settlement units is determined by
their functions, forms, architectural styles and constructional materials,
as well as by their spatial arrangement. So in an agricultural economy,
the main elements are the barn, the corral, the farmhouse, the grain
store, the silo, the labourer's cottage, the stable and the equipment
shed. They may be spatially distinct units, but grouped together in one
place they will form a farmstead. This is the universal element of rural
settlement. It is to be found in various forms and in varying degrees of
sophistication in all agriculturally active areas. It may, as for example in
much of North America and Western Europe, stand on its own surrounded by its field units, or it may be grouped with several other farmsteads
into hamlets. There are various definitions of the hamlet (and even more
of the village), but as a grouping of several farmsteads it occurs in many
regions. With larger nucleation of farmsteads the arbitrary boundary to
the status of village is crossed.

In addition to the farmsteads, the village will contain buildings
housing the services required by the local population, as well as the

dwellings of those engaged in these non-farm occupations. In some areas, the village may be only a provider of services and a centre for local industry, and therefore will be predominantly or entirely a non-farm settlement. In this role is verges on urban status, but more of that question later.

In short these are the essential elements of settlement of an agrarian society. In some regions the hamlets and villages will be composed of the dwellings and associated buildings of fishing rather than farming folk. Or they may be the focus of more specialized activities such as forestry or mining. There will be regional and even local variations in building styles, in materials and in contemporary society; the elements may be the framework of settlement for an economy which no longer exists. Recent trends in Europe and North America, for example, have turned many villages and hamlets into residential settlements for urban workers, or into vacation centres for second-home owners. In some areas, isolated farmsteads have been abandoned or adapted for residential use. Traditional elements such as the mills and the local workshop have largely disappeared in industrial societies. Even in the agriculturally-dominated societies of the so-called underdeveloped world, certain changes in the character of rural settlement elements are beginning to occur as agriculture experiences modernization. New elements, too, are being added, some associated with modern technology, others with residential and recreational activity in rural areas. These will be examined in detail in later chapters, but it is important to stress here that, while the basic elements of rural settlement remain, in many areas their function and appearance are experiencing important changes.

The Classification of Settlement Types

The recognition of this complexity in settlement elements has led, inevitably, to the construction of a large number of classifications of rural settlement types. Much of this work has been carried out by German and French geographers whose concern for a more scientific approach to settlement studies has been expressed mostly in terms of typological research. The origins of this are to be found at the very heart of German human geography in the mid-nineteenth century, when the study of the creation of settled human landscapes was considered the essence of the subject. So, as early as 1845, Kohl proposed a typology of rural settlement and initiated a field of research which has preoccupied German rural settlement geographers until the present day.[27]

At the most basic level, rural settlement typologies distinguish between nucleated and dispersed settlements, and so base classification upon the relative location of individual buildings. Meitzen has had a remarkable influence in this respect, for his division of rural settlement into various forms of nucleated village (*haufendorfer*) and isolated dwelling (*einzelhofe*) has been followed by many other typologies.[28] Demangeon's classification of French rural settlement, for example, distinguished initially between agglomerated and dispersed settlements.[29] Christaller identified the three basic elements of the isolated farm, the hamlet and the village, as has Thorpe in his classification of British rural settlement.[30] Despite the widespread acceptance of the nucleated/ dispersed settlement dichotomy, it remains a concept which is based more upon general statements about grouping and non-grouping of buildings than upon any rigorous definitions. There is, therefore, no agreement on the minimum spacing of dispersed settlements, nor on the number of buildings required for a nucleation.

Beyond this basic distinction between agglomerated and dispersed forms, four criteria are used by typologies. These are the forms, or morphology, of settlements; their location, particularly in relation to the physical environment; their genesis; and their function. Most typologies have delineated the different types of settlement in terms of their morphology, location and genesis, and where function has been considered it is in the context of the relationship between the settlement and its associated field system. Only recently have more broadly-based, functional criteria been employed.

The central concern with settlement morphology is well illustrated by the classifications proposed by Christaller and Demangeon. Christaller considered not only the internal shape of nucleated settlements but the differences in the spatial arrangement of hamlets and isolated farms. Demangeon's classification is somewhat simpler than that of Christaller, for he recognized in the rural settlement structure of France three types of villages: linear villages (*villages longs*), squared villages (*villages masses*) and star-shaped settlements (*villages en êtoiles*). Dispersed farmsteads were arranged linearly, randomly, or clustered into hamlets.[31] Along with other taxonomists, Demangeon and Christaller produced classifications which were concerned with morphology in terms of the compactness, shape and regularity of settlements.

Yet reference is also made to the location of particular settlement forms. Christaller's linear villages are classified according to the physical environment in which they are set. This is a recurring theme in German settlement typologies, so that such categories as forest villages

(*waldhufendorfer*), marsh villages (*marschhufendorder*) and mound
villages (*terpen*) have been the standard diet of traditional settlement
geography. The shape of settlements has been seen also as being
controlled by other landscape features. Thus Demangeon's linear
villages are aligned along roads, or rivers, or constricted by their
location in narrow valleys. His star villages are seen as the result of
location at a convergence of routeways. The implication of the relationship of morphology to environment is that the manner of their
evolution strongly influences the variations in types of settlements.

   This is the fundamental assumption of taxonomies which have
related settlement forms to field systems. Meitzen associated the
nucleated village with open-field systems of communal agriculture
and the dispersed settlement with individual cultivation and enclosed
fields. Variations in types of nucleated village were a function of
morphology, the location of settlement and of differences in open-
field systems. Although Meitzen's hypothesis of the relationship
between village forms and open-field systems has been largely dis-
credited, subsequent classifications have stressed the importance of
field systems in influencing settlement form. In his first attempt to
classify French rural settlement, Demangeon saw three types of village:
those associated with open fields, those with contiguous fields, and
those separated from their fields. He also defined dispersed settlement
in strongly historical terms, referring to primary, secondary and recent
dispersals.[32]

   This brief and selective examination of attempts to classify rural
settlement elements reveals several severe limitations which restrict the
usefulness of most of the better known and more widely used typologies.
Firstly, they have been devised within a particular regional context,
Christaller's in eastern Germany, Demangeon's in France, Thorpe's in
Britain. None, in fact, is applicable outside Europe. Secondly they are
essentially historical approaches for they are classifications of agricultural
settlements set in the context of nineteenth- and early twentieth-century
land use patterns. Thirdly, they place excessive emphasis upon the
morphology of settlements and deal insufficiently with the functional
bases of modern rural settlement.

   Recently a serious attempt has been made to produce a general
typology of rural settlement which overcomes these limitations. The
International Working Group for the Geographical Terminology of the
Agricultural Landscape has produced a typological framework 'according
to which all rural settlements can be registered and classified and existing
terminology uniformly arranged and defined'.[33] Drawing heavily upon

the approaches of existing classifications, four basic criteria are employed: function, physiognomy and topography (that is morphology and location), genesis, and future development. These are subdivided into 66 sub-criteria, which appears to permit the categorization of virtually any type of settlement. The application of this system to the study of the rural settlement of any particular region however promises a complex result. For example, a single settlement must be defined functionally in terms of its topological and chronological position, its degree of permanency, its employment, industrial, commercial and social structure and its level of socio-economic development. Physiognomically and topographically, it must be defined in terms of its size, and its morphological and functional development must be considered, and finally it must be classified according to its prospects for future development.

In principle the work of the IGU Commission permits the identification of the whole range of rural settlement types. The taxonomic approach, however, is technical and abstract and gives little insight into the distinctive reality of rural settlements as human habitations. Even at their most sophisticated, rural settlement typologies are based upon the recognition of a number of basic elements— the village, the small town, the hamlet, the isolated farmstead, the individual dwelling. These are the elements which universally give distinction to rural settlement. With few exceptions, they are the primary subjects of rural settlement research. This is because they are the centres of human activity in rural areas; the foci of continuity and change in rural society.

In the next three chapters we shall investigate the broad framework of rural settlement in terms of these major elements, looking firstly at the elements themselves and then at the landscapes created by their varied spatial arrangement. We shall neither follow nor attempt to construct a classification of settlement, for the aim is to investigate the processes and relationships which influence the distinctive characteristics of rural settlement, rather than to catalogue its enormous complexity.

Notes

1. C.A. Doxiadis, *Ekistics* (London: Hutchinson, 1968), p. 81.
2. R.H. Best and A.W. Rogers, *The Urban Countryside* (London: Faber and Faber, 1973), p. 55.

3. Doxiadis, *Ekistics*, p. 82.

4. United Nations, Department of Economic and Social Affairs, *Human Settlements: The Environmental Challenge* (New York: Macmillan, 1974), p. 17.

5. Ibid., pp. 22-3.

6. This has been thoroughly discussed in R. Williams, *The Country and the City* (London: Chatto and Windus, 1973).

7. Lewis Jones, 'The Hinterland Reconsidered', *American Sociological Review*, Vol. 20 (1955), pp. 40-44.

8. C.J. Stewart, Jnr., 'The Urban-Rural Dichotomy: Concepts and Uses', *American Journal of Sociology*, Vol. 64 (1958), pp. 152-8.

9. R.C. Bealer, F.K. Willits and W.P. Kuvlesky, 'The Meaning of Rurality in American Society, Some Implications of Alternative Definitions', *Rural Sociology*, Vol. 30 (1965), pp. 255-66.

10. United Nations, *Demographic Yearbook* (New York: 1975), p. 31.

11. The definitions of rural and urban areas by the various national censuses are collectively published in the UN Demographic Yearbook, p. 31.

12. B.J.L. Berry, K. Cooke and D.M. Ray, 'The Identification of Declining Regions, an Inductive Approach', in *Areas of Economic Stress* (Queen's University, Kingston, Industrial Relations Centre, 1965).

13. Bealer *et al.*, 'Meaning of Rurality', p. 257.

14. Helen Buckley and Eva Tihanyi, *Canadian Policies for Rural Adjustment*, Economic Council of Canada, Special Study No. 7 (Ottawa, Queen's Printer, 1967).

15. R. Dewey, 'The Rural-Urban Continuum: Real but Relatively Unimportant', *American Journal of Sociology*, Vol. 66 (1960-61), pp. 60-6.

16. P. George, *Précis de Géographic Rurale* (Paris: Presses Universitaires de France), 1963; and J. Bonnamour, *Géographie Rurale* (Paris: Masson, 1973).

17. A. Meitzen, *Siedlung und Agrarwesen der Westgermanen und Ostergermanen, Vol. 1.* (Berlin, 1895); R. Dion, *Essai Sur la Formation du Paysage Rural Francais* (Tours: Anrault, 1934); M.A. Lefêvre, *L'Habitat Rural en Belgique* (Liége, 1926).

18. E. Jones, 'Settlement Patterns in the Middle Teify Valley', *Geography*, Vol. 30 (1945), p. 106; S.W. Wooldridge, 'The Anglo-Saxon Settlement', in H.C. Darby, *An Historical Geography of England* (Cambridge: Cambridge University Press, 1936), pp. 88-132; and R.C. Harris, *The Seigneurial System in Early Canada* (Madison: Wisconsin University Press, 1966).

19. F. Seebohm, *The English Village Community* (Cambridge: Cambridge University Press), 1883; and M. Bloch, *Les Caractêres Originaux de l'Histoire Rurale Francais* (Oslo, 1931).

20. H.C. Darby and I.S. Maxwell, *The Domesday Geography of Northern England* (Cambridge: Cambridge University Press, 1962); and B.K. Roberts, *Rural Settlement in Britain* (Folkestone: Dawson, 1977).

21. James T. Lemon, *Best Poor Man's Country: A Geographical Study of Early Southeastern Pennsylvania* (Baltimore: Johns Hopkins Press, 1972).

22. K.H. Stone, 'The Development of a Focus for the Geography of Settlement', *Economic Geography*, Vol. 41 (1965), pp. 346-55.

23. A. Demangeon, 'La Géographie de l'Habitat Rural', *Annales de Géographie*, Vol. 36 (1927), p. 13.

24. M. Aurousseau, 'The Arrangement of Rural Population', *Geographical Review*, Vol. 10 (1920), pp. 223-40.

25. J.C. Hudson, 'A Location Theory for Rural Settlement', *Annals*, Association of American Geographers, Vol. 59 (1969), pp. 365-81; and E. Bylund, 'Theoretical Considerations Regarding the Distribution of Settlement in Inner North Sweden', *Geografiska Annaler* (Series B), Vol. 42-44 (1960), pp. 225-31.

26. Demangeon, 'L'Habitat Rural', p. 13.

27. J.G. Kohl, *Der Verkehr and die Ansiedlung der Menschen in ihrer Abhangigkeit vander Gestaltung der Erdoberflache* (Dresden and Leipzig, 1841).

28. Meitzen, Vol. 1.

29. A. Demangeon, 'Types de Villages en France', *Annales de Géographie*, Vol. 48 (1939), pp. 1-21.

30. H. Thorpe, 'Rural Settlement', in J.W. Watson and J.B. Sissons, *The British Isles: A Systematic Geography* (London: Nelson, 1964), pp. 358-79.

31. Demangeon, 'Types de Villages', p. 15.

32. Demangeon, 'L'Habitat Rural', pp. 15-17.

33. H. Uhlig, (ed.), *Rural Settlements*, International Working Group for the Geographical Terminology of the Agricultural Landscape, Vol. II (Giessen, 1972).

2 THE VILLAGE

The bulk of the world's rural population lives in or close to villages and few people have origins which do not go back to a village community. Indeed it is not only a widespread form of settlement, but one which has had a powerful influence upon the development of many societies, and attained a revered status in many cultures: the subject of rural literature, the source of morality and the utopian form of community. This is not entirely surprising for it has been, and in many regions remains, the primary focus of political, social and economic activity for rural people. There is, then, considerable justification for devoting a chapter to the essential features of the village as a settlement element. In this chapter we shall, in the main, examine the village as a traditional settlement form, emphasizing the processes by which it has developed. Recent changes in its characteristics will be the subject of later chapters.

It is difficult to arrive at a satisfactory definition of the village. The *Oxford Dictionary* defines it as 'a collection of dwelling-houses and other buildings, forming a centre of habitation in a country district'.[1] Clearly it is much more than this, although the concept of centrality and nucleation expressed by this definition is important. What is more important is how the buildings are arranged, what their relationships are with the surrounding land, what people and functions they contain, how they evolved, how they are organized politically. All these vary temporally and spatially, hence the impossibility of general definition. But underlying this variation are universal characteristics which distinguish the village as a settlement form.

Village and Land

That there is a remarkable degree of continuity in the basic framework of the village in the rural landscape of many areas, is primarily a function of the intimate relationship between the village and its land. The significance of this relationship is to be found in the very origins of human settlement itself. Our knowledge of early society is still remarkably limited and continues to be the subject of academic controversy. Yet, in general terms, it is clear that early *Homo sapiens* and its immediate ancestors were not settled peoples. As small, dispersed groups of hunters and gatherers, the impact of their settlement on the land was negligible.

For the most part, the habitation sites of early and middle Paleo-lithic groups, living between 50,000 and 100,000 years ago, were occupied only ephemerally. Dwelling places were natural shelters such as caves, crude ditches and sleeping hollows. In the late Paleolithic increasing specialization in European hunting and gathering economies led to greater permanence of dwelling sites, with some evidence of hut construction in summer. These were the precursors of the village. Yet there is no evidence of continuity in the occupation of sites and certainly no significant attempt was made to construct buildings on any permanent basis.

By the Mesolithic period increased sophistication in hunting and gathering had led to some permanence in settlement, a greater amount of construction and possibly some type of village form in parts of east Africa and the Near East. Yet this economy alone could not facilitate the development of the basic elements of rural settlement. What led to the consolidation of Mesolithic settlements was a revolution in the means of acquiring food and other materials. The great Neolithic revolution conceived of by Childe involved the domestication of plants and animals which marks the origins of agriculture.[2] As Mellaart has shown, permanent settlements were not necessarily created by agriculture for there is evidence of permanent hunting settlements in the Middle East which gradually became agricultural. Mellaart claims, too, that there is evidence for the establishment of cities prior to the development of sedentary agriculture.[3]

What is more likely is that agriculture assisted in stabilizing patterns that were already beginning to appear. Hunting and gathering people began to become farmers; to herd animals, to demarcate pastures, to cultivate the soil and to lay out fields. Inevitably this provided both the stimulus and the means for fixing settlement more permanently on one site and for making the fabric of settlement more substantial. The archaeological consensus is that agriculture originated in the Near East, although other less widely accepted hearthlands have been proposed.[4] What is certain is that the Near East contains much valuable evidence for the establishment of early forms of rural settlement. The evidence that exists suggests that, in various forms, the nucleated village is the oldest type of rural settlement. The cereal cultivating communities of Palestine, such as Jericho, 'Eynam and Nahal Oven, existed as early as 8850 BC and consisted of, at that stage, open settlements of oval or circular huts'.[5] What is more important, however, is that these sites experienced centuries of continuous occupation and marked the establishment of sedentary rural society.

Over the next four to five millenia, sedentary agriculture spread west and east, into southern and then central Europe, across the Caucasus into northern India, and, as far as is known, into northern China. The distribution and timing of migrations does not concern us here, but what is important is that they resulted in the clearance and colonization of land for agricultural purposes.

Thus by 5000 BC, as Piggott has explained, 'from Anatolia and Levant eastwards to Persia and Turkmenia there was a well-established pattern of peasant communities with villages and small-towns.'[6] With the Bronze Age came advances in technology which resulted in the expansion of the use of the plough in Europe and the spread of mixed farming with fixed fields.[7] This gave further impetus to the establishment of loosely organized nucleations such as that on the site formed at Perleberg shown in Figure 2.1.

The formation of villages, then, depended in large measure upon the establishment of new relationships with land as a resource. Along certain shorelines villages have been based on fishing economies, but we shall not consider these separately, for the water resource of a fishing community can be treated analogously to the land resource of an agricultural community. In fact, the origin of most villages can be traced to the grouping of individuals for the purposes of exploiting the surrounding land. For this reason our primary concern is with the village as a nodal point of an agricultural territory in which settlement and land are fundamentally integrated.

In this sense, the traditional village can be viewed as a settlement of both buildings and the lands with which they are associated. The elements which comprise the village are therefore more than just the nucleated settlements but include fields, wells, irrigation ditches, track-ways, fences and other items which lie within village territory. Villages, too, are more than the sum of these elements, for the integration of settlements and land has been achieved through the development of villages as organized societies. Organization of village territory occurs at three levels: communality and co-operation in agriculture, continuity in land tenure and control of population and land.

Communality and Co-operation

The simplest forms of organized villages are those which exist to facilitate communality and co-operation in the use of agricultural land. This is the

Figure 2.1: Bronze Age Village Site: Perleberg, East Germany

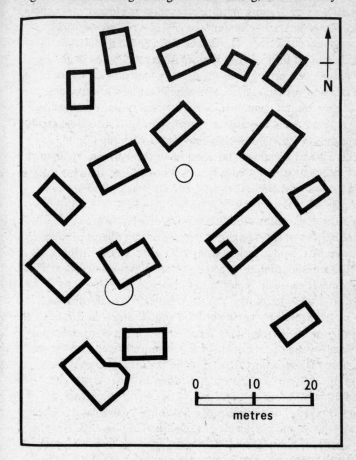

Source: Piggott, *Ancient Europe*, p. 43, with permission of Edinburgh University Press.

essence of the peasant village: a settlement of cultivators which cannot farm successfully independently of each other. We can imagine the early forms of village evolving in this way, with the needs of agricultural co-operation reinforced by the requirements of defence of group territory. This type of village is common today in parts of Africa, southern Asia and southeast Asia.

The type and extent of communality varies considerably from one to another. In most villages, co-operation in the use of labour, of agricultural equipment and of pastures is the predominant form of communal activity. In both shifting cultivation and intensive cropping systems, the need for large amounts of labour is met by exchanges between family cultivators. This can be a simple arrangement as, for example, amongst Burmese paddy rice farmers, where the main role of the village is as a structure in which co-operation in the use of labour can be achieved with minimum difficulty.[8] Or it might be a more sophisticated form of communality such as that of the Yoruba village in Nigeria. Here the main purpose of the grouping of individual family compounds is to facilitate an elaborate system of group farming in which lineage and agnatic relationships are used to arrange communal labour.[9] Brooke has indicated similar types of villages amongst the Galla in Ethiopia, where land clearing and the care of land are com-munal tasks.[10]

Among fishing communities, too, the role of the village as a co-operative settlement is important. Many fishing villages produce food from agricultural land as well as from fishing, but peasant fishing economies are labour intensive and, in some ways, require more co-operation at particular times of the year than is necessary in agriculture. Some villages base this upon extended family structures which provide labour for fishing boats, a good example of this being the fishing villages of Newfoundland. In others there can be co-operation which goes beyond these groupings. For example in southern Thailand, fishing in the Malay villages depends upon the maintenance of large crews of up to 14 men and of shared equipment.[11]

In addition to labour co-operation, village structures permit, as Ahmad has said of Punjabi villages, 'a host of collective habits'. These include exchange and borrowing of agricultural implements, draught animals, even seeds and fodder.[12] In some villages a focus for group activity is the management of communal land. This is important in some Mexican villages where *ejido* (community) lands form a significant proportion of village territory, and in many Indian villages where the care of communal pastures and wastes is a focus for co-operation amongst pastoralists. However, of greater significance in village collect-ivism is the supply of water for both human and agricultural consumption. As Brooke has pointed out in his study of an Ethiopian village, the importance of maintaining an adequate and clean water supply for the whole village is something which must involve co-operation. The digging and the daily use of village wells and the control of water supply are communal activities.[13]

Continuity

Co-operation in peasant society is essential for long-term survival. It is for this reason that the village has certain strengths which are not shared by isolated compounds or farmsteads. Yet it is doubtful whether communality alone has ensured the perpetuation of the peasant village. A second aspect of village organization is the guarantee of continuity in the use and tenure of village lands. There is a bewildering variety of customs and laws of land tenure and inheritance, and the picture is made more complex by changes that occur as societies evolve.

Yet, in general terms, the evolution of institutional controls over land titles and transfers has been, and in many cases remains, an important aspect of village society. Most land tenure arrangements have evolved from tribal and clan customs and are the basis for self-government that characterizes many peasant villages. Village councils, local chiefs and tribal courts are the guarantors of land tenure laws. The role of the village is therefore to ensure the cohesive management of its territory. The primary aim usually is to preserve continuity in land tenure in order to keep village lands under the control of the village. For example, in Javanese villages, any transactions involving land must give priority to blood relatives in the village and then to other members of the village community.[14] Among the Yoruba and the Ibo in Nigeria, village councils and chiefs retain ultimate authority over the disposal of land such that, in a sense, each household has only an inherited right to use or occupy particular parcels.[15]

The role of village authority can extend beyond the enforcement of inheritance laws to total control over the allocation, tenure and use of village lands. Thus group solidarity is achieved by locking the individual villager into a set of laws and customs which determine who shall have rights to land, how much land each person shall have, where the parcels shall be located and how the land shall be used. In many instances this level of village authority has occurred because of the need to use village lands as efficiently as possible. In his study of South Indian villages, Beals illustrates this point well by describing the village as an ecological unit whose structure is designed to establish successful relationships between settlement and environment.[16]

This may manifest itself in the form of various restrictions on the actual use of the village's agricultural lands. In the Punjab, for example, farmers still follow customary rotation patterns which originated in a village concern for essential food supply and compatability between the land uses of the various land parcels.[17] The same situation applied to open-field villages of Europe, and remains important in parts of Africa where multiculture on village plots requires conformity in cropping. Village authority is essential also in areas where irrigation is necessary. In paddy rice growing regions the use and maintenance of irrigation ditches is generally subject to village law, which is also important in ensuring that land is allocated in such a way that the maximum amount of agricultural productivity can be achieved. This may have been, in fact, a major force for the nucleation of rural settlement, a point which Ayrout makes about Egyptian villages, where, 'in order to give the fields the largest possible cultivable area the unproductive space is reduced to a minimum'.[18]

Control and Authority

What has been presented so far is a view of the village as a self-acting, self-perpetuating community. Rituals, traditions, customs and laws governing the use and tenure of village lands exist to maintain group solidarity. This is the 'little community' described by Redfield in which territorially organized life gives social stability.[19] Agriculture is seen as a way of life carried on under the institutional arrangements which are commonly accepted and understood. Yet, as Redfield has shown, few agricultural villages have been established as autonomous land-using communities. Rather they have evolved as part of a political hierarchy in which land use rights are subject to a superior and external authority.

The nature of this authority exhibits great regional and temporal variation but its effect has been universally the same: the institution-alization of the territorial management of the village. This has intensified the role of the village as a political unit controlling agricultural land and the population that cultivates it. Authority may come in the form of tribal (or clan) rule which determines the inheritance laws and cultivation customs of the villages occupied by its members. This is common in parts of east and west Africa where the local chief or village council act as the administrators of tribal or clan authority. Invariably this has had the effect of stabilizing rural settlement patterns. In some areas of Africa and of southern and southeast Asia villages have become established under the jurisdiction of petty kingdoms. In the ancient kingdoms of south India, of Dahomey, and of Buganda, for example, the village has assumed a fundamental political role for, in a sense, it has acted as the trustee for lands which belonged ultimately to the monarch.

This arrangement can be described quite simply as feudal. Needless to say it is one form of feudalism, but it contains an essential ingredient which has been a strong force in the development of agricultural villages. In some areas, notably in Africa, Polynesia and parts of southern Asia such as Burma and Thailand, the village has retained a degree of freedom in the running of its own affairs. Elsewhere, however, across most of Europe, Asia and Latin America, the concept of village settlement was consolidated primarily under feudal systems with autocratic and hierarchical control of land.

The central feature of a feudal system is the elimination of individual ownership of land by the peasant cultivator and its replacement with ownership by a landlord. In Europe, the relationship between the village and its land was formalized as monarchs assumed title to all the lands in their kingdoms and in turn granted it to nobles, knights and the church. By AD 1000 much of the northern and western European population was settled in villages, the lands of which were the property of estates. As Bloch has emphasized, the primary object of the powers enjoyed by the local lord was to furnish him with revenues by securing for him a portion of the produce of the soil. This was ensured by granting the lord a real property right or title to the cottage, arable and meadow of the villein. This title was expressed by the right to demand a new investiture every time these elements changed hands, a right to appropriate them by lawful confiscation, and, above all, the right to impose taxes and demand services.[20] Inevitably this resulted in the entrenchment of the village as a political organization in which property rights and cultivation duties were recognized in law, and enforced by manorial authority.

Communality and continuity were therefore ensured to the advantage of the landowning groups and the rural population became firmly fixed in village territories. The open-field system which accompanied most feudal arrangements demanded strict observance of cultivation laws and restricted the dispersal of peasant dwellings. It was impossible for the peasant to dwell in the centre of his fields and so he was forced to occupy a site in that part of manorial territory that was set aside for buildings. Indeed there are many instances in Europe of village settlements being planned and built by manorial lords to replace existing settlements and thus gather the rural population into one, conformist, nucleation.

There was considerable variation in the nature of feudal villages, particularly in the relative freedom of sections of the peasantry. Nevertheless, as Smith has suggested, the bulk of today's villages in western Europe were founded by the mid-fourteenth century.[21] They were established under a political system which inevitably led to the nucleation of population into highly organized agricultural communities. In the centuries succeeding the heyday of feudalism in Europe, village organization underwent significant changes. In Britain, for example, the last remnants of the feudal system disappeared by the end of the eighteenth century, but the perpetuation of village settlement is a legacy of that system. In Russia, of course, the breakdown of the feudal village has been dramatic and complete. Yet in parts of southern Europe, in Spain, Greece, southern Italy, the landlord often still dominates the settlements and fields of dependent peasants.

The European village, then, evolved as a hierarchical, political organism and became the official political entity which governed the lives of most rural inhabitants. Similarly the entrenchment of the village as the predominant form of rural settlement on much of the Indian subcontinent, in China, Japan and in parts of Latin America, can be traced to feudal influences. In India, the development of a complex and hierarchical caste system has encouraged elitist control of land and ensured the establishment of a durable village society. This is not the place to examine the caste system, but an important aspect of it for understanding the Indian village is the increasing dominance of various landowning classes. Thus the village became the form of settlement that ensured these classes of a ready supply of tenants and labourers who could cultivate land. Bétaille has suggested that the landowning castes were grafted on to villages by giving them title to remission of revenue or ownership of land.[22]

Under this system, between the fifteenth and seventeenth centuries, the bulk of today's villages were formed. The arrival of the British saw the formalization of land titles and the proliferation of landowning groups. In recent years, particularly in southern parts of India, and with government land reform legislation, some large estates have been broken up. Yet in many villages studies have revealed the continuation of the power and authority of dominant families which control a good proportion of village land.[23] Their control of land places them in the position of 'master to their clients, landowner to their tenants, creditor for village debtors and main employer of a retinue of dependents'.[24] In short, they remain a strong force for the centralization of territorial organization.

The feudal basis of the European and Indian village is an intensively researched subject. Much less has been written about other areas. Yet in China, until the 1949 revolution, villages persisted under a more or less institutionalized system of landownership and tenancy.[25] In Japan, too,

from the twelfth to the nineteenth centuries, feudalism left a deep
impression upon Japanese culture. Village lands were controlled by
manorial lords, estate managers, local agents of powerful court families
or religious institutions.[26] The picture in Latin America is more
confused than elsewhere for there has been considerable regional
variation and temporal fluctuation in the organization of village society.
Ford has claimed that in Peru, the patterns and values of feudalism
were transferred from the Old World without significant alteration.[27]
This is an overstated claim, yet the latifundia-minifundia structure of
rural landholding resulted in *most* Latin American countries in the
development of village-based concentrations of dependent small holders
and landless labourers.

The Territorial Village

We have dwelt at some length upon the village as an integration of land
and settlement in order to illustrate the fundamental processes underlying the development of the village as a settlement concept. This is a
normative, or traditional view of the village which explains the structure
within which subsequent adaptations have occurred. It is a view, too,
which is relevant to most peasant villages which survive in the modern
world. Yet the concept is incomplete without a consideration of its
spatial expression. The pressures of communality and co-operation and
the undoubtedly strong influence of various types of feudal control of
land and population have given the traditional village a territorial form.
The village is therefore an area with an apparent boundary within
which the spatial arrangement of the various elements of land and
settlement are functionally related. Thus, following Doxiadis, we can
see that the characteristic parts of a village consist of the 'homogenous
parts', consisting of the fields; the central parts, or built-up settlement;
the circulatory parts, consisting of roads and paths within the fields
and between the settlement; and the special parts, such as wells,
monasteries, burial grounds, and so on.[28]

In reality the territorial village is more complex than this simple
scheme. Firstly there are many variations in the spatial distribution of
village elements. Secondly the organizational relationship between the
elements strongly influences the spatial arrangement of village territory.
Let us deal first with the relationships between the built-up settlement
and the agricultural land. Two fundamentally different forms of land
parcel arrangement appear to have a strong influence on the differences
in the spatial pattern of these relationships. The most widespread type
of arrangement is the one in which the land parcels of the peasant

farmer are, in various ways, separated from his dwelling place. Generally
this system incorporates a fragmented distribution of individual strips,
blocks or fields in areas of village land institutionally designated for
agricultural purposes. In many instances it involves also distinct areas
of communally held land for grazing, lumber, and hunting and gathering. Examples of this form of territorial arrangement are shown in
Figures 2.2 and 2.3. In Gende Hogalo, the Ethiopian village, the settlement compound is defensively located on a hill with agricultural land

Figure 2.2: Village and Territory: Gende Hogalo, Ethiopia

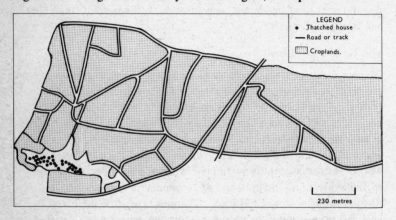

Source: Brooke, 'The Rural Village', p. 66, adapted from the *Geographical Review*,
Vol. 49, 1959, with the permission of the American Geographical Society.

sloping away from it. The use of the land by the villagers is predominantly communal, hence the structural arrangement of land use areas.
The existence of a multitude of small land parcels of the Indian villages
in Figure 2.3 in fact obscures a repetition of the structuring of agricultural
land use. Blaikie has shown how the effect of distance between field and
settlement necessitates an ordered arrangement of cropping patterns,[29] and
and Chisholm provides a number of examples of similar organization
from southern Europe.[30]

A second type of land parcel arrangement is one in which the parcels
are contiguous with the dwellings and farmsteads of the village settlement.
The parcels extend from the individual farmstead so that the relationship between settlement and land is closer and less formal than in
villages with scattered plots and open fields. It is a structure which is
common in certain areas where a degree of control of land tenure may

Figure 2.3: Land Parcels in Indian Village Territory

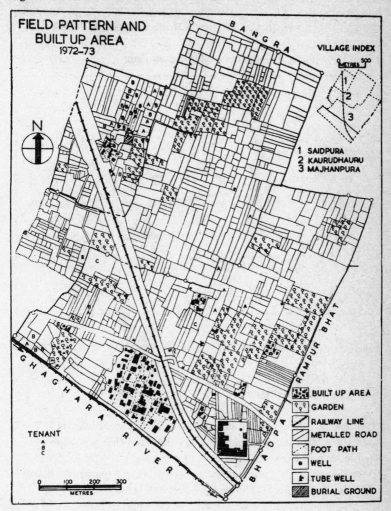

FIELD PATTERN AND BUILT UP AREA 1972–73

VILLAGE INDEX

1 SAIDPURA
2 KAURUDHAURU
3 MAJHANPURA

BUILT UP AREA
GARDEN
RAILWAY LINE
METALLED ROAD
FOOT PATH
WELL
TUBE WELL
BURIAL GROUND

TENANT
A
B
C

0   100   200   300
METRES

Source: Rana P.B. Singh, *Clan Settlements in the Saran Plain, A Study in Cultural Geography* (Varanasi: National Geographical Society of India, Res. Pub. No. 18, 1977), with permission of National Geographical Society of India.

occur but where the total control of feudal or communal organization is absent. In the post-medieval colonization villages of northern and eastern Europe the village territory generally comprised a linear settlement of farmsteads with contiguous fields extending to the village boundary (Figure 2.4). Similar arrangements are to be found in the independent villages of wet-rice growing areas of South-east Asia.

Figure 2.4: Linear Village on North German Plain

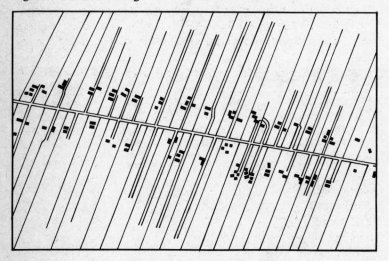

Source: Germany, Series M841 (G.S.G.S. 4414), Sheet 2318, Scale, 1:25,000.

Villages as Communities

'The [Indian] village communities', wrote Sir Charles Metcalfe in 1882, 'are little republics, having nearly everything that they want within themselves and almost independent of any foreign relations.'[31] Even today this might be a popular notion of the village; one which, however, has never been realistic. Politically, as we have already seen, most villages are controlled in some degree by external authority. Economically and socially, too, contact between villages and between village and town has always been a traditional rather than an innovative fact of rural life. Yet the role of the village as the organizational focus of man-land relationships that has been described in the preceding pages has resulted in strong community identity if not in autonomy and self-sufficiency.

To a large extent the village is a community from political necessity. We have seen the significance of this in the development of territorial organization, and, in particular, in the need for co-operation and communality in agriculture. However, the persistent strength of the village is due also to its ability to provide most of the material, spiritual and cultural needs of its inhabitants. This is achieved through the dependence of villagers upon each other – perhaps the best interpretation of the term 'community'. Thus, even today, many peasant villages can provide most of the services needed to sustain daily life. This is well illustrated by the breakdown of occupational structure shown in Table 2.1. Some of these activities directly serve the needs of farmers,

Table 2.1: Occupational Groups and Castes in Rájpur, Northern India

Caste	Rank	Persons	Per cent of total population	Per cent of total cultivated land
Ját (landed farmer)	1	149	16	33
Bhágbán (vegetable grower)	2	76	8	5
Dhimar (water carrier)	2	49	5	1
Kumhár (potter)	2	60	6	3
Dhuná (cotton carder)	3	32	3	2
Chamár (leatherworker)	4	332	35	18
Barhái (carpenter, Muslim)	4	41	4	1
Lohár (blacksmith, Muslim)	4	8	1	2
Nai (barber, Muslim)	4	33	4	2
Téli (oil presser, Muslim)	4	133	14	8
Bhangi (sweeper)	5	25	3	0
TOTAL	–	938	99	75
Outsiders	–	–	–	23
				98

Source: J.W. Elder, 'Rájpur: Change in the Jajmáni System of an Uttar Pradesh Village', in K. Ishwaran, *Change and Continuity in India's Villages* (New York, Columbia University Press, 1970).

others serve the general demands of the village population. In the traditional peasant village the strength of the community is emphasized by the provision of services on an exchange basis, where one service is paid for with another. Beals describes this practice in south Indian villages where, for example, farmers obtain services by providing grain at harvest time.[32] Yet even where cash economies prevail, the existence of key services at one place is a major force for community solidarity.

Services available in the village also satisfy the social and cultural needs of the population. Thus even today the public house, and various social organizations such as the Woman's Institute, provide important foci of community in many British villages.[33] In the Greek village it is the coffee house which is the centre of, at least male, social life. And in varying degrees scholars, schoolteachers, lawyers, physicians, medicine men, and even moneylenders are key figures in active village communities. Perhaps the most widely influential role in village life throughout the world is played by the religious institution. The mosque, the church, the temple, the shrine, the holy place in different ways perform the fundamental function of sustaining the culture and ritual unity of the community. Thus the village priest is as important a village servant as the innkeeper. In fact, historically, those vested with religious authority have been as powerful as the landowning class in the control of the village as a community. In some cases the religious institution and the landowner are one and the same thing. This is true in parts of Latin America, it was true of feudal Europe and certainly continues to be apparent in village India. The priest and other equivalent religious figures have the extraordinary power to exploit fear and superstition and to provide for human welfare, and therefore to ensure village loyalty. In Christian areas the church has been a prime organizer of village life and major authoritarian force.

However, the perpetuation of the village as a community has depended also upon relationships between inhabitants. In some cases these may be informal. Often the village community is interpreted as one in which the frequency of internal social and economic contact is greater than that which occurs externally. The village is therefore the place for visits between individuals and families, for quarrels and disputes, for discussions around the well or in the coffee house, for gossip and intrigue; in short for all the daily activities of any society. The solidarity of the village community, however, has frequently been controlled more by formal social structures than by informal arrangements. Raymond Firth has explained more clearly than most writers the significance of the relationship between social structure and economy in peasant society. As Firth points out, the control of permanent land rights is a major determinant of rural social structure.[34] So the formalization of land use organization that we have already discussed, becomes reflected in the structure of village society. In some villages, particularly in tropical Africa, kinship and lineage are the basis for this structure. They influence land tenure arrangements and therefore many aspects of village economy.

In other villages, however, the community is characterized by a social structure which is based upon a class system which itself reflects economic status and function. The European feudal village was and, where it continues, is a good example of this, for the community is founded upon a social order in which each group performs a predetermined role. An even better example is the Indian village, where the caste system represents the functional as well as the ritual position of people in Indian rural society. The caste system is complex for it has evolved over eight centuries of Hindu culture. Recently, too, government reforms and modernization have caused some breakdown in the system. However, in one form or another, it remains the basis of the Indian village community. Each caste group fulfils a role, particularly in the economic life of the village. So, as Bétaille has shown, village life depends upon the 'complement of crafts and services in the agrarian economy'.[35] This results in strongly interdependent relationships which bind inhabitants to the village as firmly as do their relationships with land.[36]

The durability of the village as the basis for rural society in so many areas of the world, has been achieved through the strong sense of solidarity that the various forms of community create. Perhaps this has been best expressed by Yang in his description of the Chinese village, which for centuries the Chinese have come to call *t'ien, ynan, lu, mo* (fields, gardens, houses and graves). This is a classical expression signifying 'homeland' or the roots of life. The village, therefore, developed as the *Ku hsiang* or 'old homeland' with which the traditional Chinese associates his entire social existence.[37] This spiritual and symbolic identification with the village underlies the strong sense of identity with place that has been a widespread factor in village development. Tangible expressions of this can be elusive but as Relph has said, 'the relationship between community and place is indeed a very powerful one in which each reinforces the identity of the other'.[38] Thus the village is the locus of work, play, life and death: the place of the society to which the individual primarily belongs. It is common in many areas for rural people to be known by the village from which they came. In Peru, migrants from rural to urban areas form clubs based upon village affiliation and through them retain strong links with their home village.[39] Mandelbaum has pointed out that in India, too, even in the more dispersed forms of villages the inhabitants 'know who belongs to their village and what it takes in'.[40]

Attachment to the village as a place and as a community is expressed through gestures of loyalty: support for a village sports team, defence of even a local rival against external criticism, and, most commonly, loyalty to the village as a political entity. The strength of many villages rests upon the recurrent ritual expression of loyalty. This can be in the form of festivals which honour village saints or deities, or through rituals that confirm village solidarity, such as the Indian cattle-curing rite known as *Akhta*. In this the whole village is sealed off for 42 hours, an act which symbolizes the village as a defensive unit against malevolent forces.[41]

Community and Village Morphology

An important manifestation of the village as a community is the morphology of the built-up area. A number of scholars have linked the existence of clustered or nucleated village settlements to a strong community structure. Students of the European village have gone further and suggested that the degree of nucleation of the village has varied directly with the level of manorial authority.[42] The same relationship has been identified in India where the compact village invariably is one with a well-developed caste system.

The spatial expression of community has been achieved through varying degrees of formality. The basic form involves the clustering of village buildings for mutual protection, convenience, social cohesion, economy and, sometimes, solidarity. DuBoulay describes this in a Greek mountain village where houses are oriented towards the main square, and the morphology of the village reflects 'a way of thinking according to which, after his own individual house the village looks to the community rather than to selected components'.[43] This kind of arrangement need not be formal, for in many areas the natural tendency to seek neighbourly proximity and community identity has led to an informal arrangement of buildings and pathways which focus upon the centre of the village settlement. In Indian compact villages, the irregular arrangement of buildings is often inward-facing, which creates, at the same time, a windowless barrier to the surrounding land. Connections with the fields are made by a restricted number of openings in this 'wall', but routeways within the settlement aim at maximum inter-connectivity. Similar objectives are apparent in the concentrated arrangement of compounds and huts in some African villages (Figure 2.5a). In the large agricultural villages of southern Italy, Spain and north Africa the intense crowding of buildings into a compact nucleation is also an indication of the concentration of the village community.

Figure 2.5: Examples of Common Village Morphologies

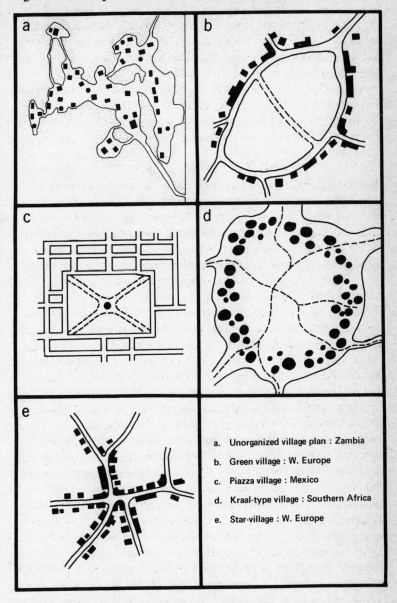

a. Unorganized village plan : Zambia

b. Green village : W. Europe

c. Piazza village : Mexico

d. Kraal-type village : Southern Africa

e. Star-village : W. Europe

The inward-facing cluster has been expressed somewhat more formally through various fashions in village morphology. Indeed it is likely that regional and cultural norms have exerted a strong influence on this aspect of village design. Meitzen and others have suggested the importance of village morphology as an indicator of cultural diffusion in Europe. Thus clustering has taken on various standardized forms of which the most widespread are the village surrounding a green, square or other central open space, the street orientated cluster (which has varying forms) and the radial village. The central open space plays an important role in the physical expression of village community. Buildings are usually grouped around the green or the square into which major route-ways lead. By this arrangement, households look inwards, they are connected by a common space and use it for communal activities (Figure 2.5b). Outside Europe, the central space is also an important design feature. The piazza village of the Iberian peninsula has been transferred to Latin America (Figure 2.5c). Some African villages often involve a quite formal arrangement of huts and compounds around a central area in which such communal structures as the grain store and the threshing floor are usually situated (Figure 2.5d). This is a wide-spread pattern in areas of tropical peasant cultivation, particularly in southeast Asia. Clustering, however, has been achieved with other morphological arrangements. Indeed, in many areas, the most common village layout is one which has simply evolved in a nodal form. The layout of the example of Figure 2.5e illustrates a village form which can be seen in many parts of northern and western Europe. The nodal role of the settlement is achieved with buildings built along unevenly spaced routeways which lead to the village centre.

Conformity to particular morphological styles has tended to be greater in areas where villages have been planned. It is, in fact, often difficult to distinguish between the planned and the unplanned, for even though many villages may not have been laid out in a formal way, their evolution has invariably involved some organization. However, in areas where systematic colonization of new land has occurred, villages have been laid out according to a preconceived plan, and as a result tend to be more formal expressions of the forms described above. In Europe, the colonization of reclaimed marshland and of forested areas in the post-medieval period led to the construction of many new villages. The most common form focused on a single street which, with successive extensions probably resulted in a diminution of a community where elongation was involved. However, Gutkind has given an excellent account of how the street village became more stereotyped and rigid as the colonization on new land in eastern Germany progressed. The construction of houses around squares and along streets created not only the elongated form but also 'the circular or square open space in the centre that became the indispensable prerequisite for the layout'.[44]

Thus village planning adopted the central space and the interconnectivity of streets as morphological instruments of community identity. In some ways the regularity of street layout was influenced by the human grid pattern, and is therefore a relative of the large, squared, grid village of southern Europe. Other European planned village layouts, however, emphasize the value of the radial form. The circular and oval villages of marshland and reclaimed areas of Holland, north Germany and parts of eastern Europe, have a regular pattern of radiating roads meeting an encircling road which forms a distinct boundary to the settlement (Figure 2.6).

Figure 2.6: Influence of Planning on Village Morphology: North Germany

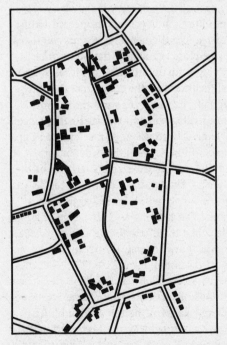

Source: Germany, Series M841 (G.S.G.S.) Sheet 3324, Scale, 1:25,000.

The planned settlement has been an almost universal feature of the New World. The strongest influence is clearly that of the classical grid, so that village communities were housed within square or rectangular envelopes when new territories were laid out. Lewis describes the Iberian influence on the Mexican village: a large, sprawling rectangle with a central plaza,[45] and in the Guianas the typical layout of villages is that of a narrow rectangle surrounded by dams and ditches of the irrigated farmland.[46] A widespread alternative to this is the achievement of nodality through the interconnection of side streets with a main street in which major social and commercial activities occur. This is a form typical in North America.

Morphological expressions of community in villages are usually intensified by the strategic location of the various functional elements of settlements. So the gravitational influence of the village centre is, to a large extent, created by the various services which are available in the piazza, around the village green, along the main street or at the meeting of roads. Where religious authority and beliefs are strong, religious buildings are prominent in this part of the village, as is shown by the generally central position of the church in Catholic Europe and Latin America and of the mosque in Islamic settlements. The symbolic focus of the church is augmented by the close spatial association of other services, such as the village market, retail outlets, meeting houses, coffee shops, inns and by institutional facilities like the communal threshing-floor, the grain store, the town hall, the post office and the school.

The structural manifestation of villages as communities has occurred also through designs which have recognized the need for defence against external influence and even attack. In most areas the concern for defence has long since vanished but the defensive characteristics of the settlements remain. As Rowlands has shown, these do not necessarily involve fortification nor a concern simply with physical aggression.[47] Siting of a village in isolated valleys, on hilltops or on the edge of a forest can satisfy defence needs, while the internal morphology of the settlement, in particular the compact or clustered form, can act as a defence against the breakdown of the community.

To a lesser extent the desire for defence has been explicitly expressed by the existence of various methods of fortification. In some instances this has been achieved by perching villages at the top of high bluffs. Such naturally fortified positions were sought by rural population in the Mediterranean region during periods of widespread insecurity and remain as active settlements today in southern France, Italy, Spain and north Africa. The construction of fortifications around villages is, if less spectacular, a more common defensive technique. Long after the original need for defence has disappeared these structures remain along with the influence they have had on the shapes of the enclosed settlements. Walled villages occur in the Po valley and in parts of north Africa and the Middle East, and are a traditional form of rural settlement in China and Japan. In India, it is common for villages to be surrounded by a mud or earthen barrier, a feature which can be found surrounding west African compound settlements.

There is a danger in overemphasizing the extent of morphological and other physical expressions of the village as a community. Many villages have, in fact, developed with rather sprawling, irregular layouts which may have little to do with community solidarity. Sternstein gives an example of Thai villages in which settlement stretches for several miles along irrigation ditches and community identity is maintained through social networks.[48] Nor is the Indian subcontinent without a number of regions, particularly in the southwest, where village communities are spatially fragmented. The dispersed Indian village consists usually of a central settlement and several satellite hamlets which are often inhabited by 'untouchables' or pastoralists. In the southern Indian province of Kerala, with greater independence in the ownership and use of land, villages characteristically extend in ribbon-like fashion along rural roads. The community is maintained less by the physical compactness of the settlement than by its social space. Furthermore, if we recollect that the village consists of its settlement and surrounding land, there is reason to believe that a compact nucleation is not a prerequisite for a village community. In some areas of the world, in fact, villages are often quite sprawling, rather chaotically-laid-out settlements. Frequently this is because they consist of properties settled, sometimes at different periods in time, by individual families without any control by some village authority.

Just as the community of the village need not be expressed in strong morphological terms nor should we assume that all villages are necessarily unified and cohesive communities. The space occupied by both land and settlement can be viewed also as a social space which in many instances is composed of distinct but related social units. Thus the village may be a functioning community in which each group plays a fundamental role, but it need not be one with social unity. A good example of this is the traditional Indian village where both territory and settlement have an internal spatial structure which reflects the importance of ritual distance between various castes. In some villages individual inhabitants will have a fair degree of independence from the community. This is true particularly where cultivation of land proceeds independently of the community; in other words where cultivators have

some freedom over the control, ownership, use and disposal of their
holdings. This became characteristic of agricultural land use in much of
western Europe by the beginning of the nineteenth century. In some
areas it led to the movement of farm families out of the village settlement and occasionally even in the abandonment of nucleated
settlements altogether.[49] In other areas, for example in Bavaria, it
merely involved more independent forms of land tenure within a
continuing fragmented land parcel framework. In west Africa, too, in
recent years, the traditional territorial structure of villages has been
broken down by the dispersal of family compounds into individually
owned and operated agricultural land.[50]

The Non-Peasant Village

The major effect of these trends is to alter the relationship between the
village and its territory. This is a process which has gathered momentum
over the past few centuries, beginning with the weakening of feudalism
in western Europe and culminating in the often radical transformation
of village structure in the twentieth century. The nature of recent
change is examined in a later chapter, in which the impact of socialist
transformation and the commercialization of agriculture upon peasant
villages is stressed. Here the concern is with the evolution, predominantly
in western Europe and North America, of the non-peasant, non-
agricultural village.

The adaptation of the village in northern and western Europe to
post-feudal land tenure systems and then to massive urban growth did
not result in major changes in the physical structure of village settlements.
It is true that the enclosure movement in Britain caused the destruction
and even disappearance of some villages when serfs were dispossessed
of land rights and farmsteads were dispersed. Yet many villages with
feudal origins remain. It is notable, too, that in the colonization of parts
of northern and eastern Europe, the traditional form was adopted even
where independent systems of land tenure and cultivation prevailed.
However, the modern village in much of Europe is one which has lost
much of its influence over land and community while at the same time
retaining certain of its original characteristics. In some regions, for
example Britain, northern France and Scandinavia, the enclosure of
open fields led to a physical dispersal of farmsteads and farming people
which led the village to become the political, social and economic focus
for a population which was more independent of the authority of the
village community. There are villages which precede this process by
many centuries, particularly in southern France and the Celtic fringes,

where independent cultivation made villages more like central places than peasant communities. In other parts of Europe, such as in central and southwest France and much of Germany, the farming population is independent of seigneurial authority but still remains residential in the village. Here the sense of an agricultural community may remain strong, but again the ingredient of village authority over agricultural land is lost.

With or without the physical dispersal of the farm population, many European villages have become settlements in which community identity is achieved through the various services it provides, rather than through a singularity of purpose and organization. This does not mean that the administrative function of the village necessarily has been lost. Indeed, long after the disappearance of the feudal and communal village, most larger European villages have retained some administrative responsibility for their surrounding territories. In most cases this involves variations on the theme of the English parish. This institution has origins which coincide with the decline of the feudal system, and throughout the seventeenth, eighteenth and nineteenth centuries the village was the locus of parish authority. Its power declined proportionally with the decline in the power of landowners and the Church. By the end of the nineteenth century the parish was a vestigial element of English local government. Yet, in some ways, the parish council still provides an identity with the village, for it is a means of dealing with controversial problems and of initiating involvement at the local level.

If the organizational role of some later European villages is at best symbolic, then the most influential factor in the maintenance of village settlements has been the diversification of social and economic structure. Even during the Middle Ages, many villages in Europe aspired to small-scale, cottage-based manufacturing activities. In northern and western regions in particular they supplied the growing urban market with their products and provided employment, often on a part-time basis, for an expanding village population. In England, as Thirsk has shown, the combination of rural industry and farming played an increasingly important role in the village economy. Weaving, knitting, woodworking, mining and quarrying, charcoal-burning were foremost among village activities until mid-nineteenth-century urban industrialization made them redundant.[51]

A more enduring impact of diversification in European villages has come from the growth of commercial activities. As a result of the increasing affluence of rural society, particularly during the eighteenth and nineteenth centuries, larger villages began to expand the number and range of services provided to the local population. By the mid-nineteenth century, most English villages contained a wide range of services and other commercial activities.

Subsequent improvements in personal mobility caused villages to surrender much of their service role to the towns. Yet the social and economic basis of many villages remains a diverse one. From its agricultural peasant beginning the village in industrialized Europe has evolved into a small-scale residential social and commercial community. We shall see in a later chapter how villages continue to experience changes which alter their character, but many villages which have ceased to be merely peasant communities have a physical structure which owes a great deal to the growth of functional diversity during the sixteenth, seventeenth and eighteenth centuries. The great period of village reconstruction in England occurred during this period as the widespread occurrence of Tudor and Georgian village architecture testifies.

The organizational separation of village settlement from agricultural land use is most apparent in the rural regions of the New World. For the most part, rural settlement began with a dispersed farm population and nucleated settlements grew up as places which served the economic and social needs of that population. The result is that even the use of the word 'village' to describe these settlements is problematical. Functionally they tend to be small trade centres and for those who have used them as such since their establishment they have been referred to invariably as towns. New Zealand villages, as Anderson and Franklin have said, are 'rural, but non-farm, urban but not wholly urban'.[52] North American terminology for these settlements is utterly confused. The use of village or small town appears to depend upon the cultural background of a particular area and of the user of the word, and upon the relationship which an individual has with the place. Even academics cannot agree on which term is appropriate. For example, in independent studies of small trade centres in Wisconsin, Hart and Salisbury call them villages, while Fuguitt and Deeley use the term 'small town'.[53] The confusion mounts when Fuguitt refers to the same places as villages in another study.[54]

The problem is that, as trade centres, these settlements are part of the urban system and therefore town-like. As such we shall examine them in another context: as small towns, which is one of the subjects of the next chapter. Yet the village in North America cannot be dismissed so easily, for in other ways it is very much a reality, with the same kinds of community and place identities as villages elsewhere. In both the

United States and Canada 'village' is an officially recognized term for rural places of certain sizes and status. Thus an incorporated village is a recognized political entity with its own local government. This is clear evidence that such settlements play the social and cultural role that characterizes villages generally.

In some areas the village is more easily identified as a distinct element of settlement because it has traditional origins. A good example of this is the *puebla* of New Mexico which comes closest to being a peasant village in North America for, as a traditional agricultural settlement its structure is strongly influenced by the relationship between society and land. This is true also of the fishing communities of Newfoundland which grew up as independent villages based entirely on a local resource base.

Elsewhere, however, villages have developed as places which depend upon a rural hinterland. One study which illustrates this particularly well is that by Brown of Upsala, Minnesota.[55] This incorporated village, with a population of 356 in 1960, is the focal point for those who inhabit the village and the surrounding farms. In addition to being a trade centre (or small town) in a rural area, it is, like so many villages in modern Europe, the centre of the local community. In 1960, as well as 27 economic establishments, it had eight political and eight social institutions. Of particular importance in shaping people's identity with the village are schools, churches, baseball leagues and various societies and clubs. The social significance of the village is illustrated by the growing number of retired farmers moving in to take up residence. All this suggests a village which is a strong rural community. And, as Brown's examination of the relationship between the incorporated village and its agricultural hinterland shows, it is a village which has a clearly demarcated territory. Thus, despite its different origins, this typical Midwest village has important similarities with its European counterpart, for in its own specialized way it reveals territorial characteristics.

The importance of the village as the focus for rural community may be more immediately apparent in the eastern regions of North America. Here, particularly in areas such as New England and Quebec, the village is an important part of the cultural heritage of the rural population. Furthermore, a number of villages have traditional origins as farm settlements. In New England, in fact, this has found expression in the layout and physical appearance of some villages. The grouping of village buildings around a village green is not uncommon and, as Duncan has suggested, much of the local identification with the village depends upon the 'village-like' atmosphere of its colonial architecture.[56]

In Quebec, the transfer of certain aspects of the French seigneurial system resulted in the retention of some of the more traditional features of village communities. After an initial period of universal dispersal of the rural population, villages grew up in the latter half of the eighteenth century around a church and around basic commercial activities. Generally aligned along a single street but occasionally laid out by a seigneur in a grid pattern, the villages now serve as the parish centre, as a residential location for the elderly and as the base of operations for tradesmen and professionals.[57] Just as some villages in New England may be reminiscent of their English ancestors, those in Quebec are suggestive of the typical French village with the cultural centre of the community, the church, dominating the settlement.

Summary

This examination of the village has aimed to provide a conceptualization of this particular element of rural settlement. It has done so by stressing the evolution of the peasant village as a structure for organizing a productive relationship between population and basic resources. The village is viewed therefore as a territorial unit, a community, an economic, social and political centre with regionally varied but distinctive geographical manifestations of these characteristics. The peasant village is the fundamental form which remains in many areas, but which in others has undergone adaptations to societal change which have diminished the importance of settlement-land relationships. Two issues remain: the significance of rural settlement elements which lie outside this conceptualization of the village, namely dispersed settlement, hamlets, small towns and specialized settlements; and, secondly, the recent changes that have occurred in both peasant and non-peasant villages.

Notes

1. *Shorter Oxford Dictionary* (Oxford: Oxford University Press, 1959).

2. V.G. Childe, *Man Makes Himself* (London: Watts, 1965).

3. J. Mellaart, *The Neolithic of the Near East* (London: Thames and Hudson, 1975), p. 277.

4. Sauer's thesis was that it originated in the fishing economies of the Far East with the domestication of animals such as the dog; C.O. Sauer, *Agricultural Origins and Dispersals* (Cambridge: MIT Press, 1969).

5. S. Piggott, *Ancient Europe* (Edinburgh: Edinburgh University Press, 1965), p. 43.

6. Ibid., p. 43.

7. C.T. Smith, *An Historical Geography of Europe Before 1800* (London: Longmans, 1967), p. 32.

8. D.E. Pfanner, 'A Semi-Subsistence Village Economy in Lower Burma', in C.R. Wharton (ed.), *Subsistence Agriculture and Economic Development* (London: Cass, 1970), pp. 47-60.

9. C.J. Ojo Afolabi, *Yoruba Culture: A Geographical Analysis* (London: University of London Press, 1966), pp. 57-8.

10. C. Brooke, 'The Rural Village in the Ethiopian Highlands', *Geographical Review*, Vol. 49 (1969), pp. 58-75.

11. T.M. Fraser, Jr., *Fishermen of South Thailand, The Malay Villagers* (New York: Holt, Rinehart and Winston, 1966), pp. 32-4.

12. N. Ahmad, 'Rural Settlement Types in the Uttar Pradesh', *Annals*, Association of American Geographers, Vol. 46 (1962), pp. 388-98.

13. Brooke, 'The Rural Village', p. 63.

14. S. Soemardjin, 'Influence of Social Structure on the Javanese Peasant Economy', in Wharton, op. cit., pp. 41-77.

15. W. Bascom, *The Yoruba of South-West Nigeria* (New York: Holt, Rinehart and Winston, 1969), p. 24.

16. A. Beals, *Village Life in South India* (Chicago: Aldine, 1974), pp. 23-4.

17. P.M. Blaikie, 'Spatial Organisation of Agriculture in some North Indian Villages, Part I', *Transactions of the Institute of British Geographers*, Vol. 52 (1971), pp. 1-40.

18. H.H. Ayrout, *The Egyptian Peasant* (Boston: Beacon Press, 1963), p. 87.

19. R. Redfield, *The Little Community* (Chicago: University of Chicago Press, 1955).

20. M. Bloch, *Feudal Society*.

21. Smith, *Europe Before 1800*, p. 32.

22. A. Bétaille, *Caste, Class and Power* (Berkeley: University of California Press, 1965), p. 111.

23. This is well documented in Beals, op. cit.; D.G. Mandelbaum, *Society in India*, Vol. 2 (Chicago: University of Chicago Press, 1970).

24. M.N. Srivinas, 'The Social System of a Mysore Village', in M. Marriott (ed.), *Village India* (Chicago, 1955), pp. 1-35.

25. C.K. Yang, *A Chinese Village in Early Communist Transition* (Massachusetts: Technology Press, 1959), p. 40.

26. R.K. Beardsley, J.W. Hall, and R.E. Ward, *Village Japan* (Chicago: University of Chicago Press, 1959), p. 42.

27. T.R. Ford, *Man and Land in Peru* (New York: Russell and Russell, 1971).

28. C.A. Doxiadis, *Ekistics* (London: Hutchinson, 1968), p. 27.

29. Blaikie, 'Spatial Organization', pp. 15-17.

30. M. Chisholm, *Rural Settlement and Land Use* (London: Hutchinson, 1963).

31. Quoted in, Mandelbaum, *Society in India*, p. 327.

32. Beals, *Village Life*, p. 56.

33. R. Blythe, *Akenfield* (London: Penguin Books, 1969).

34. R. Firth, 'Social Structure and Peasant Economy: the Influence of Social Structure upon Peasant Economics', in Wharton, *Subsistence Agriculture*, pp. 28-9.

35. Bétaille, *Caste, Class and Power*, p. 137.

36. Beals, *Village Life*, pp. 62-3.

37. Yang, *Chinese Village*, p. 9.

38. E.C. Relph, *Place and Placelessness* (London: Pion Press, 1976), p. 34.

39. R. Skeldon, *Migration in Peasant Society: the Example of Cuzco, Peru,* Unpublished Ph.D. thesis (University of Toronto, 1974).

40. D.G. Mandelbaum, *Society in India*, p. 337.

41. Ibid., p. 333.

42. Smith, *Europe Before 1800*, pp. 269-70.

43. J. DuBoulay, *Portrait of a Greek Mountain Village* (Oxford: Oxford University Press, 1974), p. 10.

44. E.A. Gutkind, *International History of City Development*, Vol. 1 (New York: Free Press of Glencoe, 1964), pp. 119-20.

45. O. Lewis, *Tepoztlán, Village in Mexico* (New York: Holt, Rinehart and Winston, 1965), p. 4.

46. D. Lowenthal, 'Population Contrasts in the Guianas', *Geographical Review,* Vol. 50 (1960), p. 46.

47. M.J. Rowlands, 'Defence: A Factor in the Organisation of Settlements', in P.J. Ucko, R. Tringham and G.W. Dimbleby, *Man, Settlement and Urbanism* (London: Duckworth, 1972).

48. L. Sternstein, 'Settlement Patterns in Thailand', *Journal of Tropical Geography*, Vol. 21 (1965), pp. 30-43.

49. M. Beresford, *The Lost Villages of England* (Leicester: Lutterworth Press, 1954).

50. R.K. Udo, 'Disintegration of nucleated settlement in Eastern Nigeria', *Geographical Review*, Vol. 55 (1965), p. 53.

51. Joan Thirsk, 'Industries in the Countryside', in F.J. Fisher (ed.), *Essays in the Economic and Social History of Tudor and Stuart England in Honour of R.H. Tawney* (Cambridge: Cambridge University Press, 1961).

52. G. Anderson and H. Franklin, 'The Villages of the Manawatu', *New Zealand Geographer*, Vol. 11 (1955), pp. 53-71.

53. John Fraser Hart and Neil E. Salisbury, 'Population Change in Middle Western Villages: A Statistical Approach', *Annals*, Association of American Geographers, Vol. 55 (1965), pp. 140-60; Glenn V. Fuguitt and N.A. Deeley, 'Retail Service Patterns and Small Town Population Change: A Replication of Hassinger's Study', *Rural Sociology*, Vol. 3 (1966), pp. 53-63.

54. Harley E. Johansen and Glenn V. Fuguitt, 'Changing Retail Activity in Wisconsin Villages', *Rural Sociology*, Vol. 38 (1973), pp. 207-18.

55. R.H. Brown, 'The Upsala Community: a case study in rural dynamics', *Annals*, Association of American Geographers, Vol. 57 (1967), pp. 267-300.

56. J.S. Duncan, Jnr., 'Landscape Taste as a Symbol of Group Identity: A Westchester Country Village', *Geographical Review*, Vol. 63 (1973), pp. 334-55.

57. R.C. Harris and J. Warkentin, *Canada Before Confederation* (New York: Oxford University Press, 1974), pp. 75-6.

3 BEYOND THE VILLAGE

The village is an ancient and widespread settlement form and, indeed, is the dominant element in many rural societies. Yet in most rural regions, settlements have also evolved which represent a divergence from the centrally-organized village community. Since ancient times, the dispersal of settlement beyond the village has reflected a need or desire for some degree of independence from the nucleated village. Out of this has developed a variety of dispersed elements, the most widespread of which is the dispersed farmstead. Yet, in addition, increasing cultural and economic specialization in rural areas has led to the diversification of rural settlement so that as well as dispersed forms, various non-village nucleations have become established. The most common of these are the hamlet and the small town.

The Process of Dispersal

The evolution of dispersed rural settlement is often explained in terms of two types of dispersal processes. Primary dispersal is that which occurs during the initial phase of the occupation of a territory, while secondary dispersal involves the spread of settlement from existing nucleations. The purpose of this model is to distinguish between regions in which dispersed elements are the original form and those in which they are the result of a spread from a village base.

However, in the application of this model to any particular region it is often difficult to distinguish between these processes. Firstly, it is not always possible to establish with certainty that dispersed elements are the original settlement form. Secondly, the products of primary and secondary dispersal frequently exist side by side. Finally, the colonization of new territory may be described in terms of primary dispersal, yet the population involved may have originated from village settlements. Therefore rather than adhering closely to the primary/secondary dichotomy, we shall examine the dispersal process in terms of the various conditions under which it has occurred.

In certain areas there is evidence to suggest that dispersed settlement has ancient origins, and that these forms have persisted until the present day. Parts of Ireland, Wales, the Highlands of Scotland and Brittany, for example, retain dispersed forms which can be traced to early Celtic settlement. Recent discoveries suggest that hamlets and scattered farm-steads existed side by side in early Wales, where freemen lived outside the small nucleations on independently cultivated land.[1] Johnson, too, claims that in Ireland some present-day dispersed farms are of great antiquity for their origin can be traced to Celtic heritage.[2] Of particular importance in this influence was the emphasis on pastoral farming and the ubiquitous water supply. Yet we cannot discount the effect of the limited amount of community organization among Celtic groups which tended to permit the existence of independent farmers within an infield-outfield system.

The evidence for Celtic settlement evolution is somewhat flimsy, and the scattered farmsteads of the Celtic fringes may be due to more recent dispersal. In other parts of Europe, however, there are areas of dispersed settlement whose evolution is easier to trace. For this we can thank Smith, whose detailed elaboration of Demangeon's classification distinguishes three groups of early dispersion.[3] The first involved the expansion of settlement on to poorer land in England, France and western Germany during the Middle Ages. Thus the scattered farmsteads of the boulder clays of northeast Hertfordshire, and the Pays de Caux in France, originated in late medieval piecemeal clearing and the creation of enclosures by individual peasants. A second type of primary dispersal has more recent origins. The extension of the cultivated area by irrigation or drainage was often accompanied by the establishment of dispersed farmsteads, as in the English Fens and the Netherlands. The third form of settlement dispersal identified by Smith is that associated with frontier colonization after the feudal period in northern Europe. So scattered farmsteads of central and northern Sweden evolved through the gradual extension of pastureland beyond village boundaries.

The analysis of early dispersal of rural settlement in Europe favours both culture and economics as the motivation for primary dispersion. Thus Celtic social organization permitted independent location of farms, while the weakening of the feudal system in Europe allowed individuals to enclose land when new areas were colonized at the end of the Middle Ages. At the same time the economic advantages of independent farming on consolidated land parcels are cited as reasons for dispersal especially where newly occupied land was used for pasture. In some areas it is difficult to establish with any confidence why the dispersed form was favoured. However, it is clear that the establishment of farmsteads and homesteads outside of villages meant a new relation-ship between settlement and land. So the characteristic layout of the isolated farmstead in these areas which were occupied by dispersed settlement from the beginning is of the farm buildings of an individual family surrounded by a contiguous land parcel which is cultivated independently rather than communally.

It is this independence from the territorial and economic organization of the traditional agricultural village which is distinctive of the isolated farmstead. In Europe, the colonization of new land must have created welcome opportunities for some peasants to break away from the communal farming system. For others the chance to farm more efficiently, particularly where livestock was concerned, offered added benefits in terms of standard of living and social status. This close association between independent cultivation and dispersed settlement is apparent in other areas of the Old World. Over most of the East Bengal plain in Bangladesh the traditional village of the Indian sub-continent is absent. In a region which is criss-crossed by rivers and streams, with large areas subject to complete inundation during the rainy season, the ubiquitous availability of water and the necessity of building on every piece of raised land has resulted in a dispersed pattern. Unlike the social organization of the land-owning peasants cultivating land parcels which surround their homestead. The *bari* (homestead) houses the extended peasant family which works the paddy rice fields independently of any communal organization.[4]

This relationship between early dispersal, method of cultivation and social organization has been recognized also in parts of west Africa. In Ghana, north of the Black Volta, the overwhelming majority of rural settlements are dispersed, and this is directly related to traditional social organization. Communities are loose-knit and divided into a number of discrete extended family cells. Each group has its own land and therefore builds its household in the middle of this land.[5] In south-eastern Nigeria, hoe cultivation predominates, meaning that farming tends to be small-scale. The Ngwa people have developed a social organization to match this farming system such that there are not villages in the accepted sense. Rather, settlement consists of scattered, extended family compounds linked by pathways. Each family cultivates its own compound land.[6] As Morgan has shown, however, within the same region and using hoe cultivation, the Diobu people organize cultivated land into large blocks associated with nucleated settlements. This indicates the importance of the degree of individual freedom in the dispersal process.

In the evolution of rural settlement in the Old World the dispersed element has been significant in initial colonization in only relatively few areas: pockets within larger regions where the village soon became the predominant form of settlement. It is in the New World that the colonization of land by scattered settlement has had such a widespread and remarkable impact upon the landscape. As we have noted already, the agricultural village is not characteristic of North American rural settlement. In both the United States and Canada the dispersed farmstead and other scattered structures are the most common forms. For the most part, these dispersed elements have their origin in a dispersal which occurred when land was first settled by European migrants.

The model for rural settlement in North America was set by the early settlers of the eastern colonies who quickly rejected proposals for agricultural villages. Quebec and Pennsylvania, whose settlement patterns we shall examine in detail in the next chapter, illustrate a process which strongly influenced subsequent settlement on both sides of the border. In eschewing the village, settlers sought the organizational independence and economic efficiency of the farmstead set in its own contiguous fields. To some extent this reflected the growing trend in Europe towards the dispersal of farmsteads. A more general factor, however, was the spirit of individualism and independence which underscored immigration to North America.

As settlement spread, this spirit was officially recognized and the generally unplanned dispersal of the east was replaced by survey systems which distributed farmers across the land in an orderly fashion. In both Canada and the United States this ensured the establishment of the independent family farm as the central element in North American rural settlement. The dispersal of farmsteads was often accompanied by the scattering of other settlement elements, particularly schoolhouses and churches, and sometimes mills, blacksmiths' shops and other agriculturally related services.

During the nineteenth century, too, the opening up of other colonial territories, in Australia, New Zealand and southern Africa, involved the establishment of scattered homesteads. This was associated for the most part with the drive to colonize new land for specialized commercial agriculture such as wheat and sheep farming in Australia. However, the homesteading of the Boers in South Africa, and of settlers in New Zealand, was a process similar to the pioneering of the United States; that is involving small-scale family farm enterprises. In some areas, such as the Argentine pampas, parts of Mexico and the White Highlands of Kenya, large European commercial farms and ranches added a new, dispersed dimension to traditional rural settlement.

To a large extent, the trend towards immediate dispersal in the New

World was consistent with developments in European rural economy and society which had been going on since late medieval times. It involved the partial breakdown of the village-based feudal system which resulted, in some areas, in the physical separation of farms from villages. Two factors were responsible for this process. Firstly, the decline of the feudal system, the reasons for which are too complex to discuss here, resulted in greater freedom for the peasantry. At one and the same time it permitted and was stimulated by the establishment of individually cultivated and enclosed parcels of land on which the farm family resided. Secondly, the enclosure movement was stimulated by the recognition that consolidated farms in separate tenure was a more efficient way of farming than open-field agriculture.

As a result of the pressure, then, for both social and economic independence, the settlement fabric of much of rural northwest Europe, in particular of Britain, parts of France, northern Germany, the Low Countries and Scandinavia, was transformed. The fact that the enclosure movement was at its height during the great emigration to North America suggests that it was a major influence in the predominance of dispersal on the new continent. Some settlers came from farms which were already separate from the village settlement. The example of Gordon Sellar who settled in Ontario in 1824 is typical of many emigrants. Sellar came from a small tenant-farm in the Scottish lowlands. In his diaries he describes his experience on a dispersed farm unit and his desire to increase this independence by owning as well as living on his own land in the New World.[7]

The European enclosure movement is a well-documented example of the establishment of dispersed rural settlement. It was widespread and, during its later phases, formalized by government policies. In southern Italy, for example, the abolition of feudal rights during the nineteenth century resulted in a steady increase in albeit small and often poor peasant farmsteads. More recently, however, land reform programmes have helped peasants to move from overcrowded villages to viable compact holdings.[8]

One condition which has often led to the dispersal of the rural population is a rapid increase in village population. This is a situation in which it becomes impossible for new generations to cultivate within village boundaries and thus are forced to move out, often as squatters, on to unorganized land. This has happened intermittently in a number of tropical areas. Parts of west Africa have experienced periods of intense population pressure. In one area of eastern Nigeria, recent increases in rural population have placed considerable pressure on land resources. Traditional block-farming methods have had increasing difficulty in supporting the growing population. The result has been a gradual occupation of farmlands by younger generations.[9] Mabogunje has attributed the proliferation of dispersal with minute holdings to 'a mad scramble for land' resulting from intense pressure of population.[10]

However, in eastern Nigeria and in other parts of rural Africa such as Kenya and Zambia, a combination of political and social events has also led to the setting up of dispersed homesteads and compounds. The introduction of colonial administration led to village abandonment in east and west Africa as villagers moved to escape from the authority of colonial officials. In east Africa the break-up of villages was often physically enforced by colonial administrations who sought to reduce tribal authority. During recent years, dispersal has intensified as a result of social changes in which village authority has declined. This has been associated by Long in his studies of Zambia with the desire on the part of some villagers to acquire a higher standard of living which can be achieved only by breaking away from the circle of village kin and 'setting up on one's own'.[11] In Nigeria this tendency is intensified by the independence of the young married men who wish to take advantage of a more diversified and market-orientated agricultural economy. The result is an increase in small, self-contained compounds set amidst garden plots. To some extent dispersal from African villages is more complex than this, for, as Cowie has shown in Zambia, villagers can be forced out of the village for nonconformist behaviour as well as choosing to leave for the reasons described above. In one village studied by Cowie, a woman was banished for witchcraft and another individual for rowdyism![12]

The Elements of Dispersal

The process of dispersal involves the creation of particular forms of settlement. The most widespread of these is the farmstead, but the creation of dispersed patterns in many areas has involved the establishment of other elements. These include non-farm residences, institutional buildings, and commercial and industrial structures.

Farmstead and Farms

As a dispersed element, the farm is usually a consolidated land unit in which the most obvious settlement feature is the farmstead. This is the centre of operations for the farm enterprise, yet the farm is more than its buildings, for settlement includes the fields and associated elements which are its *raison d'etre*. In examining the dispersed farm, then, we must see the farmstead and farm as functionally related elements.

Geographical research on the farmstead has often emphasized its physical form. Initial consideration of it in these terms would appear to present little difficulty, for to most of us the farmstead is a compact collection of buildings. In reality, however, there is little similarity between the farmsteads of different regions beyond the existence of this general theme of the grouping of farm residence and agricultural buildings. The particular style of a farmstead is a function of three interrelated factors: the structure of the farm family, design conventions and type of farming. The relationships between these factors can be extremely complex, and so we can do little more than illustrate how these factors have influenced farmstead structure in selected cases.

Where the dispersed farm is operated by a family unit, as it is in most areas of the world, the size and structure of the family has influenced both the size and composition of the farmstead. The predominantly nuclear farm family structure has led to the dominance of the single farmhouse as the residential centre of most farms. Larger families have resulted in larger farmhouses, while generational expansion has often led to the addition of extra wings or of separate dwellings. In contrast to the nuclear farm family, extended family structures generally result in more elaborate residential arrangements. Extended family structure is common in many peasant societies, and although they usually occupy villages and hamlets, there are some examples of dispersal of extended family farmsteads. Where this has occurred in Africa it generally involves the establishment of a few huts with associated grain stores, threshing floors and other structures such as the homestead schematically illustrated in Figure 3.1.

Considerable emphasis in the study of farmsteads has been placed upon the influence of design conventions. A major reason for this is the interest in rural building styles as an indicator of cultural variation. Rapoport explains this approach by showing how important folk traditions have been in the vernacular architecture of so much of the peasant world.[13] This is apparent, as we have seen in village morphology, but it is more easily seen in individual buildings and in small groupings of buildings such as the isolated farmstead. This has been an important theme in European studies which have tended to concentrate on farmhouse and barn styles. Publications such as that by Barley illustrate how cultural diffusion is apparent in farm buildings and how various design conventions have been adapted to local environmental circumstances.[14]

Figure 3.1: Extended Family Homestead, Ghana

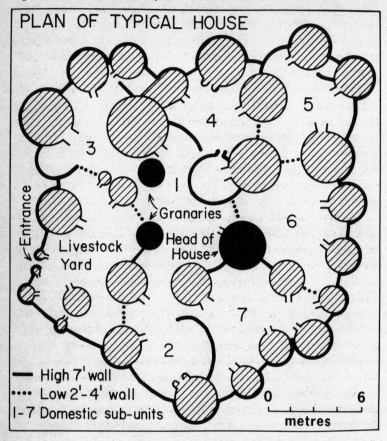

PLAN OF TYPICAL HOUSE

Entrance

Granaries

Livestock Yard

Head of House

— High 7' wall
•••• Low 2'-4' wall
1-7 Domestic sub-units

0   6
metres

Reproduced by permission from the *Annals* of the Association of American
Geographers, Vol. 57 (1967), pp. 339-49, J.M. Hunter.

This process has been important in North America and this has led to a
number of studies of the impact of cultural conventions on barn styles.[15]
Barns have played a highly visible role in the development of the North
American farmstead. Ennals has shown how different barn styles can be
linked to the cultural background of settlers in Upper Canada, while
Hart has produced an admirable summary of the barn as a culture
form.[16]

The main concern here, however, is not with the details of farm
building design, for that is a topic in its own right and one which has

been well treated elsewhere. Furthermore, as the operational centre of the farm, farmsteads have been influenced in their structure as much by the nature of the farm enterprise as by broad cultural factors. So the type and arrangement of farm buildings and also of other elements such as fences and woodlots have been developed in most areas in response to the needs of particular types of farming. Design conventions, in fact, have experienced major modifications because of the largely personal and increasingly commercial nature of dispersed farming. This means that, for the most part, farmsteads are highly functional elements of settlement. They are designed to accommodate living quarters for those who work the land, shelter for livestock and equipment, storage facilities and processing space for farm produce, fences for security, roads and paths for access: in short, a host of structures to support an agricultural operation.

Thirty years ago, Trewartha published a study of basic American farmstead types, which showed the major changes that can occur on farmsteads from one farming type region to another.[17] While one might question Trewartha's notion of 'typical' farmsteads, his study showed clearly how structures vary according to specialized agricultural needs. This can be well illustrated by examining the mixed livestock-crop farm which, in various forms, has been the conventional type of family farm in so much of western Europe and North America for the past 150 years or so. The basic elements of the farmstead of the mixed farm reflect first of all the variety of products. Generally this had led to all-purpose types of farmsteads in which a large barn with fodder storage space and livestock accommodation predominated. The amount of space needed depends upon the size of the farm and, of course, upon the extent to which local climate increases the need for winter protection. For example New England barns tend to be much larger than their counterparts in southern England where the open farmyard fulfills a wide range of functions in a milder climate. Depending upon the type of livestock and the level of technology, other structures such as hen-houses, pig-pens, equipment storage sheds and milking parlours complete the composition of the farmstead.

The traditional mixed farm produced a farmstead designed to meet a variety of operational needs. Yet in both Europe and North America this type of farmstead frequently contains elements which were designed for past rather than present needs. Furthermore, major changes in technology have added new structures. Kiefer has traced changes in farm settlement in Indiana and shown that, while the basic structure of the old mixed farmstead has remained unchanged, a variety of new elements have been added, including silos, feedlots, broiler houses and hogpens.[18] It is the fairly rapid changes that now occur even on the small family farm which make farmstead analysis more complex.

With the trend towards greater specialization many dispersed farmsteads in various parts of the world have been designed to meet quite specific requirements. This is as true of the cash crop wheat farm of the Prairies as it is of the modern smallholding of the Ghanaian cocoa farmer. In these circumstances certain structures fulfil special functions. A few examples will serve to illustrate this point.

One example is that of the dry-lot livestock farm which has become increasingly important in modern livestock production. The basic system involves the feeding of cattle in feed barns and corrals rather than by the conventional pasturing method. One version of this is the Californian dry-lot dairy farm, the layout of which is illustrated in Figure 3.2. Here farm and farmstead are one and the same space, for feed is purchased off the farm. The arrangement of milking barns, feedbins, corrals, calf pens and feed barns is designed for maximum efficiency and large herds. Little space is allocated to the farm residence which is set-off in a corner of the farmstead. The dry-lot farm is one example of various forms of industrialized agriculture which are having an increasingly important impact upon the farmscape of many economically advanced regions. They include mechanized feed-livestock operations such as broiler chicken, beef cattle and hog enterprises, as well as vegetable production under modern climate-control and irrigation systems. Lounsbury, in his study of Puerto Rican commercial farms, has analyzed the relationship between farmstead structure and the type of enterprise.[19] His farmsteads are indicative of the type of agricultural economy and of the level of agricultural technology. The variation in size, composition and layout of Puerto Rican commercial farms is clearly shown in Figure 3.3. In A and C, the sugar-cane and dairy farmstead illustrate just how large and organized these settlements can be, with labourers' dwellings neatly planned as part of a farmstead which is like a self-contained hamlet. In B and D, the prominence of specialized structures, such as the packing house and drying floor, shows the close relationship between function and farmstead form.

To a large degree it is the commercial scale of this type of farming which makes the farmsteads such distinctive elements of settlement. This is obvious in tropical plantations and in the extensive agricultural regions of the New World, where the isolation and independence of such operations as the Australian sheep ranch, and the Argentinian *estancia* has resulted in large, virtually self-sufficient farm settlements.

Figure 3.2: Dry-lot Dairy Farmstead, Southern California

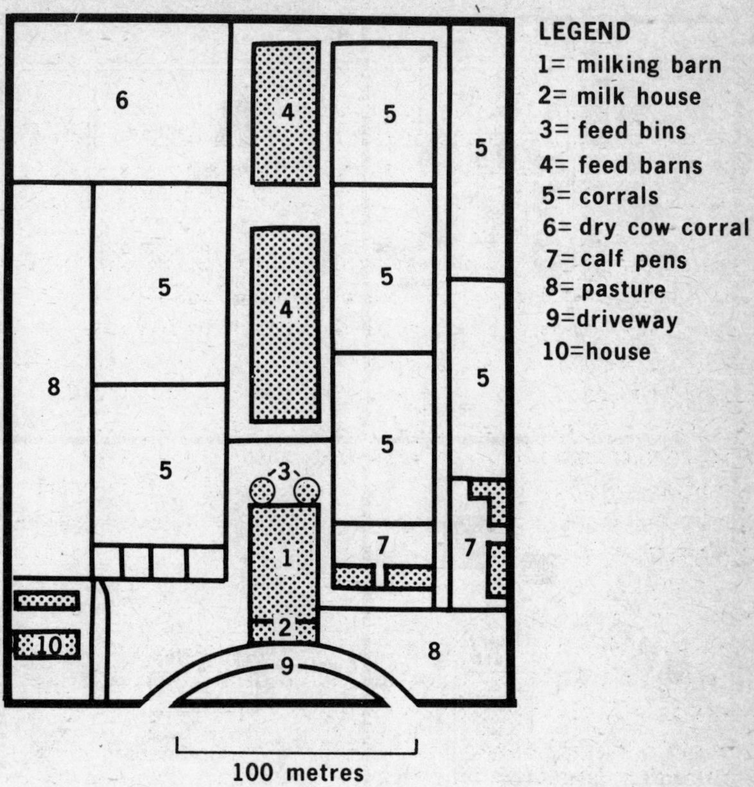

LEGEND
1= milking barn
2= milk house
3= feed bins
4= feed barns
5= corrals
6= dry cow corral
7= calf pens
8= pasture
9=driveway
10=house

100 metres

Source: H.F. Gregor, 'Industrialized Drylot Dairying: An Overview', *Economic Geography*, Vol. 39 (1963), with permission of the Editor, *Economic Geography*.

In fact, colonial exploitation of the tropics and subtropics has produced structures of dispersed settlement which are in marked contrast to farmsteads of peasant farmers. Dispersal of peasant farms invariably results in the division of land into small parcels so that the farms are effectively smallholdings of only a few hectares. In southeastern Nigeria, for example, individual farms are little more than garden plots and many are less than 0.5 hectares in size. In these circumstances even the growing of a commercial crop does not require the construction of an elaborate farmstead. The typical farmstead of peasant smallholders everywhere is one in which the family dwelling is the main if not the only structure. In many cases these are simple structures and in some

Figure 3.3: Specialized Farmstead Layouts, Puerto Rico

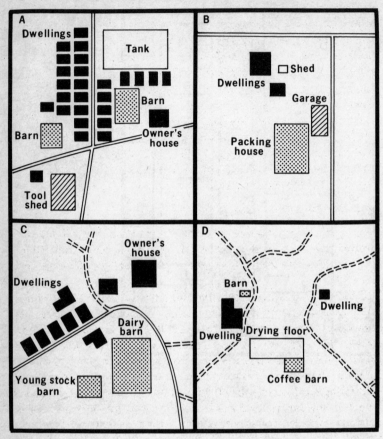

Key to Farmsteads:
A. Sugar-cane B. Pineapple C. Dairy D. Coffee

Source: Lounsbury, 'Farmsteads in Puerto Rico', p. 161, adapted from the *Geographical Review*, Vol. 45, 1955, with the permission of the American Geographical Society.

areas they are tangible evidence of the poverty of small farmers. Lounsbury describes the contrast in Puerto Rico between the large commercial farmstead and the 'small and flimsy' dwelling of the peasant smallholder.[20] The size and simplicity of this farmstead, in various architectural forms, is repeated in many areas of the tropical world where small, individual holdings are often the main form of farm settlement.

The methods of peasant farming, however, can be sufficiently specialized to produce unique farmstead structures. A good example of this can be seen in the relationship between transhumant livestock farming and the location of farm buildings in Alpine areas. Here the traditional method of agriculture represents an ingenious adaptation to local environmental circumstances which results in a dispersed rather than compact farmstead. In winter, cattle are fed and sheltered at the farm headquarters, usually a combined house and byre located in a valley village. In summer, lowland fields are used to produce hay and other crops, while cattle are moved up the valley sides to upland pastures. On these the rest of the farmstead is built, including milking sheds, chalets for herdsmen and simple shelters for cattle. In some cases the dispersal of a single farmstead can be over several kilometres.

Non-Farm Elements in Dispersed Settlement

In many areas where dispersal of rural settlement has occurred it has involved only the separation of the farmstead from a nucleation. Non-farm activities have tended to remain in village and town. However, in certain areas, dispersed settlement contains non-farm elements. In the New World, where villages and towns were slow to develop after initial settlement, various institutional buildings were often distributed across a township. In early Ontario, for example, this was frequently influenced by the scattered nature of church and crown land parcels, so that churches and school rooms were built where land provision was made for them. In the opening up of the American Midwest it was a means of minimizing the distance which farm families had to travel to church and school. In some areas it was a reflection of the independence of various religious groups. Whatever the cause, the effect has been to leave a legacy of school houses, churches, chapels and meeting houses along rural roads and frequently at road junctions. Some survive intact and functional, others are derelict, and still others have been converted to new uses. More recently rural regions in the vicinity of expanding metropolitan areas have experienced a proliferation of dispersed settlement. This phenomenon poses problems which are discussed in a later chapter. However, it is important to stress that it represents a further stage in the dispersal process. Punter has plotted the distribution of residential estates in the metropolitan Toronto region and shown that much of this new dispersal is associated with a fragmented pattern of farmland severance.[21] Associated with residential development are the scattered buildings of commercial enterprises such as service stations, restaurants and garden centres.

Hamlets

Of the American hamlet Trewartha has written, 'it is neither purely rural nor purely urban, but neuter in gender, a sexless creation midway between the more determinate town and country'.[22] Trewartha's metaphorical description sums up the difficulty of defining precisely what a hamlet is. In general terms it is a rural settlement consisting of a small collection of buildings but without the formal organization or complexity of the village.

Central-place studies generally place hamlets at the bottom of the settlement hierarchy, and in this way they can be seen as the first stage of population concentration. Yet hamlet formation has also accompanied the dispersal process, so that it is a form frequently associated with separation from village settlement.

Probably the oldest types of hamlet that exist are those associated with early clan groupings of agriculturalists. These can still be found in Ireland where they originate from small kin groups. For the most part these settlements are simply small groupings of farms and cottages. Ancient hamlets made up primarily of clusters of farmsteads belonging to individual clan groups or sometimes simply extended families are to be found in other areas. They are the predominant form of rural settlement in the more remote areas of the Balkans, and are common in western Brittany where, again, Celtic influence is strong.

The failure to develop into larger, more diversified settlements is a common feature of many hamlets which have a long history. There are various reasons for this. It may, as in west Africa, be due to the nature of tribal and family organization, or, as in the Balkans, to the persistence of an essentially subsistent local economy. In other cases, as in Ireland and Brittany, it is simply that not all small clusters of farmsteads could grow to acquire the political and economic status of the village. Indeed, during periods of rural depopulation villages in many areas of Europe have been reduced to the size and status of hamlets. Although they have a shorter history, the hamlets of the Appalachian hollows have experienced the same fate. Established by small groups of settlers, frequently members of extended family or immigrant groups, the 'hollows' hamlets have been by-passed by modern commercial development or abandoned after a short period of strip mining and remain a cluster of small farms.[23] Few have developed the political and economic status that brings sewage facilities, piped water, electricity, schools and so on, so they continue as hamlets in the strictest sense of the term: dominated by one or two families, unserviced and unincorporated.

It is their unincorporated status that is a basis for Trewartha's identification of the hamlet in the Midwest.[24] Trewartha's work provides important clues about the distinctive nature of the hamlet in North America. Contemporaneously with the agricultural settlement of the United States west of the Appalachians and with the occupation of much of Canada, small, compact nucleations grew up as minor service centres amidst dispersed farm settlement. Some originated through the activities of promoters selling subdivisions for development and remained hamlets because they failed to become large enough to qualify for incorporation. More commonly, they are the result of the accretion of small-scale commercial activities at strategic locations in rural townships. Trewartha illustrates a variety of hamlet forms. Most of these settlements however cluster in various layouts around cross-roads, and, less commonly, ribbon-fashion along rural roads, where a couple of farmsteads have been added to by a general store, a gas station and perhaps a church or a school house. The combinations of commercial activities vary from place to place, and, with the uncertainties that face small business, from time to time.

The commercial North American hamlet, with its counterparts in other areas of recent European settlement, has developed directly from the initial phase of settlement. Yet in some regions hamlets are the clustered version of the move to greater independence from the village which characterizes much of the general dispersal of settlement. The satellite hamlet, set up beyond the village core, but usually still within its political jurisdiction, can be the result of a group's desire for economic or social independence. In some instances it is the village which forces groups to live outside its boundaries, while in others it is sheer pressure on land which results in new settlements being established.

As with the dispersal of individual farms, an important factor in the development of satellite hamlets can be the pressure to farm more efficiently. Satellite hamlets are common in parts of India and many have been formed by kin or caste groups moving from the village to take up residence amongst their fields. This is particularly common among pastoralists. So in hamlets, *dhani*, as they are called, the predominantly homogeneous groups of farmers gain the economic advantage of being close to their fields, so that livestock can be better cared for, land adequately manured and time saved in agricultural operations.[25]

The same problems of village land shortage which stimulates the dispersal of individuals on to independent farms, has led also to the

establishment of hamlet settlement. This is common where whole
families break away from an expanding village. In Turkey, for example,
rapid growth of rural population has traditionally resulted in the hiving-
off of individual families into *muhtarliks*: hamlets of three to four
homesteads which expand as the growing families add new houses to
the original settlement.[26]

Economic factors in hamlet development cannot be distinguished
easily from social and cultural influences. The fission of village communities is often escalated by the emergence of new forms of power
and social status, such as the decline in authority of the village headman
and the shifting emphasis of power within kin groups. Pressure to be
physically separate from the village can, however, come from the village
organization itself. A good example of this are the hamlets of lower
caste groups which lie outside the main settlement of many Indian
villages. These are tiny communities consisting of households belonging
mainly to untouchable and other low castes. Because they have no
service caste members there are no stores, religious establishments,
schools, post offices or resident government officials. They are
unofficial settlements with few of the social and economic activities of
the village, but, as Beals comments, 'Thefts, quarrels, fights and party
conflicts rarely occur in hamlets!'[27]

Small Towns

The dispersal of rural settlement is part of the general increase in the
diversification of rural settlement structure. In Europe and the New
World in particular this has been accompanied by increasing functional
specialization as well as by the socio-economic disintegration which we
have traced so far. Christaller and other central-place theory disciples
have stressed the importance of commercial specialization in the
establishment of a hierarchy of rural settlements.

The most commercial of all rural places are the small, urban centres
usually referred to as small towns or market towns which have long
been essential elements in many rural areas. The study of small towns
is not well developed, perhaps because they represent a number of
conceptual difficulties. Are they urban or rural? How small are they?
When does a village become a small town? There are no clear answers to
these questions, for, as with all other settlement, the term 'small town'
has evolved through common usage rather than precise definition. If
one accepts the notion of an urban system they are indeed part of it,

for places referred to as towns will have the political and economic status of a municipality. Yet their urban role is played in, and on behalf of the rural economy. As to their size, there are small towns in rural America with no more than 1,000 people and market towns in Europe with over 20,000. Size is variable (in space and time) and not a useful indicator below a population even of 50,000. The distinction between village and small town is fairly clear when one is dealing with agricultural or peasant villages. However, as we saw at the end of the last chapter, the development of non-farm villages, particularly in North America, confuses the distinction.

The most useful approach to a consideration of small towns is to recognize that, historically, they have played a distinct role in rural areas. This has been as centres of exchange and services for a rural hinterland. Their origin can be traced to the rise of commercialism in parts of medieval Europe and Asia, when the development of some rural economies beyond local subsistence agriculture led to increasing trade between city and country. Prior to this, and indeed this remains true of modern areas of peasant subsistence, towns in rural areas had been established with special institutional relationships with rural society. Many were built by monastic orders which were landlords of surrounding rural estates. Others developed at the site of castles and fortresses from which local barons or princes exercised often arbitrary authority over the surrounding rural population. To these places, rural people went to pay taxes and homage, to be tried or seek justice, and sometimes for refuge in times of strife. The physical signs of this function can still be seen in medieval castles which dominate many small towns in Europe and also in Japan.

In western and southern Europe during the Middle Ages, the gradual relaxation of feudalism, accompanied by increasing commercialism in agriculture, led to a change in the role of the small town. It became dependent upon a reciprocal relationship with its rural hinterland: a market centre, its size closely related to the local density of the rural population. The market town evolved, therefore, as a new force in rural society, for it provided a permanent point of exchange between agricultural commodities and non-agricultural goods and services. By the end of the Middle Ages it has been estimated that there were in the Holy Roman Empire 3,000 corporate towns. This, as Smailes suggests, reflected the fragmentation of the medieval political and economic structure.[28]

However, as population expanded and regional economies diversified after the Middle Ages, at least in western Europe, the small market town proliferated, frequently through the growth of existing villages. And these precursors of the modern small town were not only the point of exchange for the farming population, but also played an intermediary role in the folk-urban continuum. In other words they facilitated a political and economic relationship between metropolis and country-side. The result is that, even today, European market towns are compact urban places set in a rural landscape. They contain a surprisingly large array of services and small industries, which serve the hinterland not only commercially but also through the provision of employment to rural people.

With generally less commercialism in agriculture, small towns have not been as important in the rural settlement structure of most Asian and African regions. Peasant farming societies, as we have seen, are village orientated and in many areas trade through moving, periodic markets. However, there is evidence for a hierarchy of village service centres in India, some of which are large enough to perform the role of small market and administrative towns.[29] Smaller urban centres in Malaya have developed from early colonial administrative centres into service towns with a strong retail emphasis.[30] Morgan has identified similar, but more recent, small towns in Kenya where administrative centres, often the place of residence of prominent chiefs, provide a net-work of settlements in which commerce can be located. Local trading towns have developed also in the White Highlands where a fully developed cash economy present opportunities for trade in a wide range of agricultural supplies and produce.[31]

The relationship between town and country in many peasant areas, however, is not always established through trade in the tertiary sector, but through a worker-peasant society which is occupied in small-scale town industry but which also farms in the surrounding rural area. Local manufacturing of agricultural implements, household necessities and clothing have long been essential to peasant economies, and so, in some regions, the peasant is also a town-based craftsman. Franklin has identified the worker-peasant phenomenon in parts of Europe where members of villages commute to the nearby small town in order to supplement their cash income.[32] This is the fundamental reason for town development in Yorubaland, in Nigeria, where 'small towns' are in fact large by world standards, containing up to 50,000 people. The major role of these places is as craft centres, but, as Bray has shown, as much as 80 per cent of the craftsmen also engage in farming. One of the reasons for this is that the Yoruba town is generally the product of a coalescence of villages and hamlets, and retains the low level of economic specialization and division of labour of the traditional village settlement.[33]

The North American small town has a somewhat different history, function and form compared with its Old World counterpart. In a sense it is a less complex settlement for the term 'small town' is very much a North American one and is used to describe the many commercial centres which serve rural populations. The small town was immediately essential to the expansion of rural settlement in North America.

The colonization and settlement of each new region depended upon the speedy establishment of strong local economies. In New England dispersal from early agricultural villages saw many of them become service centres for a scattered farm population. The spread of settlement along the Ohio Valley illustrates the early significance of the small town. Between 1800 and 1860 a network of 148 urban centres developed to service the frontier economy: entrepôt towns along the Ohio river, merchant and milling centres at the interior junctions of smaller streams and local roads, which were service centres for what must have been small hinterlands.[34] Similar developments have been described by Lemon in southeastern Pennsylvania during the eighteenth century when over 100 small urban places were founded. These, too, were service centres for an agricultural hinterland. As they grew and were incorporated they featured regular agricultural markets, shops, inns, and merchants who were a valuable source of capital for farmers as well as town businesses.[35]

The small town spread westwards as land on both sides of the US-Canadian border was gradually settled. But these nineteenth- and early twentieth-century places were smaller, more uniformly functional than the towns of the east and certainly those of Europe. One observer has suggested that the small town of the Canadian prairies is 'an incidental by-product of an economy dominated by farming'.[36] It is doubtful whether all such towns were merely by-products and certainly few that survived did so incidentally. Indeed we have considerable evidence that across much of rural North America, the type of small town which we are considering has depended upon a precise functional relationship with the surrounding rural population.

Much of the evidence for this comes from central-place studies which show how small towns serve local needs and do so in an hierarchical framework of settlement based upon various levels of service provision. Berry's study of rural Iowa reinforces this point. Within a radius of no more than eight miles and serving approximately 5,000 consumers each, smaller towns contained such activities as grocery, gas station, restaurant, post office, farm elevator, church, hardware store, bank, doctor, dentist and funeral parlour. Larger towns, the country seats, possessed in addition such activities as a liquor store, movie theatre, newspaper and car dealer.[37]

There is little doubt that many North American small towns manifest their small-scale commercialism in highly functional layouts and townscapes. This is true of even quite small places and is why what might otherwise be thought of as villages have an urban atmosphere which turns them into small towns. The commercial structure of Cannington, a small town in southern Ontario, is a typical illustration of this point. As Figure 3.4 shows, the orderly, straight main street contains a wide range of commercial outlets, evidence of the town's role as the functional service centre for the surrounding area.

Figure 3.4: Commercial Diversity on a Small Town Main Street: Cannington, Ontario

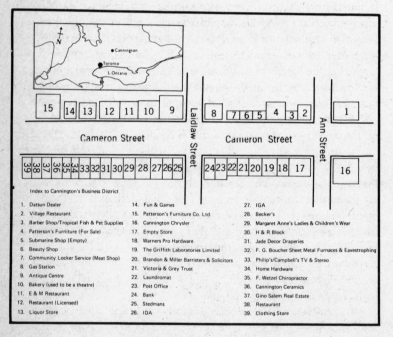

Index to Cannington's Business District

1. Datsun Dealer
2. Village Restaurant
3. Barber Shop/Tropical Fish & Pet Supplies
4. Patterson's Furniture (For Sale)
5. Submarine Shop (Empty)
6. Beauty Shop
7. Community Locker Service (Meat Shop)
8. Gas Station
9. Antique Centre
10. Bakery (used to be a theatre)
11. E & M Restaurant
12. Restaurant (Licensed)
13. Liquor Store
14. Fun & Games
15. Patterson's Furniture Co. Ltd.
16. Cannington Chrysler
17. Empty Store
18. Warners Pro Hardware
19. The Griffith Laboratories Limited
20. Brandon & Miller Barristers & Solicitors
21. Victoria & Grey Trust
22. Laundromat
23. Post Office
24. Bank
25. Stedmans
26. IDA
27. IGA
28. Becker's
29. Margaret Anne's Ladies & Children's Wear
30. H & R Block
31. Jade Decor Draperies
32. F. G. Boucher Sheet Metal Furnaces & Eavestrophing
33. Philip's/Campbell's TV & Stereo
34. Home Hardware
35. F. Wetzel Chiropractor
36. Cannington Ceramics
37. Gino Salem Real Estate
38. Restaurant
39. Clothing Store

Even smaller places can take on an urban air. Rees illustrates this in his study of small Saskatchewan towns whose chief functions have been the distribution of goods and the shipment of grain. The commercial street is central to the gridiron plan. The false fronts of the buildings, the grandiose design and the strategic location of the bank, the hotel and the church, exaggerate the metropolitan notions of these places. Yet the result is, as Rees says, 'a bleak and depressing environment'.[38] Optimo City, J.B. Jackson's imaginary but typical Midwest town, is:[39]

> The blur of filling stations and motels you occasionally pass; the solitary traffic light, the glimpse up a side street of an elephantine courthouse surrounded by elms and sycamores, the brief congestion of mud-spattered pickup trucks that slow you down before you hit the open road once more.

In the east, particularly in New England, small towns have a richer townscape because their local service function attracted entrepreneurs who often saw in the towns which they laid out metropolitan meccas for rural society. Impressive main streets, public buildings in imposing, frequently neo-classical styles, and graceful, tree-lined boulevards serve as a reminder that they are more than merely places to come for the groceries. Peirce Lewis sees such towns developing as 'havens against recalcitrant and often hostile country' and places which presented 'opportunities for economic betterment'.[40] In the competition to become the county seat, these towns used the commercial opportunities of an agricultural economy to establish an urban, mercantile middle class which was economically dependent upon but culturally distinct from rural society.

Notes

1. E.G. Bowen, 'The Dispersed Habitat of Wales', in R.H. Buchanan, E. Jones and D. McCourt (eds.), *Man and Habitat: Essays Presented to E.E. Evans* (London: Routledge and Kegan Paul, 1971), p. 70.

2. J.H. Johnson, 'The Development of the Rural Settlement Pattern of Ireland', *Geografiska Annaler*, Series B, Vol. XLIII (1961), pp. 165-73.

3. C.T. Smith, *An Historical Geography of Europe Before 1800*, pp. 287-92.

4. N. Ahmad, 'The Pattern of Rural Settlement in East Pakistan', *Geographical Review*, Vol. XLVI (1956), pp. 388-98.

5. K.B. Dickson, 'Nucleation and Dispersion of Rural Settlements in Ghana', *Ghana Social Science Journal*, Vol. 1 (1971), pp. 116-31.

6. W.B. Morgan, 'Farming Practice, Settlement Pattern and Population Density in South-Eastern Nigeria', *Geographical Journal*, Vol. 121 (1955), pp. 320-33.

7. R. Sellar, *A Scotsman in Upper Canada* (Toronto: Clarke, Irwin, 1969).

8. R.E. Dickenson, 'Dispersed Settlement in Southern Italy', *Erdkunde*, Vol. 10 (1956), pp. 282-97.

9. R.K. Udo, 'Disintegration of Nucleated Settlement in Eastern Nigeria', *Geographical Review*, Vol. 55 (1965), pp. 53-67.

10. A.L. Mabogunje, 'The Evolution of Rural Settlement in Egba Division, Nigeria', *Journal of Tropical Geography*, Vol. 13 (1959), pp. 65-80.

11. N. Long, *Social Change and the Individual* (Manchester: Manchester University Press, 1968), pp. 96-8.

12. W.J. Cowie, *Changing Settlement Systems and Economic Development in Zambia*, unpublished manuscript (Toronto, 1980).

13. A. Rapoport, *House Form and Culture* (Englewood Cliffs: Prentice-Hall, 1969).

14. M.W. Barley, *English Farmhouse and Cottage* (London: Routledge and Kegan Paul, 1961).

15. R.W. Brunskill, *Illustrated Handbook of Vernacular Architecture* (London: Faber and Faber, 1971).

16. Peter M. Ennals, 'Nineteenth-Century Barns in Southern Ontario', *Canadian Geographer*, Vol. 16 (1972), pp. 256-70; J.F. Hart, *The Look of the Land* (Englewood Cliffs: Prentice-Hall, 1975), pp. 115-36.

17. G.T. Trewartha, 'Some Regional Characteristics of American Farmsteads', *Annals*, Association of American Geographers, Vol. 38 (1948), pp. 169-225.

18. Wayne E. Kiefer, 'An Agricultural Settlement Complex in Indiana', *Annals*, the Association of American Geographers, Vol. 62 (1972), pp. 487-506.

19. John F. Lounsbury, 'Farmsteads in Puerto Rico and their Interpretive Value', *Geographical Review*, Vol. 45 (1955), pp. 347-58.

20. Ibid., p. 354.

21. John V. Punter, *Urbanites in the Countryside* (Unpublished Ph.D. thesis, University of Toronto, 1974).

22. G.T. Trewartha, 'The Unincorporated Hamlet: One Element of the American Settlement Fabric', *Annals*, Association of American Geographers, Vol. 33 (1943), pp. 32-81.

23. E. Gazaway, *The Longest Mile: the Forgotten People of an Appalachian Hollow* (New York: Doubleday, 1969).

24. Trewartha, 'Unincorporated Hamlet', p. 32.

25. A.B. Bose, 'Spatial Aspects of Rural Living', *Man in India*, Vol. 43(1) (1963), pp. 9-25.

26. N. Tuncdilek, 'Types of Rural Settlement and Their Characteristics', in P. Benedict, E. Tumertekur, and F. Mansur, *Turkey, Geographic and Social Perspective* (Leiden: Brill, 1974).

27. A. Beals, *Village Life in South India* (Chicago: Aldine, 1974), p. 87.

28. A.E. Smailes, *The Geography of Towns* (London: Hutchinson, 1964), pp. 19-21.

29. S. Wanmali, 'Rural Service Centres in India: Present Identification and the Acceptance of Extension', *AREA*, Vol. 7 (1975), pp. 167-70.

30. James C. Jackson, 'The Structure and Functions of Small Malaysian Towns', *Transactions of Institute of British Geographers*, Vol. 61 (1974), pp. 65-80.

31. W.T.W. Morgan, 'Urbanization in Kenya', *Transactions of the Institute of British Geographers*, Vol. 46 (1969), pp. 167-92.

32. S.H. Franklin, *The European Peasantry: the Final Phase* (London: Methuen, 1969).

33. J.M. Bray, 'The Craft Structure of a Traditional Yoruba Town', *Transactions of the Institute of British Geographers*, Vol. 46 (1969), pp. 179-93.

34. Edward K. Muller, 'Selective Urban Growth in the Middle Ohio Valley, 1800-1860', *Geographical Review*, Vol. 66 (1976), pp. 178-99.

35. James T. Lemon, *Best Poor Man's Country: A Geographical Study of Early Southeastern Pennsylvania* (Baltimore: John Hopkins Press, 1972), pp. 123-40.

36. Ronald Rees, 'The Small Towns of Saskatchewan', *Landscape*, Vol. 18 (1969), p. 29.

37. Brian J.L. Berry, *Geography of Market Centres and Retail Distribution* (Englewood Cliffs, NJ: Prentice-Hall, 1967), p. 15.

38. Rees, 'Small Towns', p. 31.

39. J.B. Jackson, *Landscapes: The Selected Writings of J.B. Jackson*, Edwin H. Zube (ed.) (Boston: University of Massachusetts Press, 1970), p. 116.

40. Peirce F. Lewis, 'Small Town in Pennsylvania', *Annals*, Association of American Geographers, Vol. 62 (1972), pp. 323-51.

4 PATTERNS

The emphasis in the previous two chapters is on the elements of rural settlement as separate components. Yet implicit in this is the recognition that the nature of these elements is influenced by their relationships, and, in turn has a significant effect upon settlement patterns. Indeed, the separation of the elements from the patterns of which they are a part is an essentially artificial one. Geographers in particular have stressed this by pursuing the study of settlement in spatial and regional contexts. The patterns of rural settlement are important, too, because they are an integral part of the rural landscape.

General Principles of Rural Settlement Patterns

Geographers have long been intrigued by the possibilities of establishing general principles for the explanation of spatial patterns. Settlement patterns in particular have been subject to considerable theoretical analysis. Theories of rural settlement are not numerous. Indeed, some consider rural patterns only as part of general settlement systems. Yet a few serious attempts have been made to recognize universal processes in the settlement of rural areas.

Early attempts at a theoretical analysis of rural settlement patterns grew out of the preoccupation of the nineteenth-century European geographers with the question of nucleated and dispersed settlement. Part of this, as we have seen, was concerned with explaining the reasons for village development. However, Meitzen's theories were aimed primarily at establishing a general explanation for the relative distribution in Europe of nucleated and dispersed forms. He suggested a direct relationship between the type of agricultural system and ethnic structure, which in turn determined the existence of nucleation or dispersal. Open-field cultivation was related to nucleation while dispersed patterns were associated with individual cultivation. He then traced the open-field village to Germanic influence and the independent farmstead to Celtic origin, adding, for good measure the effect of Slavonic culture on patterns in central and eastern Europe.[1]

Other attempts to establish a general explanation for the European pattern of rural settlement proposed the deterministic influence of field systems, defence and water supply. Yet, like Meitzen's theory, these failed to be generally applicable, even to the European pattern. There are two major reasons for this. Firstly the preoccupation with the dichotomy of nucleation and dispersal resulted in a failure to recognize that settlement patterns are much more complex. Secondly the early theories were essentially inductive in that they represented attempts to make explanatory generalizations from empirical observations.

Recent theories of rural settlement patterns are quite different in their approach. Firstly they are not preoccupied by dispersal and nucleation, but are concerned with the evolution of patterns in general. Secondly they have developed as part of modern spatial analysis and are therefore deductive approaches. There are two main types of theories which are relevant to the analysis of rural settlement patterns. The first are spatial equilibrium theories which set out to predict how, through competition for space, an optimal pattern of settlement will be achieved. The second group is that which examines the diffusion or spread of settlement across an area.

In North America in particular, spatial equilibrium theory has been widely used to explain the pattern of nucleated rural settlement. One of the main reasons for this is that the predominantly commercial service function of rural places conforms to the framework of the best developed of this type of theory, namely central-place theory. Christaller's work on settlement hierarchies and their spacing, supplemented by that of Lösch, aimed at devising a theory for regional settlement systems as a whole.[2] It therefore sees rural settlement as part of that system; which is one of its great strengths.

Its basic hypothesis is that competition between places for consumers will result in a hierarchy of central places which will in turn determine, through the size of their market areas, the spacing of settlements of different sizes. Rural places will be at the lower end of the hierarchy, each providing lower-order goods to smaller number of consumers within smaller market areas. Larger urban places will be successively higher on the hierarchy according to their ability to provide larger numbers of more widely dispersed consumers with higher-order goods and services. The optimal pattern of the various levels of central places is achieved by an hexagonal arrangement of market areas in which suppliers of goods and services maximize their profits and consumers minimize their costs. Rural places will therefore be located at optimal efficiency for a dispersed rural population.

Empirical tests of central-place theory are depressingly numerous, and, given the nature of much of North American rural settlement, it is hardly surprising that most support for the theory comes from studies on this continent. It is to the generally regular arrangement of small places in the Midwest and on the prairies that central-place theory is particularly appropriate. Here the supply of goods and services to an evenly dispersed agricultural population comes closest to the theory's assumptions. Thus Brush, in his study in southwestern Wisconsin, identified a three-tier hierarchy of hamlets, villages and towns with a spatial distribution which revealed close correspondence with the theory.[3] Berry's detailed investigation of consumer behaviour in Iowa indicated three similar levels of centres which formed a pattern resulting from a hierarchy of regularly spaced centres.[4]

One of the problems of central-place theory is that it assumes a modern commercial economy and considers rural settlements as part of the whole settlement system. How relevant is it in those great regions of peasant rural society? Skinner's important study of the spatial organization of traditional Chinese peasant society suggests that it conformed to central-place principles. It did so through a system of periodic markets which moved from village to village and town to town on a regular basis. Thus the settlement pattern was organized around a hierarchy of commercial and cultural centres which had achieved an equilibrium through centuries of tradition.[5]

Yet Skinner's research does not mean that central-place theory can be adapted in the same way for all peasant areas. The theory also assumes a pre-existing, evenly distributed dispersed population, and it presupposes that rational consumer behaviour is the primary factor influencing the settlement pattern. To overcome the problems of these assumptions, Siddle has proposed an alternative equilibrium solution based upon an adaptation of Von Thünen's land use model.[6] He begins with the assumption of a small subsistence village whose inhabitants cultivate the surrounding land. According to Thünian theory, activities demanding the most labour input will normally be situated closest to the settlement, those demanding less attention will be further away and the limit of village territory will be defined by the economic radius of subsistence farming.[7] With an increase in population other settlements will be established, the spacing of which will be determined by the equilibrium of boundaries of village territories. Continued population increase will reduce the regular arrangement of population envisaged by central-place theory. The notion of the spacing of subsistence villages through the demarcation of agricultural territories is logically sound. Unfortunately Siddle's own testing of his hypothesis in Sierra Leone was largely inconclusive. The main problem is that any tendency towards regularity has been broken down by recent social and economic changes, and existing patterns cannot be made to fit the theory.

Attempts to understand rural settlement patterns in terms of spatial equilibrium theory are therefore of limited value. This has been recognized by a number of scholars who have seen the need to examine the process by which settlement diffuses or spreads across a region from the initial point of colonization. Bylund has proposed, within a deterministic framework, a set of hypothetical models of settlement diffusion, based upon his study of colonization in central Lappland before 1867.[8] Waves of settlement move, as shown in the models in Figure 4.1 from mother settlements, the areas close to these settlements being settled first. The difference between the four models A to D is in the number and location of mother settlements. Settlement therefore proceeds by a number of stages, the location of each settlement being determined by the location of those of earlier stages of development.

A similar concern with the spread of settlement forms the basis of Hudson's work, which is the only attempt to develop a definitive theory of rural settlement.[9] The theory aims to explain changes in settlement distribution over time. Like Bylund's models, Hudson's theory recognizes one of the major limitations of central-place theory, that of the assumption of an *a priori*, even distribution of dispersed farms. He postulates a series of spatial processes similar to those identified in plant ecology. In these there are three phases: (i) colonization which involves the dispersal of settlement into new territory; (ii) spread in which increasing population density creates settlement clusters and eventual pressure on the physical and social environment; and (iii) competition, which produces regularity in the settlement pattern in the manner suggested by central-place theory. Empirical testing of these hypotheses over a 90-year period (1870-1960) in six Iowa counties showed that regularity in the spacing of settlements did increase with time. This led Hudson to suggest the appropriateness of his theory to areas where regular spacing occurs without any external planning.

Limitations of Theoretical Approaches

Despite the various theories that have been proposed, little real progress has been made towards the establishment of general principles of rural settlement patterns. There are certain limitations with specific theories. Central-place theory is appropriate only to the analysis of the distribution of rural service centres; the diffusion approaches consider only the question of how settlement spreads across the land. Yet there are more fundamental reasons for suspecting the value of existing normative

Figure 4.1: Bylund's Model of Settlement Diffusion

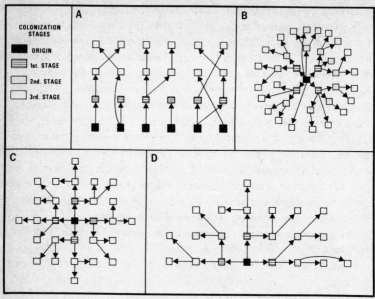

Adapted from Erik Bylund, 'Theoretical Considerations Regarding the Distribution of Settlement in Inner North Sweden', *Geografiska Annaler*, Vol. XLII (1960).

concepts. The first of these lies in the highly diversified nature of settlement evolution. So theory tends to be developed within specified regional and temporal contexts. With Grossman and Birch we can claim that Hudson's theory is neither appropriate beyond Iowa, nor even necessarily useful to understanding patterns there.[10] As Birch has shown, the position of the farmstead in Iowa was determined by its location within the farmholding. This was selected in a manner that seemed suitable to the settler's domestic and operational needs. A more serious limitation of existing theory lies in its assumption that, as a result of free economic, biological or random processes, patterns will achieve a regularity which reflects a rational use of space. In reality, where regular patterns of rural settlement have developed it has frequently been the result of conscious planning rather than of automatic adjustments towards optimality of location. Furthermore, most settlement patterns are far from regular in their spatial arrangement or normative in the manner of their evolution.

Because no general theory of rural settlement has been developed, this does not mean that some of the theoretical proposals have failed to produce some useful ideas about settlement patterns. Like most theories, their main value lies in being able to suggest the basic variables which can influence the spatial arrangement of settlement. This is particularly true of central-place theory which isolates the variables which determine the competitive relationships between places. This is of increasing importance in areas where rural settlements have become part of the whole urban system. And, despite its limitations, Siddle's notion of the relationship between the efficient use of agricultural land and settlement spacing identifies the significance of land use variables in settlement patterns. In fact, Chisholm's extensive investigation of the impact of distance upon agricultural land use includes a number of examples of village and dispersed patterns which are strongly influenced by the effect of distance from farmstead to field. This led Chisholm to the general hypothesis that the spacing of settlements is determined by the distance that peasant cultivators are prepared to travel to farm their land.[11]

An Idiographic Approach to Rural Settlement Patterns

It is sheer variety in rural settlement landscapes which has frustrated attempts to establish general explanatory principles. This suggests that while existing theory may permit generalization, it prevents a detailed understanding of the differences between rural landscapes in time and space. The alternative approach to normative analysis must therefore be idiographic: one in which the factors influencing settlement patterns are examined in the context of specific cases. This approach is central to the traditions of historical and cultural geography. Its great weakness lies in its inability to permit more than intuitive generalizations. Its great strength is that it recognizes that settlement is the result of particular decisions taken at particular times and places in particular cultural contexts. Clearly, to understand the essence of the idiographic concept we must do so within specific regional frameworks. So in the following pages the development of rural settlement patterns in a number of different areas is examined.

Southeastern Pennsylvania in the Eighteenth Century

The characteristic pattern of rural settlement along much of the eastern seaboard of the United States is that of an irregular arrangement of farmsteads, hamlets, villages and towns. This pattern is the result of the adaptation of the ideals and objectives of the early settlers to local conditions. It is particularly well illustrated in southeast Pennsylvania, the early settlement of which has been documented by Lemon.[12]

Penn's original plans for settlement were for an orderly scheme in which townships would be dominated by agricultural villages organized along almost manorial lines. Yet the general pattern of rural settlement that developed after 1700 represents a direct rejection of Penn's philosophy, by settlers who held a quite different view of the New World. Their ideology was an independent, liberal one which represented a desire to break away from the already declining authority of the European village. Some groups, such as the Quakers, had religious reasons for avoiding Penn's villages, but most settlers saw both economic and social advantages in living at the centre of their newly acquired land. Society in eighteenth-century Pennsylvania was pluralistic and individualistic. This led to a steady process of irregular dispersal of settlement, much of it involving squatting and land speculation, in which settlement preceded the official survey.

While these ideological factors had a strong influence on the establishment of an irregular dispersed pattern of settlement, two other factors determined the spatial arrangement of dispersed elements. Firstly, in the occupation of land, settlers showed a strong tendency to congregate along ethnic, national and religious lines. These created focal points of settlement from which subsequent settlement extended. Yet there was an overlap of various groups in many areas and it is clear that local environmental circumstances played a stronger role in creating the detailed settlement mosaic. The quality of land was certainly a consideration for the ambitious settler and this influenced the size and shape of farms and therefore the spatial arrangement of farmsteads. Many settlers initially sought out the better lands of areas like the Lancaster Plain with its gently rolling relief and fertile soil, and avoided the hilly tracts. But accessibility to water supply had a stronger influence on the particular location of farmsteads. Lots were often located first along streams so as to avoid the digging of wells. Lemon, however, stresses that the availability of land at various times was probably more important than its physical aspects. So farmers located next to already occupied sites, near neighbours, markets and water, and allowed the quality of land to have its own effect.

The impact of these factors in the early settlement of Pennsylvania remains clearly imprinted on the present-day patterns of rural settlement (Figure 4.2). The irregular distribution of farmsteads and hamlets, the preference for sites on valley terraces, along rivers, and resultant

Figure 4.2: Settlement Patterns in Lancaster County, Pennsylvania

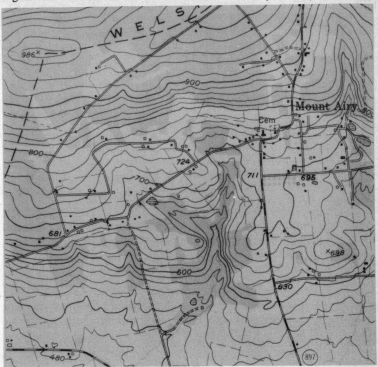

Source: US Geological Survey, Topographic Series, New Holland Quadrangle, scale, 1:24,000.

complexities in the configuration of roads, is in sharp contrast to the patterns which occur to the west of the Appalachians.

Settlement and the Survey System in the Midwest

The most striking feature of the pattern of settlement in the rural Midwest of the United States is its regularity. This might suggest that it is a pattern which can be explained by some of the theoretical frameworks which were discussed earlier. Yet the major influence on all settlement west of the Appalachians is the survey system. The settlement patterns in the Midwest reflect the government's desire for order and equity in the occupation of new land. Land division proceeded according to the township and range system. The standard scheme was a township of six miles (9.6 kilometres) square, subdivided into square mile sections, which were then further reduced to quarter sections of 160 acres (64 hectares) and quarter quarters of 40 acres (16 hectares). The actual pattern of land holdings is more complex, yet the development of settlement through the nineteenth century involved a remorseless spread of an orderly grid across the land. This grid deviated from the points of the compass only when it was adjusted to roads, railroads and streams.

More detailed studies of the effect of this on settlement patterns have been carried out in Indiana by Hart and Kiefer.[13] Hart indicates that within the general survey framework, the spatial arrangement of farmsteads was determined primarily by the size of holdings new settlers could afford to buy. As population increased its pressure on land through the early nineteenth century, the minimal mandatory purchase unit was reduced to 80, and in some cases 40, acres. This obviously had a significant effect on the distribution of farmsteads and on the density of rural settlement. In Rush County, Indiana, for example, Kiefer found that most of the land was purchased in 80 acre tracts. This is in contrast to the situations on the Great Plains where the 160 acre farms provided under the later free land grants have resulted in a lower density of dispersed settlement.

The physical environment has had some influence on the pattern of settlement, but only at the local level, in that the selection of farmstead sites has been strongly influenced by drainage conditions and local topography. However, in general terms, environmental factors have operated only to facilitate a wide range of choice in agricultural productivity. This has led to an intense commercialism and efficiency amongst the farming population. It has also meant that the agricultural economy has had a significant influence on the evolution of farm settlement. This has been admirably illustrated by Hart's comparison of the patterns of different farming-type areas.[14] The corn-hog farming areas of the eastern Middle West tend to be occupied by small farms with simple farmsteads. This reflects the persistence of the original settlement pattern with six to eight farmsteads per square mile and an average farm size of 80 to 100 acres. In contrast, the corn-cattle-hog areas to the west contain large, complex farmsteads, and because of large farm size have only about four farmsteads per square mile. The basic grid of the survey system, then, was adapted to local circumstances and the needs of individual farmers. The diversification of economy and society added further elements to the landscape, including small towns and villages, usually located at the crossroads and conforming to the regularity of the grid. This is illustrated by the example from Illinois in Figure 4.3, which reveals a pattern reflected in much of the present-day rural Middle West.

Figure 4.3: Grid Pattern of Rural Settlement, Illinois

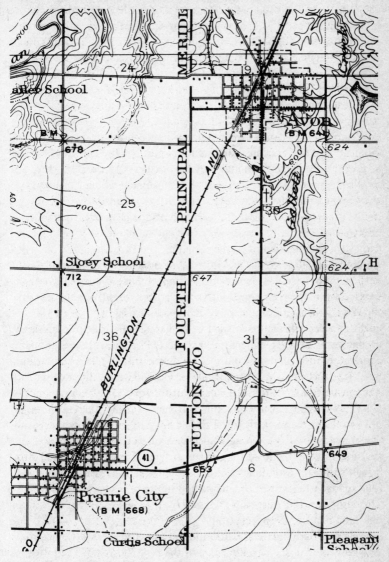

Source: US Geological Survey, Topographical Series, Avon Sheet, scale, 1:24,000.

Settlement and Conflict in Corsica

The history of rural settlement in Corsica is, like many other parts of the Mediterranean, a tormented one. Thompson has examined in detail the interrelationships between the factors which have influenced the settled landscape.[15] The most important single influence on the settlement pattern has been concern for defence and security. In Thompson's words, 'A history of almost incessant conflict has led Corsicans to evaluate terrain and land resources in a manner consistent with maximum security of settlement sites from both internal and external attack.'[16]

Yet the problem of security has been fostered by a combination of physical, economic and social circumstances. The role of the physical environment is evident in the difference between the settlement conditions of the crystalline mountains which occupy two-thirds of the island, and the folded mountains of the northeastern quarter. The crystalline mountains present a harsh environment which confines movement to the narrow valleys, and limits the availability of fertile soil. A pastoral economy therefore has been the basis of settlement, and this has tended to encourage group and family independence. The mountainous relief led to further isolation and the patriarchial society perpetuated village rivalry and mistrust of outsiders. The resulting settlement pattern was one of large, compact villages, located where terrain permitted their construction and with a careful eye for security.

The northeastern mountain system presents a less hostile environment, but deep dissection has led to similar isolation of communities as in the west. However, Italian influence in the northeast has resulted in a more developed economy and society. Furthermore, this is the chestnut zone (the Castagniccia). The high density of villages in this area reflects the previous importance of the chestnut for food, construction and tannin. While the density of settlement may be higher than in the hostile mountains of the west, the rural settlement pattern of the whole island is dominated by large, strongly nucleated villages. Thompson traces this to three factors: the need for security from attack, for communal effort in self-sufficient economies and the extended family basis of society. The spatial arrangement of villages undoubtedly has been influenced by the desire for a defensive site, but also by the need to obtain maximum insolation and good spring water.

The peculiarly isolated distribution of Corsican rural settlement has been reflected in the developments of the past 200 years. The introverted, subsistent village society had the effect of preventing the development of market towns, and urban growth was restricted to the coastal areas. The result has been steady depopulation of the rural areas and the decline and often abandonment of villages.

Cultural Transfer and Adaptation in Quebec

The early settlement of North America involved the transfer of a number
of cultural influences: Spanish in Florida and the southwest, Dutch in
the Hudson Valley, English on the eastern seaboard, and French in
Louisiana and Quebec. The most durable of these influences in terms
of the present-day settlement pattern is that of the French settlement
of the lower St. Lawrence lowlands in Quebec.

The distinctively linear arrangement of settlement in this region, can
be understood only by examining the early history of its settlement. It
was first occupied by the French in the early seventeenth century and
it was their system of land division and the way that it was adapted to
the particular conditions of the St. Lawrence Lowlands which has had
the greatest influence on the present-day pattern. Initially, the French
crown decided to settle New France by granting land to *seigneurs* (lords)
according to the French feudal system. However, as Harris has shown in
his classic study, the seigneurial system was not transferred intact to
New France.[17] The independence of the *habitants*, the general poverty
of the *seigneurs*, and the pioneer environment of the St. Lawrence
limited the social and economic influence of the *seigneurs*. Yet the
method of land division which accompanied the seigneurial system did
have a fundamental impact upon the settlement pattern.

The land division system was cadastral and based upon the long-lot
rôture, or parcel, which, conventionally, was 20 to 40 hectares in size
and approximately rectangular in width. The rôtures were to be laid out
along the rivers and then in parallel rows behind them, as shown in
Figure 4.4. In reality, the general pattern of rôtures conformed to this
model, but rôtures quickly amalgamated, and tributary streams and
stretches of infertile land interrupted the regular arrangement of long,
narrow land parcels. Nevertheless, allowing for these distortions, the
system resulted in a relatively even dispersal of farmsteads along river
frontages, and later along the roads which demarcated the subsequent
rows of long-lots (Figure 4.5). The cadastral system and the shape of
the land parcels encouraged the regular dispersal of settlement, while
the narrow strips of fertile land along the St. Lawrence and its
tributaries resulted in the strongly linear pattern. Villages did not
develop to any great extent, despite the wishes of the authorities, for
the habitants immediately saw the benefits of independent settlement,
particularly when illegal participation in the fur trade offered useful
remuneration.

By the time of the British conquest, the basic settlement framework

Figure 4.4: Typical Survey Pattern, Quebec

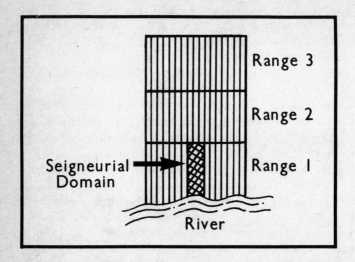

had been established. During the nineteenth century the orientation and dimensions of lots and rows became more or less standardized. Increased commercialism in agriculture and a growing rural population became the main factors in the pattern of rural settlement. The long-lot remained the skeleton of the pattern, but with successive generations subdivisions of rôtures has been widespread. In addition, the growth of the grain trade during the nineteenth century led to more affluence in agriculture. This encouraged the appearance of villages and hamlets as service centres. It is likely, too, that village development was influenced by the formalization of parishes which increased the social role of the church in rural Quebec. A few villages were laid out in compact form, but most followed the existing dispersed pattern and became the straggling linear settlements which are the predominant element in Quebec.

Environment and Village Siting in northeast England

At the local level, or micro-scale of analysis, the spatial arrangement of settlements is usually the result of decisions which have been taken in the past over the choice of settlement site. An interesting example of where this has had a strong influence in the rural landscape is in the Vale of Pickering in Yorkshire, northeast England.

The Vale of Pickering is a wide, relatively flat valley which is bounded by two high escarpments to the north and south. It is covered by alluvial and lacustrine post-glacial deposits, and is therefore badly drained

Figure 4.5: Farmstead Pattern in Contemporary Quebec

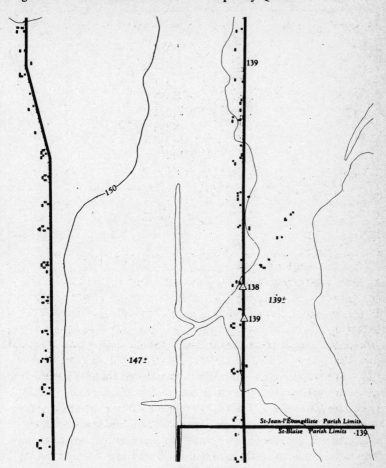

Source: Canada, National Topographic Series, scale, 1:24,000.

except by artificial means. The early settlement history of the Vale
involved the gradual formation of villages during the period of Anglian
and Scandinavian influence of the eighth and ninth centuries. There is
evidence that many villages conform to a standard layout and were
therefore planned. If this is so, then serious thought would have been
given to the selection of settlement sites.

In Figure 4.6 the arrangement of villages in relation to topography
and drainage is clearly shown. In fact considerations of relief, drainage

Figure 4.6: Village Siting in the Vale of Pickering, Northeast England

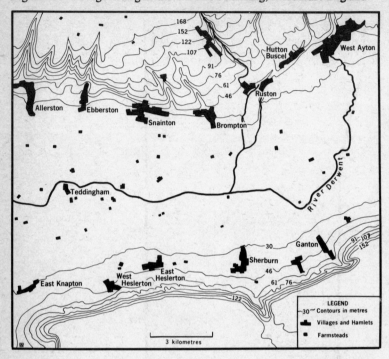

and water supply were dominant factors in the choice of village site in the Vale. An important concern in the construction of villages would have been the availability of fairly level land. Villages therefore avoided the steep slopes of the southern edge of the Vale and the heavily dissected slopes to the north. But the problem of water appears to have been a more fundamental constraint. Firstly, a fresh, regular water supply was a prime necessity and the only source of this was from the springs and, to a lesser extent, small streams which appear at the geological junctions of the escapements and the Vale. Indeed most villages are spring-line settlements sited at the point where steep slopes change fairly abruptly to the relatively flat land of the Vale. A second problem with water was the marshy, badly drained nature of the Vale itself. Villages therefore avoided this land, particularly because of its tendency to flood and the unsavoury quality of its water supply.

This combination of factors produced a line of villages on each edge of the Vale of Pickering. An added advantage of their locations comes from the availability to each village of land both in the Vale and on the slopes and tops of the bordering escarpments. Being on convenient lines of east-west communication also helped to fix villages at or near their original sites. The modern settlement pattern has involved the extension of villages along the edges of the Vale, but intense inertia reveals the importance of original site decisions in determining even present-day locations.

While the pattern of village settlement reflects the impact of early locational decisions, the arrangement of dispersed farmsteads illustrates how important economic and social events can lead to alternative responses to the physical environment. The impetus for the dispersal of farmsteads which came from the enclosure movements led in many areas of Britain to the reclamation of both moorland and marshland. So in the Vale of Pickering, the possibility of enclosure in the eighteenth century terminated the avoidance of the marshy lowlands and led to major drainage schemes which permitted both settlement and farming across the width of the valley. And on the hill land above the villages, moorland and common pasture was enclosed and occupied, particularly to the north by small, isolated hill farms.

Factors and History in Settlement Patterns

While an idiographic approach recognizes the importance of uniqueness in the development of settlement patterns, this does not prevent some generalizations being made about the factors which influence these patterns. Indeed the examination of regional and local settlement patterns indicates the prevalence of certain factors. Cultural influences play perhaps the strongest role. The way in which society is organized; its ideals, its objectives and its traditions determine the forms of settlement organization and the systems of land division. This occurs through both institutional and individual decisions. Insofar as they are distinct from the culture of society, economic factors play a role, largely through the central significance of agricultural land use. The system, relative commercialism of agriculture and the type of farming affect the size and distribution of farms, the spacing of service centres and the density of rural population. Variations in agricultural land use are influenced by the physical environment, which also has a strong effect on the detailed spatial arrangement of settlement.

However, we should be wary of predicting a deterministic role for these factors, for it is clear that the ways in which they influence settlement patterns vary according to local conditions and the impact of

historical events. In some cases the settlement pattern is affected by
one powerful influence at a particular period in time. One good
example of this is the impact of communist ideology on the reorganization of rural Soviet Union. The patterns which have resulted from
this reflect the trend towards economic rationalization of settlement in
rural USSR and the steady enlargement of collective and state farm
settlements.[18] Another quite different example is the impact of sudden
population pressure in eastern Nigeria, which has led to what one
observer has described as a 'mad scramble for land'.[19] The resultant
landscape is one of a dense pattern of dispersed homesteads and the
disintegration of traditional nucleation.[20]

Yet population pressure and political ideology occur in particular
regional and temporal contexts. Soviet collectivization principles have
been adapted to regional variations in environment and land use; population pressure led to massive dispersal in Nigeria because of the nature
of the traditional structure and recent opportunities for commercial
agriculture; the effects of the survey system continue to underlie the
settlement patterns of Indiana but have been altered by agricultural
modernization in Nebraska.

In many areas, rural landscapes are the result of even more complex
adaptations to local conditions. The transfer of similar ideas on
centralized settlement and land use from Europe to North America
produced different patterns in Quebec and Pennsylvania. In Quebec
the particular land division system of the *seigneuries* paradoxically
encouraged the rejection of village settlement. But dispersal would not
have occurred simply because of the long-lot pattern. The character of
the *habitants*, the poverty of the *seigneurs*, the value of involvement
in the fur trade, the importance of the rivers for transportation, the
very isolation of the region, combined to create the rural landscape of
New France. In Pennsylvania, the fierce rejection of village settlement
led to dispersal but with a quite different pattern to that of Quebec.
This was partly because land beyond the initial settlements was not
subject to a pre-settlement survey, but also because the cultural backgrounds of the settlers made them ambitious for success, and a congenial
physical environment permitted considerable freedom in the occupation
of unsurveyed land.

This brings us back to the notion of uniqueness: that settlement patterns
are the product of the area which they occupy. This view is most
relevant at the local level. Rural settlement on Corsica reveals special
interrelationships of factors. The clannish and isolated nature of village
communities has caused, but in turn has been intensified by, a concern

for security. Yet the mountainous terrain must have accentuated isolation and insecurity, as well as providing settlement sites which were naturally defensible. The location of the island in a region of long-term instability added to its unique situation. The example of the Vale of Pickering illustrates, too, how cultural and economic determinants of settlement can be constrained in such a way that settlement patterns directly reflect the natural features of the area.

This approach to the study of rural settlement patterns is one which accepts the concept of the cultural landscape. In this, present-day patterns are seen as a palimpsest or series of layers of the past, which is composed of decisions and events which have taken place within a particular regional context. Sauer called this landshaping and argued that the explanation for a particular human landscape lay in its history.[21] Harris has recently taken this view further and argued for the central importance of what he terms the 'historical mind' in the interpretation of processes which have created settled landscapes.[22]

Notes

1. A. Meitzen, *Siedlung und Agrarwesen der Wesgermanen und Ostergermanen*, Vol. 1 (Berlin), 1895.

2. For a full explanation of Christaller's central-place theory and its modern applications see, B.J.L. Berry, *The Geography of Market Centres and Retail Distribution* (Englewood Cliffs, NJ: Prentice-Hall, 1967).

3. J.E. Brush, 'The Hierarchy of Central Places in Southwestern Wisconsin', *Geographical Review*, Vol. 43 (1953), pp. 380-402.

4. Berry, *Market Centres*, pp. 5-23.

5. G.W. Skinner, 'Marketing and Social Structure in Rural China', *Journal of Asian Studies*, Vol. 34 (1964), pp. 3-43.

6. D.J. Siddle, 'Location Theory and the Subsistence Economy: the Spacing of Rural Settlements in Sierra Leone', *Journal of Tropical Geography*, Vol. 31 (1970), pp. 79-90.

7. For a detailed account of Von Thünen's theory see P. Hall (ed.), *Von Thunen's Isolated State* (New York: Pergamon, 1966).

8. Erik Bylund, 'Theoretical Considerations Regarding the Distribution of Settlement in Inner North Sweden', *Geografiska Annaler*, Vol. XLII (1960), pp. 225-31.

9. J.H. Hudson, 'A Location Theory for Rural Settlement', *Annals*, Association of American Geographers, Vol. 59 (1969), pp. 365-82.

10. Birch and Grossman have criticized Hudson's theory on a number of counts: B.P. Birch, 'On a Theory for Rural Settlement', *Annals of Assoc. of American Geography*, Vol. 60 (1970), pp. 610-13; and D. Grossman, 'Do We Have a Theory for Settlement Geography? The Case of Iboland', *The Professional Geographer*, Vol. 23 (1971), pp. 197-203.

11. M. Chisholm, *Rural Settlement and Land Use: An Essay in Location* (London: Hutchinson, 1962), pp. 43-67.

12. James T. Lemon, *The Best Poor Man's Country* (Baltimore: Johns Hopkins Press, 1972), pp. 42-70 and 98-117.

13. J. Fraser Hart, 'The American Mid-West', *Annals, Assoc. of American Geographers*, Vol. 62 (1972), pp. 258-82; and Wayne E. Kiefer, *Rush County; a Study in Rural Settlement Geography*, Geographic Monograph Series, Vol. 2 (Dept. of Geography, Indiana University, Bloomington, 1969).

14. Hart, 'The Mid-West', pp. 269-71.

15. I.B. Thompson, 'Settlement and Conflict in Corsica', *Transactions of Institute of British Geographers*, Vol. 3 (1978), pp. 259-73.

16. Thompson, 'Corsica', p. 259.

17. R.C. Harris, *The Seigneurial System in Early Canada* (Madison: Wisconsin University Press, 1966).

18. S.A. Kovalev, 'Transformation of Rural Settlements in the Soviet Union', *Geoforum*, Vol. 9-12 (1972), pp. 33-45.

19. A.L. Mabogunje, 'The Evolution of Rural Settlement in Egba Division, Nigeria', *Journal of Tropical Geography*, Vol. 13 (1959), pp. 65-80.

20. R.K. Udo, 'Disintegration of Nucleated Settlement in Eastern Nigeria', *Geographical Review*, Vol. 55 (1965), pp. 53-67.

21. C.O. Sauer, *Land and Life* (Berkeley: University of California Press, 1965).

22. Cole Harris, 'The Historical Mind and the Practice of Geography', in David Ley and Marwyn S. Samuels, *Humanistic Geography* (Chicago: Maroufa Press, 1978), pp. 123-37.

5 STAGNATION AND DECLINE

The evolutionary interpretation of rural settlement in the previous chapters recognized the importance of long-term trends and adjustments to social, economic and environmental conditions. Throughout the history of rural settlement persistent continuity in elements and patterns has co-existed with major and often quite sudden changes. This situation continues today with the result that some of the world's rural settlements are dominated by traditional structures while others are undergoing radical transformations.

However, recent history has seen a radical shift in urban-rural relationships caused by the increasing concentration of power and wealth in urban centres and industrial enterprises. With the acceleration of this trend in the post-war era, change in rural settlements has taken on dimensions and characteristics which are in many ways quite different from previous developments. In a predominantly urban world, rural areas and communities have been infiltrated and often transformed by modern, industrial society. Some have benefited from this and remained in the economic and social mainstream. Others have not been fully absorbed into the urban sphere, and have fallen behind the material growth of metropolitan culture.

This chapter deals with the problems created by the inability of many rural communities to match urban growth rates. This has resulted in widespread stagnation and decline in rural settlements, which is both relative and absolute. In the first part of the chapter we shall examine the symptoms of this in general terms, indicating the problems common to many rural areas. Then we shall discuss the main causes of these problems in the context of the particular circumstances of stagnating and declining rural settlements and regions.

General Symptoms

In the analysis of rural stagnation and decline it is difficult to distinguish between symptoms and causes. As processes, both growth and decline tend to be self-perpetuating: symptoms have effects which generate further symptoms. This circularity has been widely recognized in rural areas in which the 'vicious circle of poverty' is seen to be particularly problematical. The logic of the downward spiral is simple yet realistic. Low incomes and limited employment opportunities weaken the community infrastructure and lead to reductions in local investment and to the exodus of population. This causes further decline in economic, social and demographic structure and a slide further down the spiral. The most direct symptoms and, at the same time, causes are personal and institutional poverty, economic and community limitations in many rural settlements which are cast in stark contrast to the growth opportunities of the cities. Direct results are decay in physical structures and facilities, and depopulation.

There are, however, complications to this scenario, for stagnation and decline can be selective rather than general. Thus poverty, whether it be urban or rural, is notorious for affecting only certain groups in society. But hardship can exist for one sector of a rural settlement while at the same time the settlement as a whole may be supported by the prosperity of another. This is characteristic of what has happened to many farming areas of the United States. The departure of the poorer members of agricultural society has coincided with a great expansion in the size and affluence of the remaining enterprises. Certainly the great loss of population has led to the contraction and abandonment of farmsteads and other settlements. Yet one could hardly claim that the Corn Belt was poor as a consequence. Another complication is that stagnation and decline in certain elements of settlement structure need not be accompanied by depopulation and general economic decay. The best example of this is where rural services contract, while an active population remains because it can satisfy its retail and cultural needs in nearby urban centres.

In considering the symptoms of stagnation and decline, therefore, we should conceive of them operating in two ways. Firstly, interdependently and circularly so as to reflect the general deterioration of communities and regions, and, secondly, as independent symptoms which involve decline in only certain aspects of settlement.

Economic Symptoms

Poverty is regarded by many observers as a widespread problem in rural settlements. In 1964 rural poverty in one of the world's most affluent countries was considered to be so serious that a presidential commission was established to examine it. The commission reported in 1967 that rural poverty in the United States was widespread and that most of the rural south was 'one vast poverty area'.[1] In Canada, a report to a Senate Committee on poverty has claimed that 'the greatest incidence of poverty

and the highest percent of poverty is definitely found in rural areas'.[2]
Of rural poverty in the underdeveloped world, Ahluwalia has written:
'The basic fact that the poor are disproportionately located in the rural
areas and are engaged in agriculture or allied rural occupations is well
established in conventional wisdom and easily verified.'[3] He estimates
that 56 per cent of the Asian and 47 per cent of the African population
have annual *per capita* incomes below an arbitrarily established poverty
line of $75 US, and that at least 70 per cent of this group live in rural
areas. A World Bank study has proposed an annual income equivalent of
$50 *per capita* as one below which even minimum standards of nutrition,
shelter and personal amenities cannot be maintained. In all underdeveloped
countries with populations of more than one million it is estimated that
85 per cent of those living below this level occupy rural areas.[4]

This is a view which sees poverty in absolute terms, as a state of
deprivation in which the basic necessities of life cannot be secured.
However, any measure of deficiencies in nutrition, clothing, shelter,
sanitation, education, and so on, is necessarily arbitrary. Minimum
levels of income will vary according to levels of economic, social and
political development, and even with personal circumstances. For
example, median poverty level for a family of four in the United States
in 1977 was $6,191.[5] If this was applied to many rural areas elsewhere
it would represent a staggeringly high income.

There can be little doubt that rural poverty is real and, in many
areas, endemic. However, for the purposes of analysis, it is probably
better to see it as a relative condition in which poverty changes its
dimensions with the changes in the expectations of society as a whole.
In the context of rural poverty, this is best expressed by the concept
of rural-urban disparity, in which rural people are classified as poor
simply because they are at the bottom of the economic heap.

The use of income levels to measure economic disparity between
rural and urban areas involves a number of problems. Firstly, income
statistics are not readily comparable at the global scale because they are
not available for all countries in the same years, nor are they based
upon similar earning units. Secondly, the distribution of income between
urban and rural populations will depend very much upon how these
groups are defined. Thirdly, cost of living variations affect the compar-
ability of incomes. Finally, rural cash income is often supplemented by
non-cash items which are not measured in monetary terms.

The comparison of rural and urban incomes is based therefore on
crude measures. Yet there is general agreement that average rural
incomes in most regions of the world fall below those of urban

populations. In the United States, for example, the average income of
metropolitan households in 1977 was $14,611, while that for non-
metropolitan households was $11,861.[6] In Canada the gap was wider,
for in 1971 average annual income for males over 15 was $4,857 for
rural and $7,050 for urban areas.[7] Studies of the distribution of income
across populations have shown the disproportionate concentration of
the lowest income groups as well as lower average incomes in rural areas.
In much of the world the concentration of economic growth in the
urban sector has resulted in great income disparities between agricultural
and non-agricultural populations. Even in a relatively affluent country
like Venezuela the average income in the large cities is two to three
times that in rural areas which depend upon traditional agriculture.[8]

Low incomes in both wages and the net returns of farmers and
entrepreneurs are serious impediments to the development of a local
economy. A major economic problem in many rural communities is the
low level of consumption and investment. This is the direct result of low
incomes and a low propensity to save which tends to perpetuate
economic limitations. This is often accompanied by limited employment
opportunities which ensure the continued depression of incomes.

Unemployment in the agricultural sector has been a persistent
problem, particularly in industrialized regions. In the United States, for
example, since 1950 it has stood at around twice the level of total
unemployment.[9] The declining demand for farm labour has led also to
unemployment amongst the non-farm rural population. In some areas
unemployment is not as serious a problem as underemployment and
lack of alternative employment opportunities. Indeed employment and
freedom from poverty for many rural people are by no means
synonymous. Seasonal fluctuations in employment are a major
problem for rural people and in the United States there is 'evidence that
underemployment is widespread in rural areas, and is as acute a problem
as unemployment'.[10] The rate of underemployment estimated in 1960
was 18.3 per cent for all employed rural residents, with the highest
rates, 36 per cent, amongst rural farm residents.[11]

Problems of Community Infrastructure

A recurrent theme in the study of rural settlement problems is stagnation
and decline in community infrastructure. In some ways, this is a more
widespread phenomenon than poverty and low incomes, for the
reduction in economic, social and institutional services is not associated
only with poor rural areas. It is a process, which can be a symptom of
general decline and stagnation or of deterioration in only certain sectors

of a rural community. Three main infrastructural elements are affected: local trades and industries, institutional facilities and social and cultural services.

The closing of the general store, the blacksmith's shop, even the village inn, is representative of a general decline in local businesses in rural areas. Local economic self-sufficiency has been weakened by this process, forcing rural people to rely increasingly for goods and services upon nearby urban centres. This has aggravated employment problems as well as reducing the level of the local economy. It has been accompanied by a generally limited availability of educational, health and cultural institutions. This can mean both relative disadvantage and absolute decline.

Poor provision of educational facilities is one of the most frequently cited symptoms and causes of stagnation and decline in rural settlements. Direct evidence on the availability of educational institutions is difficult to obtain. Most studies of rural education stress lower levels of educational attainment in rural than in metropolitan areas. In the United States, the proportion of adults who have received less than eight years of formal education is as much as 40 per cent higher in rural than it is in urban areas.[12] This is, in part, a social and cultural legacy of bygone rural attitudes, but it is also a function of the relatively limited educational opportunities of most rural areas.

With the enormous increases in investment in education in the twentieth century, there is little doubt that educational opportunities in rural areas have improved. However, in virtually all regions of the world, rural communities have been able to do little more than ensure some level of primary education. Facilities for secondary, technical and post-secondary education are concentrated in urban areas, making rural communities increasingly unattractive for those who seek a full range of educational opportunities. Rural students are also at a relative disadvantage because of the distances they usually have to travel to schools. This problem has been exacerbated in Europe and North America by the steady decline in the number of elementary and secondary schools in rural areas. Consolidation and rationalization has led to the closure in many smaller communities of the local elementary school. Part of this has been due to official dissatisfaction with the educational standards of the one-room schoolhouse. But it is also a function of the declining ability of rural communities to provide financial support for schools, and in some cases even to find enough students and qualified teachers. In these circumstances, rural settlements are not only at a relative disadvantage, but also experience an absolute deterioration in

educational facilities. This is a direct symptom of community decline
for the school has always played a strong social and cultural role in
rural settlements.

In health facilities, too, the relative disadvantage of rural settlements
is readily apparent. The National Advisory Commission on Rural
Poverty summed up the effect of this on rural people, when it indicated
the high rate of disease and premature death among the rural poor.
Infant mortality is far higher among the rural than the urban poor.[13]
This situation is not unique to the United States, and in many rural
areas of the world the incidence of infant mortality, chronic disease
and premature death is much higher. This, of course, is a function of
poverty itself, but it is aggravated by the low level of health facility
provision in many rural communities. As with educational facilities, the
main problem is access to health services, for rural people are generally
forced to travel out of their own community for medical treatment. For
the more remote settlements this can be particularly problematical in
medical emergencies. Rural communities have always had to rely on
nearby urban centres for specialized hospital facilities, but there is
evidence that they now have difficulty in retaining or attracting even
basic facilities.

Limitations in the availability of educational and health facilities
represent a weakness that many rural communities have in providing
basic institutional services. Community attractiveness can be further
weakened by the inability to provide adequate social and cultural
facilities. It is difficult to establish measurable general trends in these
facilities, but stagnation and decline has certainly involved contraction
in locally-oriented social and cultural life. Economic and population
decline can lead to the closing down of churches, community centres,
cinemas and social clubs. However, it is the stagnation in cultural
provision, in contrast with its increased sophistication in urban centres,
which is a major contributor to dissatisfaction with rural life,
particularly among younger people. This may lead to out-migration,
but more significantly it is symptomatic of the relative limitations of
rural communities in an urban society.

The symptoms which have been summarized so far would not be
apparent immediately to a stranger in a depressed rural area. What
would be striking evidence of stagnation and decline would be the
physical dilapidation of settlement. Outward signs of depression do not
necessarily have a direct relationship with the incidence of poverty
and disadvantage. However, low incomes and investment, the reduction
of commercial and institutional services and, of course, the loss of

population will inevitably have some effect upon the physical fabric of settlement. In its most familiar form this means abandoned and ruined farmsteads, boarded-up stores, unused churches and schoolrooms, run-down houses, crumbling sidewalks and unrepaired roads.

The abandonment of rural buildings is often seen as the most tangible evidence of rural settlement decline. Certainly it is the usual result of the reduction in numbers of farms, of the loss of services, and the exodus of population. Yet the very weakness of a local economy can result in dilapidation of the built environment which falls short of abandonment. There is ample evidence of this in rural communities across the world which have difficulty generating enough capital to maintain, let alone improve even basic structures such as roads, drains and wells. And low levels of family income are reflected in the poor housing conditions which are often characteristic of rural areas. In the United States in 1960 (the last census for which official statistics on dilapidation were collected), 27 per cent of occupied rural housing was officially classed as substandard compared with 14 per cent of urban housing. One million were dilapidated, one in four had no piped water, and 30 per cent relied on the privy for sanitation.[14] The Canadian Council on Rural Development claims that rural housing tends to be older and more dilapidated than urban housing. It found, too, that in 1967, 22 per cent of rural dwellings were overcrowded compared with 14 per cent of urban homes.[15]

We must be cautious of assuming that poor housing conditions are characteristic of rural settlements in all regions. For example, Rogers claims that in Britain recent improvements in the rural housing stock, in particular the renovation and replacement of old buildings, have made rural areas on balance better equipped in terms of household amenities than urban areas.[16] However, as Rogers points out, there are certain regions, for example rural Wales, the Scottish Highlands and East Anglia, where housing conditions are inferior. In fact the main weakness in British rural housing is the shortage in supply of lower-cost housing, which is a symptom of local economic weaknesses and of material discomfort.[17]

Out-migration and Depopulation

The exodus of people from rural areas is seen generally as the most obvious symptom of decline. There is no reason to dispute this for the long-term effect of economic, personal and institutional disadvantage in rural communities usually leads to a search for better living conditions. Yet out-migration is not the inevitable result of the conditions which

have been described in the previous pages. Indeed the continued existence of poverty, unemployment and other disadvantages in rural
communities is evidence of the selective nature of the rural exodus. We
must be cautious also of placing too much significance on short-term
and localized population trends, for migration from a community can
often be a temporary phenomenon.

Yet rural out-migration and depopulation, though regionally and
locally variable in intensity, has been a widespread and persistent
process. Studies of rural-urban migration commonly cite lack of
employment and low incomes as the primary migratory impulses.
However, all of the symptoms which have been discussed so far should
be seen as influencing rural out-migration. Economic problems lead not
only to unemployment, underemployment and low incomes but to
perceived disparities between rural and urban levels of living. Taylor
has suggested that the achievement ideology of modern society, which
expects high values of material living, is one reason for the apparent
unattractiveness of rural communities where low incomes go hand-in-
hand with a lower level of material comfort.[18] Rural-urban migrants
may well migrate because of this relative disadvantage of rural lifestyles.
However the long history of rural exodus in many regions of the world
is also a reflection of the shift of employment opportunities to the
cities and the deterioration in the rural community.

On a global scale rural population has been increasing less rapidly
than that of urban areas in recent decades, and it is projected that by
the year 2000 the urban population will be more numerous than the
rural (Figure 5.1). By itself, however, this global trend does not indicate
wholesale rural decline for it will still involve considerable increases in
rural population. Of more significance are the rural-urban population
trends of particular regions. In fact, it is in the industrialized countries
of Europe and North America that the decline in rural population has
been most persistent. Estimates for the second half of the twentieth
century suggest that, while the rural population will still be in the
majority in less developed regions in the year 2000, that of industrial
regions will constitute less than 20 per cent of the total.[19]

Compared to the countries of Africa, Asia and Latin America, those
of Europe and North America have a long history of rural exodus, which
goes back to the earliest periods of urban and industrial expansion. Thus
in Britain, migration from rural settlements began on a large scale around
the middle of the eighteenth century. By 1851 the population of rural
districts was showing an absolute decline, a trend which continued until
1951.[20] Other European nations began to experience rural depopulation

Figure 5.1: World Urban and Rural Population Trends, 1950 to 2000

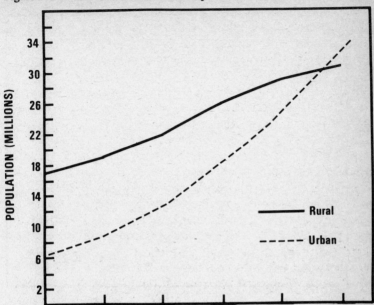

Source: Data in United Nations, Department of Economic and Social Affairs, *Human Settlements: The Environmental Challenge* (New York, United Nations, 1974), pp. 17-19.

during the nineteenth century, and this has persisted largely unabated throughout this century. In France, for example, rural population reached its maximum in 1861 and since then has declined by 37 per cent, from 26 to 16 million by 1962.[21] The rural exodus began a little later in North America where in both the United States and Canada the rate of rural population increase began to decline around the turn of the century. By 1910, rural increases in the United States had levelled off in contrast to the rapid growth of the urban population, indicating that the rural exodus had begun to have an effect on the natural increase of the rural population (Figure 5.2). For the past 50 years the American rural population has stabilized at around 54 million, although in the past decade there have been signs of a revival of population growth in many non-metropolitan and rural areas.[22]

These national statistics indicate that many rural areas have failed to retain all of their natural increase in population. In some areas and

Figure 5.2: Urban and Rural Population, United States, 1790 to 1970

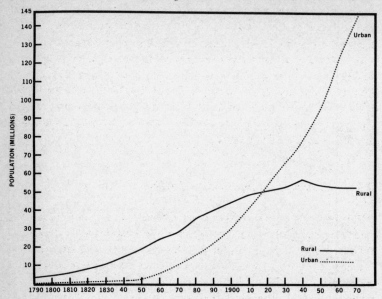

Source: US Department of Commerce, *Historical Statistics of the United States* (Washington, 1975), Series A 195-209.

settlements the rate of out-migration may not have been sufficient to cause actual depopulation. In these circumstances, it is the rate of population increase that declines. To some analysts, this is the first stage of rural depopulation. It is particularly apparent in many regions of the underdeveloped world where high rates of natural increase in a large rural population make out-migration common, particularly in Latin America, parts of Africa (where Zambia and Nigeria, for example, are among the most rapidly urbanizing in the world today) and in southeast Asia (where Indonesia is experiencing one of the highest rates of rural-urban migration).

However, even a slow reduction in the rate of population increase when this is caused by out-migration is a symptom of long-term problems for rural settlements. And this is the demographic prospect for most of the world's rural areas. With few exceptions it is those in younger working age groups who make up most of the rural emigrants. The effect of this is to reduce the fertility rate of the local population as well as to cause its overall ageing. This leads to a gradual decline in natural increase.

As this process intensifies, a reduced rate of increase changes to stagnation and then to net population loss. In this, depopulation can be seen as both a symptom and a cause of rural settlement decline. As a direct symptom it is a measure of the reduction in the population base of the community. Indirectly it reflects the limited opportunities of rural settlements. As a cause of decline depopulation frequently has been the major catalyst in a downward spiral in which the steady ageing of the population and the loss of the reproductive population combines with overall population decline further to reduce economic opportunities and depress community quality.

The Circumstances of Stagnation and Decline

So far, stagnation and decline in rural settlements has been examined in general terms and the broad symptoms of rural disadvantage identified. Yet we have said little about the underlying cause of stagnation and decline. Nor have we considered the particular regional and local circumstances in which it has occurred. Clearly it is important to recognize that the generalizations which have been made so far obscure important regional and temporal variations in the incidence of rural problems. The history of rural population in the United States is a good illustration of this point. Firstly, the decline in the population of rural America has been persistent in only certain regions of the country. And the centres of depopulation have shifted with changing economic and demographic situations. As Zelinsky has shown, early twentieth-century rural exodus was concentrated in the northeast. By the 1930s it had moved to the Great Lakes states and the Middle West, and during the post-war period was most intensive in the Plains states and in the south.[23]

The second major reason for qualifying our generalizations, is that recent trends in rural population and economy raise important questions about current problems of stagnation and decline in rural settlements. While the remoter and predominantly agricultural settlements experience problems, there is evidence of a recent upswing in non-metropolitan and rural population in some areas of Europe and North America. This indicates that long-term trends may obscure short-term variations and that stagnation and decline need not be a permanent condition in rural settlements.

The causes of stagnation and decline should be considered therefore, in the context of the regional, local and even individual circumstances

in which it has occurred. While the general shift in urban-rural relationships can be seen as the broad reason for decline in some rural settlements,
three factors in particular are worthy of detailed examination. The first
of these involves the economic resource base of rural settlements, which
in both an absolute and relative sense contains inherent and special
weaknesses. The second factor is referred to as the urban field effect:
the process of settlement and land-use competition which occurs in
metropolitan regions and which results in selective stagnation and
decline in rural settlements. Finally there is the problem of remoteness
which exacerbates the first factor and tends to lead to the worst cases
of rural depression.

Resource Base Deficiencies

A widespread reason for the fundamental problems of the rural
economy which were described earlier lies in the inherent weaknesses
of the economic resource base. Obviously for most rural communities
this has meant, first and foremost, weaknesses in the agricultural sector,
although in a few instances it has been more of a problem in other
primary resource activities such as fishing, forestry and mining. In
addition, the manufacturing and service sector of rural economies tends
to exhibit inherent limitations.

It is the weakness of the primary economic sector, particularly
agriculture, which has been traditionally at the root of low incomes,
low investment, unemployment and underemployment in many rural
areas. This has been a primary force for population decline, for the
most serious losses have tended to be from regions which rely solely
upon agriculture for a livelihood.

In some degree agriculture's problems are endemic. The basic difficulty for many farmers has been to yield adequate net returns on
investment. With growing commercialization and industrialization,
agriculture has been able to keep pace with the non-farm sector only
where it has been able to become capital intensive. This is not to say
that the small family or peasant farm cannot sustain an adequate income,
but, in the main, these kinds of operations are seriously limited in their
ability to expand in income and capital at the same levels as the
economy in general.

This is caused by four basic factors: (1) the uncertainty of decision
making in agriculture both in terms of the environment and the market-
place; (2) the tendency in many agricultural areas for there to be a large
number of small producers each of whom can hope to gain only a small
share of the marketplace or of land; (3) the generally inelastic nature of

demand for agricultural commodities which means that the total agricultural market cannot expand at as high a rate as that of the economy as a whole; (4) the increasingly high cost of inputs necessary for improving yield and labour productivity, which results in generally higher levels of investment per unit of output than in other sectors of the economy.

The combination of these factors has led to a situation in which many farmers are unable to increase their real income and, with a growing cost-prize squeeze, may actually face a decline in real income. This reduces the ability to maintain investment levels, to support all members of the farm family at adequate levels of income or direct subsistence, and to employ labour at levels and wage rates comparable to those of urban activities.

The Effect of Agricultural Rationalization

These are the economic circumstances which have led to a steady decline in the number of farmers, farm workers and farm family members. The high rate of farm out-migration across much of Europe and North America has reduced the farm population in many countries to less than 10 per cent of the total population. Apart from the effect this has had on the overall levels of rural population, it has resulted in a considerable reduction in the numbers of farms (Table 5.1). Much of this has occurred as part of the trend to larger, more specialized and more profitable farm enterprises. It is not therefore necessarily associated with general poverty in a rural region, but with a thinning-out of the rural settlement pattern.

Thus the stagnation and decline of rural settlement in areas such as the Midwest, and the Great Plains of the United States, and of the Canadian prairies, is a selective process. The absorption of smaller farms by larger ones, the introduction of dry-lot farming and the reduced demand for farm labour in recent years has accelerated farmstead abandonment and reduced both population and building densities in open countryside. Suitcase and sidewalk farming, in which the operator farms from a residence in town, has also added to the thinning out of farmsteads. The inevitable decline of rural residents where it is not replaced by an adventitious non-farm population leads to the deterioration and eventual disappearance of other dispersed settlement elements. The main casualties have been schoolhouses and rural churches. One study carried out in Missouri has shown that the loss of 69 rural churches between 1952 and 1967 occurred mostly in open country where membership of congregations had become too small.[24]

Table 5.1: Changes in Farm Numbers, United States, 1930 to 1978

| | Farms | |
Year	Number (1000)	Annual Change (1000)
1930	6,546	15
1935	6,814	54
1940	6,350	−93
1945	5,967	−77
1950	5,648	−64
1955	4,654	−199
1960	3,963	−138
1965	3,356	−121
1970	2,949	−81
1975	2,767	−36
1978	2,680	−29

Source: US Department of Commerce, Bureau of the Census, Statistical Abstract of the United States, 1978 (Washington, DC, 1978), Table 1166, p. 686.

This decline in farm population is one of the reasons why the community infrastructure of rural towns, villages and hamlets in otherwise affluent agricultural regions frequently experiences decline. The smaller settlements appear to suffer most, for there is evidence from a number of areas on both sides of the Atlantic that villages and hamlets which rely on agricultural population for support experience more persistent declines than larger rural trade centres. The problem in many of today's farming areas is that populations have declined below the minimum necessary for the maintenance of certain local services. In fact, this is not just a recent trend, for it was associated with the earliest declines in agricultural population which began on a widespread scale in the nineteenth century. This has been illustrated by Saville who shows that the decline in Britain's secondary rural population, those engaged in crafts and trades, began as early as 1850.[25] This is corroborated by a detailed study of a group of rural parishes in the Sheffield region which revealed that the number of craft and trade proprietors diminished by 43 per cent overall between 1850 and 1900.[26]

This trend has continued throughout this century in Britain as studies of rural communities in Somerset and East Anglia have shown.[27] In these studies the direct relationship between farm depopulation and service decline is only implicitly made. Studies of the North American experience, however, have analyzed this relationship more carefully, particularly in such overwhelmingly agricultural areas as the Prairies and the Middle West where small towns and villages depend so much on the farm population for their livelihood. In southern Saskatchewan extensive farm enlargement and depopulation has occurred in the past three decades. During that period the population of villages, hamlets and the tiny grain-elevator settlements declined at the same rate as that of the number of people living on farms.[28] Fast claims that a number of smaller communities have virtually disappeared in recent years and are not even used any longer for convenience.[29] Johansen and Fuguitt have presented the most recent detailed analysis of this process in an agricultural region of the United States. In their study of 77 villages in Wisconsin they discovered that between 1939 and 1970 the mean number of retail functions per village declined from 17.4 to 12.1. In 1939, 32 villages offered 20 functions and by 1970 only 12 offered this number (Figure 5.3).[30]

The paradox of the situation described in the preceding paragraphs is that the decline and even demise of certain elements of the traditional settlement structure has occurred simultaneously with the improvement of the economic position of those agricultural operations that remain. In economic terms the modern farm family is not unduly inconvenienced by the thinning out of rural population densities and the decline in local services. However, social costs can be high, particularly for the less mobile members of the population, the young and the old. For them even the most prosperous farm can be remote.

The decline in the business volume of small rural settlements under the process of agricultural readjustment tends to be cumulative. As Clawson has said, 'The decline of one kind of store or service will tend to depress the demand for the others, they are all linked together to a degree, since many trips to town are multi-purpose.'[31] According to Clawson, 'a great many of the small rural towns [of America] will wither greatly . . . some have already died and disappeared in farming areas.'[32] There is reason to suspect Clawson's statement, for at least one study shows that the number of places of less than 1,000 population has remained virtually static since 1950.[33] What Clawson's remarks really refer to is that reduction in the commercial status of small towns which is a function of what has been termed the urban field effect.

Urban fields now extend deep into rural areas. The initial effect is to stimulate the transformation of agriculture into an activity which becomes more commercialized. Its traditional ties with the rural economy are weakened and, to a degree, it becomes simply another

Figure 5.3: Changing Retail Functions in Wisconsin Villages

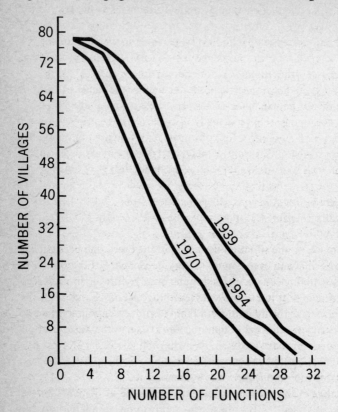

Source: Johansen and Fuguitt, 'Changing Retail Functions', p. 209, copyright 1973 by the Rural Sociological Society.

industrial sector of an urban-dominated economy. The acceleration of this trend in so many commercial farm areas has forced farmers to purchase inputs from the urban manufacturing sector and to sell directly to urban markets. This trend began early during the urbanization cycle and is one of the main reasons for the demise of rural industries and crafts which was characteristic of much of Europe and North America in the late nineteenth century. This has removed a large element of the non-agricultural resource base of rural economies in modernizing farming regions, which has added to the difficulties of providing employment, income and investment, particularly in villages and small towns. Nor was this due only to the shift in demand for farm inputs, for the demise of agriculturally-oriented industries has been matched by that of most of those activities which have been absorbed by an urban, factory system.

In Chapters 2 and 3, the evolution of European and North American villages and small towns into diversified settlements with strong local self-sufficiency was described. It is the weakening of this position as a result of the loss of their industrial sector to larger urban centres which marks the first phase of the urban field effect. The demise of rural cottage industries in Britain as early as the first part of the eighteenth century marked the first warning of a continued erosion of a broadly-based rural economy. Later this was followed by the decline of locally-oriented crafts such as shoemaking, tailoring, brewing, blacksmithing and wheelwrighting, which contributed significantly to the loss of local capital and employment opportunities. One of the most vivid accounts of this is that by George Sturt who wrote of the declining autonomy of the English village at the turn of the century.[34]

More recently, however, the influence of the urban field has been marked by the diminution of local retailing and other commercial services. Substantial evidence for this comes from a number of studies which have shown that it is competition within settlement systems which has caused this trend as much as the reduction in farm population. With the mobility created particularly by the automobile since World War II, the economic advantages of concentrating services in larger centres could be capitalized upon. This process of spatial competition between settlements in rural areas is the basic postulate of central-place theory which sees larger centres absorbing the market areas of smaller ones.

It is this trend which has led to the often false assumption that small-town America is dying. Hart and Salisbury have taken issue with this view and shown that while most villages (or small towns) have lost some of their central-place functions, the population of many continues to grow.[35] However, almost one half of the villages lost population between 1950 and 1960. The real point of this study is that the smaller and more remote villages tended to be the main population losers, while those in the more urbanized regions of southeastern Minnesota, central Iowa, southern Michigan and Ohio tended to grow in population. Yet Hart and Salisbury showed also that the average population of their sample villages experienced a slow increase in the past three decades, with only those of under 250 population showing a steady decline.[36] This trend is attributed to increased daily and residential mobility in which the decline of villages as commercial centres is unrelated to population change.

This interpretation is supported by Johansen and Fuguitt's study of Wisconsin villages which shows that, whether declining or growing in population, villages tend to lose certain retailing activities through competition from urban centres.[37] Fuguitt, in another study carried out with Butler, has concluded further that, in the Middle West, small towns which are close to or remote from urban places have grown faster than those in between. The latter have experienced slower growth because they lack the competitive advantage of more distant places and the decentralizing effect of the metropolis.[38] Hodge has predicted the probable changes in rural trade centres in North America, suggesting three trends. Firstly, the number of very small service centres serving the farming population will continue to decline. Secondly, hamlets and small villages which satisfy daily shopping requirements will lose services as a result of competition from larger centres. Thirdly, small service settlements within 24 kilometres of large towns will show substantial decline.[39] These predictions conform closely to theories of spatial competition in the tertiary sector and have been confirmed in studies such as Hassinger's who has noted the effect of 'urban dispersion'.[40]

Regional Resource Base Problems

So far we have examined the impact of problems which are character-istic of agriculture generally. They have led to a rationalization of settlement and therefore to only a selective decline in the settlement fabric. But in many rural regions stagnation and decline has been general and persistent. A major reason for this is that the intrinsic weaknesses of agriculture and other primary activities is, in these regions, intensified by their physical, economic and social marginality. The resource base itself is often the main source of problems. Land is of poor quality, there is too little of it to go round, income comes from a single source; these are the major problems of the poorer rural areas. In many regions of the world, rural settlement has been established on land which has only limited capabilities for agriculture. Where capital has been available land quality has been improved, but this option is not open to poorer societies and individuals. The main environmental problems are aridity, unreliable rainfall, poor soils, short growing seasons and difficult topography. Where these exist in combination the effect is usually to depress yields, to make production uncertain and to limit enthusiasm for innovation.

The significance of this is well illustrated by the limestone plains of eastern Ontario. This part of Canada was settled early in the nineteenth century, but, as pressure for commercial agriculture developed, it gradually became apparent that the thin, stony soil of the limestone plateau combined with a short growing season could not support a viable agricultural economy. By the turn of the century, population began to decline as farmers, and particularly their offspring, sought opportunities elsewhere. The decline in farm numbers and in productivity on the limestone plains is higher than the provincial average and, more significantly, higher than the deep soil areas of other parts of eastern Ontario. The plains therefore show signs both of abandonment and of continuing decline. Depopulation in most limestone plain townships has continued unabated since 1900, and has only been mitigated by an increase in off-farm work which is practised by as many as 60 per cent of farmers.[41]

Low incomes in agriculture and steady out-migration has, of course, led to a classical weakening of the local economy, through a reduction in the tax base and in local multipliers. Some of the poorest inhabitants are non-farm people, most of whom are the products of farm abandonment and consolidation, the drop in demand for farm labour and the lack of alternative employment opportunities. As Langman has shown, the physical signs of stagnation and decay are readily apparent in the landscape, for many former settlements are now only place names on topographic maps.[42] The disappearance of earlier farm buildings and other settlements is matched by the widespread incidence of dilapidation in the remaining occupied buildings. Farmsteads like that in Figure 5.4 are common.

The problems of eastern Ontario are in part the result of the over-extension of settlement onto land which could never have hoped to support many at adequate levels of living. This is how environmental limitations have tended to cause stagnation and decline in many other rural areas. The spread of farm settlement on to the Canadian Shield, into the western Prairies and southern plains of the United States, and into the Appalachians, has involved expansion, then contraction as settlers became aware of the marginality of their lands. In some areas, such as the Prairies, it has been aridity and unreliable rainfall combined with poor farming practices which has caused rural settlement to retreat. This remains a major reason for rural decline in other parts of the world, such as the savannah lands of sub-Saharan Africa. The most recent examples of the retreat of rural settlement in this region have been in Chad and Niger where whole villages have had their lands inundated by drifting sand.[43]

Upland areas have often posed problems for the successful

Figure 5.4: Farmstead Dilapidation in Eastern Ontario

establishment of agriculture, mainly because of the limited availability of cultivable land, cooler, moister climate, and the tendency for soil erosion on steep slopes. Yet mankind has shown a remarkable proclivity for settling upland regions, only to face subsequent difficulties. The inability of settlers to become more than marginal farmers in the hollows and valleys of the Appalachians is one reason why Kentucky has the lowest *per capita* rural income in the United States among a largely rural non-farm population. It is also contributory to the fact that the counties of southeastern Kentucky and northeastern Tennessee have experienced until very recently the heaviest depopulation in the country. Another agricultural area which has seen persistent poverty and out-migration is that of the Missouri Ozarks. Here the proportion engaged in agriculture is considerably higher than the national average yet, despite 70 years of continuous population decline, the economic status of those remaining has failed to improve. One reason for this is the limitations that the terrain imposes upon farm enlargement and mechanization. As in eastern Ontario this has resulted both in widespread farmstead abandonment and low agricultural incomes.[44]

Few studies have analyzed the economic problems of upland

farming in detail, but Raeburn's discussion of hill farming in the Scottish Highlands does indicate the difficulties of improving the productivity of the land.[45] In northern Europe generally, upland farming largely involves the use of grazing and winter feedstuffs, with a strong emphasis on hay. This type of feed is costly to produce and relatively low in nutrition. Grazing tends to be fibrous and available only over a short season. As Raeburn points out, 'These are conditions that largely prohibit commercial dairying and cattle fattening'.[46] In the Scottish Highlands they certainly contribute to the restraint of opportunity in agriculture and therefore to the steady decline in population and rural settlement.

The impact of land quality on rural settlements can, of course, be significantly intensified by land shortages. In some areas the type and amount of land available for the bulk of the rural population is as inadequate as to be the primary cause of rural depression. One reason for this situation is overpopulation. The problem of population pressure on rural land, particularly in peasant farming areas, is a well-known phenomenon. Its main influence on stagnation and decline in rural settlement has been through the increasing inability of rural societies to expand acreage proportionately with the increase in family size and numbers. Repeated subdivision of holdings, the colonization of new and often physically marginal areas by smaller and smaller farms, and the increase in numbers of landless peasantry are the inevitable results. Many of the world's peasant and village farms are smaller than five acres and large families can be supported on many of these only at low levels of income and food consumption or at the risk of serious soil exhaustion.

Severe overpopulation of this kind exists in much of the west African savanna which is now beginning to experience a major breakdown of traditional village structure and a steady drift of surplus population to urban areas. The average Nangodi farmer in northern Ghana cultivates two-and-a-half acres to support a family of 3.7 persons. With a population density of over 60 per square kilometre and the marginal nature of the savanna environment the possibilities for agricultural development are small.[47] Malnutrition runs high and the inability to produce crop surpluses limits cash income. Now that the employment and income opportunities of urban areas to the south are known, particularly amongst the young adults, the northern rural areas of Ghana face depopulation and decline. By 1960 almost 200,000, one-seventh of the total, of the north's native-born population were to be found in southern provinces.[48]

Shortages of agricultural land for many rural people are not due simply to an imbalance between population and the total amount of land available, but to serious inequities in the distribution of land tenure. Thus the most persistent examples of rural poverty are to be found in those regions where the bulk of the population is exploited by minority land-owning groups.

This has been the root cause of massive rural poverty and out-migration of the farm population of the southern states of America. Here land tenure inequality has resulted from sharecropping and a large proportion of landless labourers, both of whom experienced low incomes and insecurity. The demise of sharecropping has accelerated in recent years with massive migration of croppers and the changing structure of southern agriculture.[49] This has resulted in the abandonment of many small farm settlements and associated institutional buildings in the southeastern states. However, while some of the dilapidated shacks of the sharecropper are beginning to disappear from southern rural landscapes, many still remain and, together with the low paid — usually migrant — workers on plantations and commercial farms, form the basis of some of the poorest rural communities on the continent.

The effect of inequities in land tenure, however, remains much more significant in parts of southern Europe, southern Asia and, of course, Latin America. Feder has summed up perfectly the plight of the average rural dweller in Latin America. He lives under a *latifundio* system in which a few large landowners control most of the land while the remainder of the population are either smallholders (minifundistas) or landless labourers.[50] The land parcels of smallholders are usually too small to support the whole family, and so supplementary income is acquired by working on the local estate. In Argentina, Brazil, Chile, Colombia, Ecuador, Guatemala and Peru, Feder has estimated that minifundistas and landless labourers make up between 73 and 89 per cent of the active agricultural population.[51] Both groups suffer from un- and underemployment. One study of small agriculture in Central America has shown that many holdings are so small that farmers cannot even support themselves and their families. These are subfamily farms on which the family labour force of two people cannot be economically employed during the whole year. Supplementary employment is obtained from work on large commercial plantations, in small home industries and local services. But with peasant incomes running at around $400 per annum, and the incomes of commercial farms being spent largely in urban areas and outside the country, the possibilities for local development are minimal.[52]

The contribution of this land tenure system to stagnation and decline in rural communities has been well summarized by Whiteford. He lists five problems: peonage (debt and labour obligations to the latifundista); impoverishment; instability, insecurity and tension; ignorance and stagnation; low productivity and uneconomic operation.[53] With this pattern repeated over much of Latin America it is hardly surprising that over the past 40 years agriculture has developed more slowly than any other economic sector. 'The income, food, education, housing, and even health of rural communities continued to be the lowest in the whole social scale.'[54] Economic stagnation and demographic decline in rural areas have gone hand in hand, for Latin America has experienced a steady increase in rural out-migration in recent years. In tropical South America, the rural population declined from 64 per cent of the total in 1950 to 47 per cent in 1970.[55] Village population between 1960 and 1970 is estimated to have increased at half the rate of the population as a whole.[56]

Remoteness

One of the major problems experienced by many rural settlements is their relative isolation from the mainstream of modern life. Remoteness is indeed one of the basic causes of stagnation and decline in rural settlement. It operates at all levels from individual members of rural society to whole rural regions. Its effect is complicated by the fact that it is invariably accompanied by the resource base deficiencies described above, for it is in the nature of core-periphery relationships that the core tends to occupy the best land. Yet remoteness is also a problem in itself, for it is a locational disadvantage in which distance from the centres of economic and social activities produces extraordinary economic and social costs.

The economic effects of remoteness when combined with the intrinsic relative weakness of rural economies are bleakly apparent. High transportation costs for inputs and outputs restrict the competitiveness of local producers and limit the level of infrastructural and commercial investment. Distance from urban centres reduces the availability of local alternative employment opportunities and the chances of their development. Then there is the relative unattractiveness of a remote community: the so-called social cost of being cut off from frequent access to the cultural, institutional and political benefits of modern urban life.

The impact of remoteness on the rural economy is well illustrated by the experience of agriculture in the Scottish Highlands. Here the marginal nature of the physical environment is intensified by the distance of the region from the nearest metropolitan area and by the difficulties of access for individual farmers. According to Raeburn net income differentials between the Highlands and other regions of Scotland have widened. The result is that even older age groups have been leaving as doubts about the future of local agriculture have increased.[57] The basic economic problem for Highland agriculture and for alternative economic activities is that it creates unfavourable price relationships between products and factors. The prices of inputs in particular are high and the long-term effect of this has been to restrict the capital formation propensity of farm families and therefore their ability to remain competitive even locally.

There are many examples of this problem of market competition for economic activities in remote regions. In Zambia, for example, the development of commercial agriculture has occurred close to the main urban centres and along the main rail line, while the most depressed regions are remoter farming areas which have not had access to new markets and development possibilities.[58] A good example of the comparative advantage that the producer in a metropolitan region has over his competitor in a more remote rural area comes from potato production in Prince Edward Island in Canada. Largely because of the high cost of transporting potatoes to the Ontario market, the PEI producer has to accept significantly lower unit returns than the producer in Ontario. Government support has prevented the complete disappearance of potato farming on Prince Edward Island. Yet it has not prevented steady depopulation, particularly from farms and the general depression of agricultural communities.

The most pernicious effect of distance costs on the economy of remote regions is the prevention of the development of local economic linkages. The result is the tendency to be forced to rely on single sources of income and employment, which are linked in both investment and market terms to metropolitan centres. Thus it is that agriculture, fishing, forestry and mining, the traditional activities of remote regions, have not tended to stimulate local development. In a sense, regions such as Newfoundland, northern Maine and the southern Appalachians are examples of colonial-style exploitation by the investment centres of metropolitan regions. Thus they have been characterized by low incomes and by restricted and fluctuating employment opportunities. Above all, this has resulted in the steady depopulation of most remote rural regions, a trend which appears to be at the heart of the problems of stagnation and decline. In the Scottish Highlands, the recent exodus of older farmers has been far outweighed by the departure of those between 19 and 25 years of age who are unable to find employment locally.[59] Unemployment and seasonal employment in remote areas inevitably leads to out-migration simply because there are few possibilities of commuting to jobs in the region.

On the coasts of northern Maine and the Canadian Maritime provinces, it is the remoteness and precariousness of the economic base of the fishing communities which has stimulated out-migration. The more remote the settlement, the more likely its decline both economically and demographically. The most serious problems have probably occurred in Newfoundland where the complete reliance of the outport settlements on fishing has led to extremely low family incomes in these small communities. In a survey of over 7,000 cod fishermen's households along the north coast of Newfoundland in 1967, Lewis calculated the average income per household to be $2,797, of which $286 was in unemployment benefits and over $900 in other subsidies (this income included an estimate of non-cash income).[60] Not surprisingly, in communities where virtually the only occupation available was in-shore fishing on a family basis, the exodus of younger, and particularly female, family members has been persistent.

To a large extent, the economic cost of remoteness is matched by the social cost. We have already seen how rural settlements generally are at a relative disadvantage in providing services to the local population. This problem is intensified by remoteness because of the increased cost of providing services to scattered and frequently isolated settlements, and because of the low tax base of marginal economies. One of the major reasons for the initiation of the Resettlement Programme in Newfoundland was the increasing difficulty of providing basic public services to the outports.[61] This problem has been well explained by Thomas in his discussion of the remote rural areas of central Wales. He points out that where economic and population decline have been persistent trends, there is a danger that even the most essential services will disappear.[62] Thomas does indicate the significance of improved transportation in making services available in larger urban centres. However, the inherent problem of remote areas and settlements is that of accessibility, and one of the services which tends to be most expensive to maintain for isolated communities is transportation. Coastal and mountainous areas are notoriously difficult environments in which to maintain year-round communications. More significantly, it is the cost of maintaining road and rail links between outlying and often widely dispersed rural settlements which presents the greatest problems.

In North America the steady contraction of passenger rail service during the 1950s and 1960s may have had some influence in increasing the isolation of rural communities. After all between 1916 and 1966, 80,000 kilometres of track went out of service in the United States, while passenger kilometres dropped from 56 billion to 19 billion.[63] However, the main effect of this was to hasten the demise of trade centres along rail lines. The automobile, so much the cause of railroad decline, became, during the same period, the single means of transport for rural America. In most areas, therefore, the availability of public transport is not an issue. However, accessibility to good roads is critical, for settlements which are on poorly maintained backroads inevitably suffer from a unique form of remoteness which can exist only a few kilometres from an urban centre. For dispersed farm settlement, the main problem is the movement of inputs to and produce from the farm gate. One example of this comes from dairy farming which in recent years has switched to the widespread use of tanker collection of fresh milk. The maintenance of an efficient dairy operation under this system clearly depends on good road access.

Langman has indicated an apparent relationship between farmstead abandonment and poor road access in eastern Ontario (Figure 5.5).[64] Rafferty suggests a similar phenomenon in the Ozarks where he discovered that farms away from major roads have been abandoned with the greatest frequency.[65] Even good road access, however, may not eliminate the isolation of rural settlement for certain groups of the population. The young, the elderly and the poor in areas of dispersed rural settlement frequently experience serious transportation difficulties. For those of school age, the provision of school bus services has become a serious burden on local municipalities and school boards, particularly where school consolidation has increased the distance between students and school. Expenditure on school busing is often the largest single item in school board budgets. Furthermore, the time consumed in travelling to and from school and the spatial alienation from the school locality adds to the unattractiveness of the more isolated settlements.

The elderly and the poor, particularly the women in these groups, tend to have a lower level of access to automobile usage. These groups, of course, experience isolation in urban society too, but in rural areas this is compounded by the distances involved. The poor provision of public transport is for these people particularly problematical. This is more evident in most rural areas outside of North America, because of the lower incidence of automobile ownership. In Britain, for example,

Figure 5.5: Farmstead Abandonment in Eastern Ontario

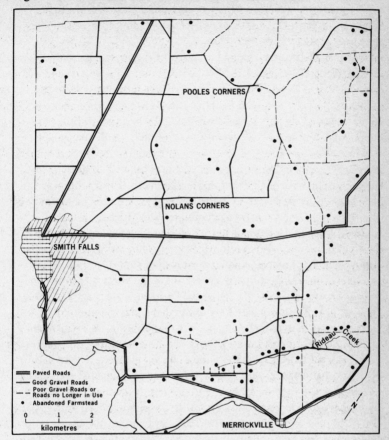

Source: *Poverty Pockets* by R.C. Langman, reprinted by permission of McClelland and Stewart Limited, Toronto.

despite an increase in car ownership in the past two decades, to the level that in some rural areas over 70 per cent of households own cars, a significant minority has restricted access to automobiles. One reason for this is that studies have shown that approximately 70 per cent of car owning households use cars for journeys to work.[66] 'It is not households but people without the use of cars that show the true extent of rural deprivation.'[67] Despite attempts to introduce public transport alternatives, such as postal buses, rural bus services have contracted at a substantial rate, particularly through the reduction of service frequency. In one study of rural Norfolk, bus usage was very limited, the major complaint being high fares and poor service which restricted shopping trips to the nearby town.[68]

The combination of low incomes, lack of employment and poor services is therefore aggravated by the difficulty of gaining regular and frequent access to the facilities of larger places. This may create an isolation mentality in which the inhabitants of remote settlements are cautious of making any personal or financial investments in the local community. In the most extreme situations, they are driven away from settlements by the absolute deprivations of unemployment and poverty. Alternatively, they remain in poverty, able to contribute nothing to the improvement of their economic environment. This situation has been graphically described by Rena Gazaway in her personal account of life in an Appalachian hollows community. For the inhabitants of Duddie's Branch, 'isolation is living in obscurity a few miles from a thriving community. The world whizzes past the turnoff into the hollow and does not even know that it is there.'[69]

Luebke and Hart's study of a community in the most remote and isolated part of the eastern edge of the Great Valley of east Tennessee, indicates the dilemma which long-term inhabitants of remote rural areas experience in modern society.[70] Isolation from the mainstream of employment opportunities led to a rapid increase in out-migration after 1940 so that by 1950 the population was little more than half of what it had been in 1900. Yet a large number of unemployed young remained at the time of study in 1957. Many of the small tenant farmers, mostly on land too steep and stony and in substandard homes, also continued to inhabit the area. This is evidence of the strong religious, community and family ties, combined with an attachment to the land and a mistrust of materialism and education, which is so characteristic of Appalachian mountain communities. Hence the dilemma for these people: the ultimate need for at least their offspring to migrate but also a strong conservatism which binds them to their land and their community.

The sad history of much of Appalachia is well known, and it is an example of the complexity of reasons why remoteness creates its own peculiar problems. The rural settlements of the southern Appalachians more than anything else are evidence of the vulnerability of remote areas to the callous exploitation of human and physical resources. Left as a marginal farming area the region might well have stabilized at low population levels before the turn of the century. However, like so many similar areas, the temporary opportunities of mining employment persuaded many settlers to stay and join the burgeoning non-farm rural population. As the mining companies moved on from hollow to hollow, they left behind forgotten communities like Duddie's Branch. From these depopulation has been steady, but many remain, mostly on welfare, returned once again to the status of marginal farmers.

The hollows settlements are an example of the existence of the absolute poverty and deprivation of remoteness and isolation in the United States. The mentality of isolation, however, has more often involved the recognition of the relative disadvantages of remoteness. Thus depopulation of remote rural areas has been attributed to a change in the values and aspirations of the people. Once content with the only life they knew, they have lost their ignorance of the outside world. Radio and television, the mobility provided by the automobile, the increasing intrusion of government officials, have combined to present alternative lifestyles.

This sense of isolation from contemporary lifestyles is, however, difficult to establish. The only methods available for doing this are surveys either of those who would like to leave a rural settlement or of those who have already left. The results of all such surveys have to be treated with caution, particularly with something as personal as lifestyle. A good example of this is Hannan's study of the migration motive in a remote rural area of Eire.[71] While dissatisfaction was expressed by the youth of these villages with the restrictions of village life, the much more tangible concern for employment opportunities was seen as the major cause of migration. The relative disadvantage of the remote community was its inability to provide employment which, in terms of status and remuneration, satisfy the individual's aspirations.

The most serious effects of remoteness, then, are a combination of factors which result in the general isolation of rural settlements and sometimes whole regions from the main currents of economic and social development. We should be cautious of assuming that all inhabitants of such settlements are discontented with their lot. The choice of remaining at low levels of income and material comfort in an outport or a Scottish croft is the only sane one for many. However, the absolute deprivations of remote rural settlements are apparent in their economic and physical poverty, while the relative disadvantages of isolation have stimulated a decline through steady out-migration.

Notes

1. President's National Advisory Commission on Rural Poverty, *Rural Poverty in the United States* (Washington: Government Printing Office, 1967), p. x.

2. The Senate of Canada, *Proceedings of the Special Committee on Poverty No. 1* (Ottawa: Queen's Printer, 1969), p. 25.

3. M.S. Ahluwalia, 'Income Inequality: Some Dimensions of the Problem', in H. Chenery *et al.*, *Redistribution with Growth* (London: Oxford University Press, 1974), pp. 10-20.

4. International Bank for Reconstruction and Development, *Rural Development* (Washington: World Bank, 1975), p. 19.

5. US Department of Commerce, Bureau of Census, *Statistical Abstract of the United States, 1978* (Washington, 1978), Table 761, p. 469.

6. Ibid., p. 469.

7. Statistics Canada, *1971 Census, Income of Individuals*, Vol. III, Part 6 (Ottawa: Queen's Printer, 1975).

8. United Nations, Economic Commission for Latin America, *Income Distribution in Latin America* (New York: United Nations, 1971), p. 106.

9. US Department of Commerce, Bureau of the Census, *Historical Statistics of the United States: Colonial Times to 1970* (Washington: US Government Printing Office, 1975), p. 136.

10. President's National Advisory Commission on Rural Poverty, p. 25.

11. Ibid., p. 25.

12. US Department of Agriculture, *The Economic and Social Conditions of Rural America in the 1970's*, Part 1 (Washington, 1971), p. 4.

13. President's National Advisory Commission, p. x.

14. President's National Advisory Commission, p. 93.

15. Canadian Council on Rural Development, p. 29.

16. Alan W. Rogers, 'Rural Housing', in Gordon E. Cherry, *Rural Planning Problems* (London: Leonard Hill, 1976), p. 103.

17. Ibid., pp. 104-12.

18. Lee Taylor, *Urban-Rural Problems* (Belmont: Dickerson, 1968), pp. 1-9.

19. United Nations, Department of Economic and Social Affairs, *Human Settlements: The Environmental Challenge* (New York: Macmillan, 1974), p. 17.

20. John Saville, *Rural Depopulation in England and Wales, 1851-1951* (London: Routledge and Kegan Paul, 1957), p. 61.

21. Pierre Merlin, *L'Exode Rural* (Paris: Presses Universitaires de France, 1971), pp. 10-13.

22. This is discussed more fully in Chapter 7.

23. W. Zelinsky, 'Changes in the Geographic Patterns of Rural Population in the United States, 1790-1960', *Geographical Review*, Vol. 52 (1962), pp. 492-524.

24. E.W. Hassinger and J.S. Holik, 'Changes in the Number of Rural Churches in Missouri, 1952-1967', *Rural Sociology*, Vol. 35 (1970), p. 365.

25. Saville, *Rural Depopulation*, pp. 20-30.

26. M.F. Bunce, *Rural Population Change in the North-East Midlands, 1861-1911*, unpublished Ph.D. thesis (University of Sheffield, 1970), p. 259.

27. H.E. Bracey, *Social Provision in Rural Wiltshire* (London: Methuen, 1952); and P.J. Drudy and D.B. Wallace, 'Towards a Development Programme for Remote Rural Areas: A Case Study in North Norfolk', *Regional Studies*, Vol. 5 (1971), pp. 281-8.

28. H.R. Fast, 'Changing Communities in Rural Saskatchewan', *Canadian Farm Economics*, Vol. 7 (2), (1972), pp. 8-19.

29. Ibid., p. 19.

30. Harley E. Johansen and Glenn V. Fuguitt, 'Changing Retail Activity in Wisconsin Villages: 1939-1970', *Rural Sociology*, Vol. 38 (1973), pp. 207-18.

31. M. Clawson, 'Factors and forces affecting the optimum future rural settlement pattern of the United States', *Economic Geography*, Vol. 42 (1966), p. 287.

32. Ibid., p. 287.

33. J.F. Hart and N.E. Salisbury, 'Population Change in Middle Western Villages: A Statistical Approach', *Annals*, Association of American Geographers, Vol. 55 (1965), pp. 140-60.

34. George Sturt, Change in the Village (London, 1912).

35. Hart and Salisbury, 'Population Change', p. 141.

36. Ibid., p. 141.

37. Johansen and Fuguitt, 'Changing Retail Activity', p. 217.

38. James E. Butler and Glenn V. Fuguitt, 'Small-Town Population Change and Distance from Larger Towns: A Replication of Hassinger's Study', *Rural Sociology*, Vol. 35 (1970), p. 401.

39. G. Hodge, 'The Prediction of Trade-Centre Viability on the Great Plains', *Papers and Proceedings*, Regional Science Association, Vol. 15 (1965), pp. 87-115.

40. Edward M. Hassinger, 'The Relationship of Retail-Service Patterns to Trade-Centre Population Change', *Rural Sociology*, Vol. 22 (1957), pp. 235-40.

41. M.F. Bunce, 'The Contribution of the Part-Time Farmer to the Rural Economy', in A.M. Fuller and J.A. Mage (eds.), *Part-Time Farming: Problems or Resource in Rural Development* (University of Guelph, 1976), pp. 249-57.

42. R.C. Langman, *Poverty Pockets: A Study of the Limestone Plains of Southern Ontario* (Toronto: McClelland and Stewart, 1975), p. 60.

43. An excellent review of the problems of desertification is contained in a collection of papers on the subject in *Economic Geography*, Vol. 53 (1977), pp. 317-406.

44. Niles M. Hansen, *The Future of Non-metropolitan America* (Lexington: Heath, 1973), pp. 83-5; and M.D. Rafferty, 'Population and Settlement Changes in Two Ozark Localities', *Rural Sociology*, Vol. 38 (1973), pp. 46-56.

45. J.R. Raeburn, 'The Economics of Upland Farming', in J. Ashton and W.H. Long, *The Remoter Rural Areas of Britain* (Edinburgh: Oliver and Boyd, 1972), pp. 3-24.

46. Ibid., p. 11.

47. J.M. Hunter, 'Seasonal Hunger in a Part of the West African Savanna', *Transactions*, Institute of British Geographers, Vol. 41 (1967), pp. 167-85.

48. John C. Caldwell, *African Rural-Urban Migration* (New York: Columbia University Press, 1969), p. 19.

49. J.R. Anderson, *A Geography of Agriculture in the United States Southeast* (Budapest: Akademiai Kiado, 1973), pp. 45-6.

50. E. Feder, *The Rape of the Peasantry* (Garden City, NY: Doubleday, 1971), p. 3.

51. Ibid., p. 9.

52. S.G. Manger-Cats and T. Berthold, 'Small Farm Agriculture in Central America: Outlook to 1985', *Monthly Bulletin of Agricultural Economics and Statistics*, Vol. 19 (5), 1970, pp. 1-8.

53. A.H. Whiteford, 'Aristocracy, Oligarchy, and Cultural Change in Colombia', in A.J. Field (ed.), *City and Country in the Third World* (Cambridge, Mass.: Schenkman, 1970).

54. N. Sanchez-Albornoz, *The Population of Latin America* (Berkeley: University of California Press, 1974), p. 228.

55. Kingsley Davis, *World Urbanization 1950-1970*, Vol. 1 (Berkeley: University of California, Institute of International Studies, 1969), pp. 123-4

56. Sanchez-Albornoz, *Population of Latin America*, p. 230.

57. Raeburn, *Upland Farming*, p. 7.

58. Mary Elizabeth Jackman, *Recent Population Movements in Zambia* (Institute for African Studies, University of Zambia, Manchester University Press, 1973).

59. Raeburn, *Upland Farming*, p. 7.

60. J.N. Lewis, *Salted Cod Fish in the Atlantic Provinces*, Report to Department of Fisheries and Forestry (Ottawa, 1969).

61. P. Copes, *The Resettlement of Fishing Communities in Newfoundland* (Ottawa: Canadian Council on Rural Development, 1972), pp. 47-53.

62. J. Gareth Thomas, 'Population Changes and the Provision of Services', in Ashton and Long, *Remoter Rural Areas of Britain*, pp. 91-106.

63. John F. Kolars and John D. Nystuen, *Human Geography: Spatial Design in World Society* (New York: McGraw-Hill, 1974), p. 167.

64. Langman, *Poverty Pockets*, p. 41.

65. Rafferty, 'Population and Settlement Changes', p. 51.

66. Ian Martin, 'Rural Communities', in Cherry, *Rural Planning*, p. 51.

67. Ibid., p. 57.

68. Hugh D. Clout, *Rural Geography* (London: Pergamon, 1972), pp. 169-71.

69. Rena Gazaway, 'The Longest Mile: The Forgotten People of an Appalachian Hollow', (New York: Doubleday, 1969), p. 64.

70. B.H. Luebke and J. Fraser Hart, 'Migration from a Southern Appalachian Community', *Land Economics*, Vol. 34 (1958), pp. 44-53.

71. D. Hanna, *Rural Exodus* (London: Chapman, 1970).

6 MODERNIZATION AND CHANGE IN AGRICULTURAL SETTLEMENT

The counterparts to the process of stagnation and decline discussed in the previous chapter are the developments of recent decades which have led to the transformation and, to some extent, revitalization of rural settlements. These developments stem from the same basic forces which have led to stagnation and decline. Yet the modernization of rural settlement is a subject which encompasses a wide range of phenomena, each of which has its own particular impact on settlement structure, land use, landscape, economy and society. Because of this breadth we shall concentrate on two aspects of modern development; aspects, it is suggested, which reflect the most important of the modernization trends. This chapter deals with the impact of recent developments in agriculture which have resulted in changes in agricultural land use and settlement. In the next chapter we shall examine the growing role in the industrial world of rural settlements as residential and recreational places.

The Spread of Commercial Farming

One of the most important recent trends in rural settlement is the spread of commercial agriculture into areas which were formerly dominated by traditional systems of subsistence production. The forerunner of present trends was, of course, the colonial plantation which resulted in the development of an essentially dualistic economy in the colonies of the underdeveloped world. There is some evidence to suggest that in the traditional agriculture of these areas, commercial and subsistence farming have been the combined objectives of rural families.[1] According to Morgan, 'the buying and selling of all manner of goods, including agricultural produce has long been established in tropical Africa'.[2] Yet the underlying principle of this has been the local nature of the markets for agricultural produce and the marketing of surpluses after subsistence needs have been met.

During this century, however, both the economic basis and the structure of rural settlement in some regions of the peasant world have shown signs of change because of increasing commercialism amongst

peasant producers. To some extent this has occurred within existing
settlement frameworks and has involved a shift in village economies.
Beals provides a good example of this from south India in a village
where the opportunities of a growing urban market have led to considerable expansion in the agricultural economy. Specialized production has
become important with a thriving village milk industry and cash crop
production.[3] The strong influence of increasing links with the urban
economy is readily apparent in this village. Indeed, the development of
market-oriented cash production in most peasant regions is only one
component of a set of urbanizing influences. The availability of urban
employment, urban markets and urban goods and services in conveniently
located villages in Zambia, for example, has had the effect of stimulating
a quite diversified cash crop economy and modernizing the settlements
through increased material possessions, more elaborate housing and,
most significantly, improved road links.[4]

However, we should be cautious of inferring that these developments
lead to a complete transformation of the traditional community
structure. Indeed the extent of modernization will be strongly influenced
by the structure of peasant and tribal society in which it occurs. Thus
Eisenstadt argues that radical changes in rural communities can occur
only when social and political structures become flexible enough to deal
with changing concepts and opportunities.[5] So the impact of increased
commercialization in agriculture on community is likely to be variable.
But, as Long has explained, cash cropping's most fundamental effect is
to increase the separation of the consumption and production activities
of the household. This tends to change the patterns of family and
communal dependencies and strengthen the role of the nuclear family
as a productive enterprise. This in turn changes village political structure
through a weakening of kinship ties. Farmers become involved in co-
operatives, political parties and capitalist ventures, thus breaking down
the traditional differentiation of community roles.[6]

In some regions, the existing frameworks of settlement and community have seriously restricted the possibilities for commercial
agriculture. This has resulted in basically two changes in settlement
structure. The first of these is the independent peasant farm which has
been created through spontaneous dispersal and land acquisition, a
process which has been described more fully in Chapter 3. The second
involves the influence of government planning which alters village
structure and creates new settlements.

Independent Commercialization

Partly because of the relative fluidity of rural settlement structure and partly because of the hiatus of colonial interference, followed by recent and rather sudden independence, it is in Africa where we find the most tangible evidence of new patterns of peasant farm settlement. In fact, colonial influence in some regions, in particular east Africa, led to the break-up early in this century of many traditional village settlements. Yet this was not accompanied by any real trends towards commercialization of agriculture and the modernization of society.

However, in her studies in west Africa, Hill has shown the effect that commercial ambitions can have on the distribution of rural settlement.[7] A good example of this is the migration of ambitious villagers from eastern regions to western Ghana to purchase land from local tribes for the purpose of commercial cocoa production. These 'rural capitalists', as Hill calls them, have a longer history than most other commercial farmers in Africa. Their capitalism is apparent in their commercial attitude to land purchase, their tendency to increase the size of their holdings, their relatively high capital investment and their treatment of coffee-growing as a business. Their settlement patterns are dispersed cottages surrounded by their plots, and what are called 'stranger towns' in which the farmers live in temporary residences, for strong links are retained with the home village back in the east.

The cocoa farmer is a rather specialized example of the influence of agricultural modernization. Recently, however, the desire and opportunity for commercial independence in parts of Africa and elsewhere in the peasant world has become more general. Unfortunately the evidence for this is fragmented because studies which have examined the effect on settlement patterns are limited in number and spatial coverage. A particularly well documented example of transformation from a traditional village structure to a landscape of dispersed, cash-cropping smallholders comes from eastern Nigeria. Here the early dispersal of homesteads has gained new momentum because of increased population pressure, declining village authority and growing agricultural commercialism. Steady increases in rural population have placed considerable pressure on land resources. Traditional methods of communal cultivation of village territory have had increasing difficulty in supporting the rising aspirations of a growing population. One result has been out-migration. The other has been the gradual occupation of farmlands by younger generations. To some extent this has been intensified by the greater independence of the young married men who set up their own

small, self-contained compound which produces cash crops, particularly
vegetables, for an urban market. The effect of this has been the creation
of smaller and smaller holdings and a densely-occupied rural landscape.[8]

There is some evidence that the commercialization process in peasant
regions has led to the development of larger-scale commercial farm
settlement more akin to the North American pattern. One example is
the expansion of livestock and vegetable farms which forms the basis
of so much of the recent success of Mexican agriculture. These farms
are usually between 100 to 150 hectares in size but some are larger.
They are an excellent example of the movement of indigenous producers
into commercial farming which is sensitive to world and, in this case,
North American markets.[9] The dispersed settlement pattern that has
resulted is not only a clear break from the village tradition of rural
Mexico, but it has also had the effect of changing traditional village
society as labour opportunities on commercial farms replace the conventional links with plantations.

Planned Commercialization

The development of commercial farm settlement in Mexico has been,
to some extent, influenced by government programmes of agricultural
development. In fact, an important influence for recent change in the
world's rural settlements is agricultural development planning in its
many forms. Virtually all countries provide some level of support for
agriculture, but some have created programmes which have had
significant, and in some cases radical, effects on rural settlement.

The primary objectives of one group of development programmes is
the alteration of economic and social structure within existing settlement
frameworks. This has been a major catalyst in the modernization of
villages in a number of regions. It has certainly been the basic philosophy
of the Co-operative Farming and Community Development Schemes in
India. This was initiated soon after independence, with the immediate
aim of increasing agricultural production, the development of villages
and the establishment of small, rural industries. The bases of the scheme
are the 'block' and *panchayat* (village council) administrative units
which were intended to supplant traditional village authority and to
encourage community self-help.

While, by 1964, virtually all Indian villages had been organized into
community development blocks of 100 villages each, the degree of
village change has been variable.[10] However, the opportunities presented
by schemes for agricultural innovation, educational improvement and
community projects like women's organizations, appear to have created

an atmosphere of change in Indian villages. This is most apparent, as would be expected, in the proximity of large urban centres, for elsewhere most villages retain traditional land tenure and social structures. Indeed, one of the weaknesses of the scheme is that village people tend to see it as a government programme of rural welfare.[11]

A contrasting approach to village community change, of course, is the Chinese commune. To treat this as the product of agricultural modernization, however, would be somewhat misleading, for it represents the impact of a whole political ideology on rural society. The main aim in the creation of the Chinese village commune was the establishment of communist society in rural areas and the creation of uniformity in the political and economic objectives of urban and rural society. However, the organization of Chinese peasant villages into communes, is representative of the most radical of changes in village society, an important objective of which was the transformation of the agricultural economy. So the modern Chinese village is part of an organization of 'teams' for working the land and for producing food as efficiently as possible for a growing urban-industrial population.[12] One effect has been the introduction of new elements, such as food processing plants, implement stations and storage buildings, to the rural landscape.

As the Indian experience would suggest, agricultural development is not always readily achieved within existing settlement structures. For this reason, there are many examples of programmes based upon resettlement schemes and the addition of new, planned elements to rural landscapes. Among the most extensive of resettlement programmes during this century have been the new agricultural settlement of the Soviet Union. The introduction of collective and state farming was, like the Chinese commune, based upon Marxist ideology, but recent developments have been very much concerned with the modernization of agriculture in conjunction with the rationalization of rural settlement into a functional hierarchy, which maximizes the efficiency of the rural economy. The Krushchev era saw the consolidation of collective farm settlements, with smaller villages being phased out and the population moved into larger, central settlements.[13] The rural settlement structure today bears little resemblance to that of 50 years ago, being a creation of modern Soviet planning. It consists of an hierarchy of 'interkolkhoz', or 'interstate' farm centres at the top, which provide transport, trade and storage facilities, followed by district centres, central farm settlements, and specialized settlements such as livestock-feeding stations and machine centres.[14]

In most other rural areas, agricultural resettlement programmes are considerably more modest than that of the Soviet Union. Largely because of the serious limitations placed by existing settlement and land use patterns upon agricultural development, Africa appears to contain more settlement schemes than most other peasant areas. Nigeria, Ghana, Tanzania, Kenya, Uganda and Mozambique all have operative schemes to establish new agricultural settlements. Some of these will be examined briefly here.

In Nigeria, agricultural development policy has placed a strong emphasis upon the establishment of settlements which can give African farmers the opportunity to increase their participation in the market-place. One element of the programme, the smallholder scheme, involves no new settlement for it provides subsidies to existing land holders to plant five acres of a commercial crop. However, two other parts of the programme have resulted in important changes in rural settlement. The nucleus plantation concept establishes processing facilities and a commercial plantation run with paid labour usually to produce palm oil. Smallholders are given small plots around the nucleus on which to construct a house, grow subsistence crops and take advantage of plantation facilities both to grow the same commercial crop and to obtain supplementary employment. A second scheme involves the resettling of a large number of dispersed peasant farmers into a consolidated planting area. In this each farmer is allocated land for housing, subsistence crops and a commercial crop, and centralized facilities for crop processing are provided.[15]

In east Africa, a major problem for rural development has been the fragmentation of rural settlement, much of which is the legacy of an exploitative and disruptive colonial period. In Kenya, for example, post-independence rural development has been dominated by the land transfer settlement programme in which over one million acres of land has been purchased from European settlers. The aim is to return to Africans some of the most productive lands of the country by laying out smallholdings for peasant farmers many of whom were previously landless.[16] By June 1965, 24,000 families had been settled in 125 separate high-density settlement schemes. Evidence of the commercial nature of many of these new peasant farms comes from the increased wealth of small towns on the Kikuyu Plateau.[17]

Further to the south in Zambia, one aspect of the rural development programme has been the attempt to regroup scattered elements of the rural population who have been squatting on public land into planned villages in which they can acquire the benefits of modern agricultural

methods and co-operative production. The formal layout of these
villages is illustrated in Figure 6.1. More recently, state farms and
ranches have been established which are aimed at increasing national

Figure 6.1: Planned Agricultural Settlement in Zambia

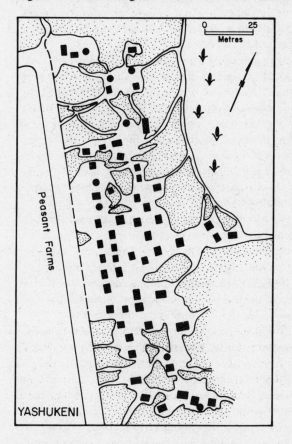

herds of dairy and beef cattle. At present there are eleven state ranches
and six dairy farms. These are in contrast to the smallholder settlement
schemes which are so common in Africa. However, Zambia also has a
programme for settling peasant farmers in schemes in which land is laid
out in 4 to 10 hectare units for the purpose of encouraging cash crop
production such as cotton, tobacco and coffee.[18] In Zambia, the various
settlement schemes are now widespread and are associated with a whole
range of new agricultural settlement elements.

Finally, before leaving east Africa mention should be made of the radical resettlement programme in Tanzania. The principle of the *Ujamaa* villages, and the villagization programme in general, is the encouragement of communal and co-operative activity and local participatory democracy. The aim is to reduce the fragmentation of rural settlement by bringing population into these new nucleated settlements in which peasant agricultural productivity, levels of living and public facilities can be improved.[19]

The common denominator of most of the schemes which have just been described is the reorganization of settlement in order to create land tenure systems which are condusive to modern commercial agriculture. This is an objective which is not limited to Africa or other ex-colonial regions, for it is an important feature of agricultural development policy in some European countries where the fragmentation of land-holdings has persisted (and often intensified) long after the demise of the feudal system by which it was conceived. Holland, France, Italy and West Germany all have programmes for agricultural land consolidation. Some aim only to redistribute land parcels around villages without changing the structure of settlement. Others involve the relocation of farmsteads and the creation of new settlements.

A well-studied example of this is that of resettlement and land consolidation programmes in West Germany.[20] A primary objective of these programmes is to cut costs in agriculture by consolidating fragmented holdings and relieving farmstead congestion in villages. The programmes aim also to improve the efficiency with which land in the low-lying, artificially drained areas of northwestern Germany are used. In the project at Mooriem, not far from the city of Bremen, the reduction of the difficulties of access and cultivation caused by the long, narrow strips of land has been achieved by a partial consolidation of holdings around newly located farmsteads.[21] In the southern half of the project, the new settlements are small groups of farmsteads of both new and resettled farmers. The new pattern is clearly shown in Figure 6.2.

Intensification, Specialization and Industrialization

The dominance of commercial farming in the agricultural settlements of advanced, industrialized regions is historically well established. Yet radical changes in agriculture and its settlement have occurred in recent years, the result of major shifts towards greater intensification and

Figure 6.2: Farm Settlement Reorganization at Mooriem, Northwest Germany

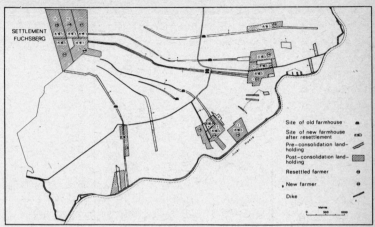

Source: A. Mayhew, 'Agrarian Reform in West Germany', *Transactions*, Institute of British Geographers, Vol. 59 (1971), p. 70, with permission of the Institute of British Geographers.

specialization of the agricultural economy. In addition the growing significance of industrialized farming systems has added a new dimension to rural settlement.

The increasing intensity and specialization of many sectors of agriculture during this century, particularly since World War II, is a function of pressure from both private and public sectors for greater efficiency and improved productivity. In simple terms this has meant significant changes in the input-mix of agricultural enterprises involving a shift from labour to capital intensity (Table 6.1). In some sectors, such as fruit and vegetable farming, the labour component is still important. Yet its use is highly specialized and is dependent upon heavy capital investment for high productivity. In agriculture generally, then, by 1980 labour may comprise only 10 per cent of total inputs in American agriculture with non-land capital making up 80 per cent of the total.[22] In part this has occurred through increasing application of machinery, fertilizers, pesticides and improved plant and livestock varieties. It has involved also the enlargement of both farm and enterprise size for the achievement of industrial efficiency in certain agricultural sectors has depended upon the inevitable economies of scale. We should

Table 6.1: Selected Farm Indexes of Inputs: 1950 to 1977, United States (1967=100 Inputs based on physical quantities of resources used in production)

Input	1950	1955	1960	1965	1970	1972	1973	1974	1975	1976	1977 (prel.)
Total	104	105	101	98	99	100	101	101	100	101	102
Farm labour	217	185	145	110	90	85	85	83	80	78	78
Farm real estate	105	105	100	99	98	95	94	93	93	94	94
Mechanical power and machinery	84	97	97	94	100	101	105	109	112	113	114
Agricultural chemicals	29	39	49	75	115	131	136	140	127	141	146
Feed, seed and livestock purchases	63	72	84	93	104	113	116	107	100	107	109
Taxes and interest	82	88	94	100	100	100	100	101	101	100	101
Miscellaneous	87	94	105	109	109	115	111	110	104	116	113

Source: *Statistical Abstract of the United States, 1978* (Washington, DC, US Department of Commerce, Bureau of Census, 1978), Table No. 1211, p. 706.

be cautious, however, of the trend towards larger farms for some modern types of farming combine high intensity and specialization with a small land base. Specialization is the inevitable result of these production efficiency objectives for it results in the use of specialized equipment, buildings, and other inputs at optimal levels.

The terminology which has been used in the preceding paragraph is, in itself, an indication of the similarity that now exists between much of agriculture and other sectors of the economy. Indeed the increases in certain types of capital investment have led to greater integration between agricultural and non-agricultural sectors. The input mix of the modern farm depends upon purchases from manufacturing and processing industries. These purchases have increased dramatically in Noth American agriculture during this century, a trend which is now matched by agriculture in parts of Europe, Japan, Australia and New Zealand. As Table 6.1 shows, the consumption of the manufactured inputs of machinery, fertilizer and seeds by United States farmers roughly tripled between 1940 and 1960.

Integration with other economic sectors has increased also on the output side, partly through changes in marketing and partly through the development of vertical integration in certain types of agriculture. The marketing sector now dominates farm production, from the processing to the retailing stage. Modern merchandizing systems depend on product control which in turn forces farm operators to standardize and specialize in order to maintain contractual arrangements with processors and distributors. In order to economize in the linkages between production and retailing, some farm enterprises have replaced an exchange relationship with an integrated one. In other words production, processing, packing and marketing are controlled by a single enterprise.

These developments suggest a move towards increased industrialization of agriculture: the expansion of the agribusiness or corporate farming which is popularly assumed to be taking over the whole of American agriculture. However, while in a 1969 survey, 21,513 farms in the United States were found to be corporations, only 1,797 of these were large agribusinesses. The rest were family operations incorporated for tax and other business advantages.[23] Large, vertically integrated agribusinesses, while they have had an impressive impact on rural settlement and food production, are restricted to certain types of specialized agriculture, such as broiler chicken and fruit and vegetable production. Change in the structure of farm settlement should be seen, therefore, in two contexts: the adaptation of the family farm to modern economic circumstances, and the introduction of new, industrialized enterprises in certain agricultural sectors.

Adaptation on the Family Farm

The transformation of many existing farmsteads in more affluent agricultural regions is obvious to any observer of contemporary rural landscapes. In the original mixed farming areas which dominated so much of western Europe and the United States, the appearance of new structures is tangible evidence of a switch from general to specialized agriculture and of increasing capital intensity in production. It is important to recognize that many crop-livestock farms contain buildings which are representative of the long-term evolution of farming practices and technology. Yet significant changes have occurred in mixed farming since World War II which have resulted in the widespread addition of structures which are quite different from any that existed previously.

These changes in the mixed farming economy of the temperate regions of Europe and North America have not, of course, affected all farms, for many remain small operations, or have been abandoned under the pressure of modernization. However, amongst farms that continue to operate, the increasing tendency is for specialization in single activities such as feedgrain production, hog and cattle fattening, egg and chicken production and cash-cropping.

In certain types of operation specialization has not necessarily involved major alterations to farmstead structure. Both dairying and smaller-scale cattle and hog fattening enterprises are good examples of this. In these, the main change in production method has come through a revolution in methods of feeding. The pressure for improved and more reliable yield of milk and meat, has resulted in specialization in feed crops, such as corn, alfalfa and soybeans, and the development of storage and delivery systems to match. The silo is probably the most familiar of these storage methods. However, a more recent addition to many farmsteads is the collection of aluminium bins which combine storage with drying, a system which is particularly advantageous where corn is used as a feed (Figure 6.3).

On many livestock farms, then, new additions are combined with existing buildings in a process of adaptation. This has been recognized by Kiefer in his study of hog farms in the United States Corn Belt. Here, modern additions of storage facilities for machinery and drying bins for corn which have come with the shift to specialized corn-hog production, co-exist with older storage methods such as corn-cribs and barns.[24] Yet, as Figure 6.3 shows, modern structures do have an

Figure 6.3: Modernization of the Corn Belt Farmstead

important impact on the physical appearance and layout of farmstead and therefore upon the rural landscapes of which they are a part. These structures reflect increased capital intensity, which is not restricted to machinery, fuel and fertilizer, but extends to the purchase of new types of buildings, most of which are prefabricated and constructed of steel, concrete, asbestos and aluminium.

There is a notable paucity of studies of new agricultural buildings, but one exception is that by Weller which discusses the problems of their impact upon rural landscapes in Britain.[25] Weller's observations are applicable to North America as well as to Britain, for he points out the importance of extensions of existing farmsteads. New buildings tend to destroy the original layout of the farmstead, particularly where a courtyard plan existed, while the modern, prefabricated buildings meet the requirements of present-day agriculture by being larger, having a wider, higher roof span, and being constructed of durable, artificial materials. In addition, they reflect the specialized uses to which they are put.

Changes that have occurred in farmsteads structure have been matched by considerable alterations to the landscape of agricultural open space and to farm layout. One aspect of this which has received probably the most attention is the enlargement of farms, which has accompanied the desire to increase economies of scale in both feed and cash cropping. The use of modern farm machinery, too, has required the expansion of field size and the removal of the permanent field boundaries which were a legacy of an era of mixed farming. In Indiana, for example, Kiefer describes the amalgamation of the small fields of one 32 hectare farm into a single field devoted solely to corn production.[26]

This process has been particularly apparent in parts of Europe, for it is there that farmers have inherited complex patterns of small fields. Yet the economic demands of efficient cash-cropping, amidst the protests of countryside conservationists, have resulted in the removal of hedgerows in Britain on a wide scale in recent years. This has been the subject of an intensive study by the Countryside Commission which illustrates the ways in which field enlargement and hedgerow removal affect the visual appearance of rural landscapes. In Huntingdon-shire, the study recorded an increase in average field size from 7.6 to 18 hectares, and the removal of 25.3 metres of hedges per hectare between 1945 and 1972.[27] This makes the large-scale use of cultivating and harvesting machinery, as well as fertilizer and pesticide spraying equipment, not only possible but also efficient. On the negative side, the risk of wind erosion because of the removal of natural windbreaks is increased.

Farm enlargement in many of the older settled areas of North America has become increasingly difficult to achieve through the addition of land which is contiguous to the original holding. Consequently a common method of expanding acreage in recent years has been the acquisition of non-contiguous parcels of land. These may be purchased or rented often from farmers who are retiring or who cannot compete in the modern agricultural economy and decide to sell their land. Diller recognized farm fragmentation as early as 1941, showing that 56 out of a total of 305 farmers in a small eastern Nebraska community operated discontiguous parcels of land ranging in size from 16 to 192 hectares.[28] In fact large crop farms in the Great Plains tend to be highly fragmented. In part this is due to the long-established practice of suitcase or sidewalk farming, which creates a clear separation between farmer and farmstead. Farming which involved the management of several or more tracts distributed over a considerable distance is evident in the Great Plains by the reduction in number of farms and the sharp increase in average size of farms.[29]

The enlargement of farms through fragmentation, however, has now spread to other regions. The most recent evidence for this comes from Smith's work in Minnesota, where in two townships he discovered that the majority of farms in both cash-cropping and feed-livestock areas consisted of fragmented holdings.[30] Smith concludes that farm fragmentation indicates that demand for land from commercial farmers exceeds the supply generated by the retirement of marginal and elderly operators. His study suggests, too, a strong positive relationship between fragmentation and farm size, which indicates that fragment-ation is an important method of increasing the scale of agricultural operations. However, in some areas, farmers seeking to enlarge their holdings are forced to accept a fragmented pattern because land use and ownership patterns prevent contiguous parcels. This is particularly evident in rural areas on the fringes of expanding urban centres, where major transformations in agricultural settlement patterns have occurred. Yet, contrary to the conventional view that farms in the urban fringe are forced to become smaller, there is evidence that large operations are made possible by the availability of scattered parcels of under-developed land. A recent survey of Markham township just to the northeast of Toronto reveals a complex pattern of farm land ownership and rental (Figure 6.4).

Figure 6.4: Fragmented Farms in the Urban Fringe

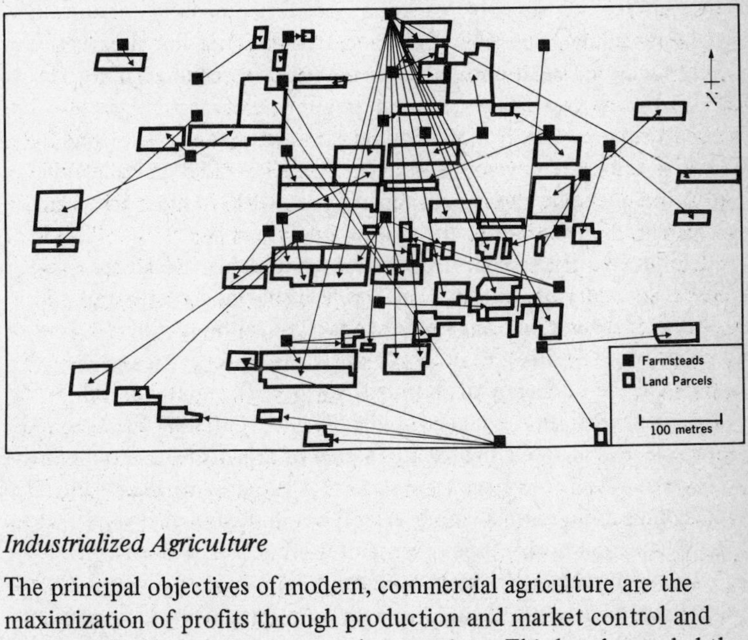

Industrialized Agriculture

The principal objectives of modern, commercial agriculture are the maximization of profits through production and market control and the minimization of environmental uncertainty. This has demanded the transfer of industrialized production methods to certain agricultural sectors: large-scale operations, large amounts of capital invested in a high technology, high energy system, vertical integration, and corporate enterprises.

This is clearly a revolution in agriculture. Not one, as we have just seen, which has led to the complete transformation of the average family farm, but one which has produced new elements of agricultural settlement in a number of regions and farm sectors. Because of the steady increase in demand for meat products in national and international markets, specialized feed grain and livestock fattening enterprizes have become an important element in North American meat production. The feedlot has a comparatively long history, having originated in the United States Corn Belt in the 1930s. However, high-energy feeding of beef cattle on a large scale using feed and yearling cattle purchased from outside the operation has spread to the south and southwest, as well as to parts of Europe and Japan. The industrialized nature of the feedlot is a function of the mass production of beef cattle through controlled and largely automated systems of feedings. Cattle are kept in regular-shaped pens and, instead of being grazed, are fed from a central feed store, the aim being to maximize output by maintaining maximum feedlot capacity year round and fattening cattle to optimum weight as rapidly as possible. The appearance of a feedlot stresses the highly functional relationship between a series of rectangular corrals, divided by service roads and surrounding the feed, machinery and administrative centre. Not all feedlots are as large as that shown in Figure 6.5. In their development in the Imperial Valley in California, Gregor has identified a range in capacity from 100 to more than 20,000, head depending on the type of operation.[31]

One version of the feedlot system which is highly specialized is industrialized drylot dairying. This has been the main method of milk production around Los Angeles for some time, although there is now evidence of it spreading to other regions where there is pressure to improve in the efficiency of fluid milk output. The southern California drylot dairy operation has been studied in some detail by Fielding and Gregor.[32] The main distinguishing feature of this type of dairying is the absence of pasture. Average farm size is 2.4 hectares. But herds are large with 100 or more normal, and over 500 not uncommon. However, the industrialization of this type of agriculture is reflected more in the level of milk production and system of management. With high-input costs milk yields have to be maximized, without placing increased demands on local land. Fodder and herd replacements are brought in from other

Figure 6.5: Beef Feedlot: Amarillo, Texas

areas, and the industrial character of the drylot is further reflected in high specialization in the use of labour. On larger operations the physical structure of the 'farmstead' is more reminiscent of a factory than a farm with large numbers of corrals, with milking barns at the centre, plus administrative offices, dormitories, cookhouses and often milk cooling and bottling plants.

An important characteristic of the feedlot system is the freeing of the 'farmstead' from dependence on its surrounding fields. This separation from land reaches its peak in contemporary methods of egg and chicken production. Modern poultry farming is one of the best examples of the industrialization of agriculture. The 'farm' itself consists generally of a long, low, factory-like structure, in which thousands of birds are fed and processed by automated systems. Scientific research has created a 'technological chicken' which depends upon prepared feeds, antibiotics and controlled breeding methods.[33] Meat and eggs from such a bird can be produced only as part of a fully co-ordinated chain of activities. Today's poultry farmer is just one stage in a vertically-integrated industry, which is dominated by national feed-processing and meat-packing corporations. These control every stage from hatching to retailing, and make the poultry farmer little more than an employee, restricted by the contract prices and production methods set by the corporation.

The development of industrialized farming systems has not been restricted to livestock production, for some types of specialized cash-crop agriculture have also undergone radical changes. One example of the effect of this on farmstead structure has been provided by Hart and Chestang, who have examined the industrialization of tobacco farming in east Carolina.[34] The main feature of this is the relatively recent adoption of mechanized methods of planting, harvesting and curing which has led to the enlargement of farm size and to the substitution of labour by capital inputs. Mechanical harvesters have reduced labour needs, but more significantly their development has been associated with the introduction of new bulk-curing barns which have replaced the traditional flue-curing barn. The new structure is 'a shiny new metal bulk barn, which looks for all the world like a trailer'.[35] The tobacco is cured by forced, heated air, and the barns are fully automated. Despite some enlargement to make optimal use of intensive mechanization, tobacco farms are not large in area. However, the modern Carolina tobacco operation would qualify as a 'large, industrialized crop farm' according to a definition proposed by Gregor.[36] In his definition, such farms have a highly rationalized farming technology, crop specialization, advanced cultivation and harvesting techniques, large operating units, management centralization, large-scale production and heavy capital investment. In addition they should have at least five resident workers with families, which is an indication of the scale of production.

The main concentrations of large, industrialized crop farms in the United States are in California where they dominate fruit and vegetable and cotton farming. But they are evident also in Texas in large cotton enterprises, in irrigated agriculture in Arizona and, more recently, in fruit production in the northeast. In southern California, much of the rapid expansion of specialized crop farming after World War II occurred on previously cultivated land and depended upon expensive irrigation systems. It was the need for irrigation and for a well-organized marketing system which favoured large industrialized operations. Irrigated rice farming is pursued on farms as large as 1,200 hectares, on which machine capital often exceeds investment in land. Self-propelled combines, land planes, contour ploughs, and even low-flying aircraft used for seeding fields bounded by plastic levées, are tangible evidence of an industrialized operation.[37] The largest of these modern enterprises, however, are among the cotton farms of the west side of the San Joaquin Valley and the specialized vegetable farms of the southwest. Ninety per cent of California vegetable farms sell $40,000 or more in products annually, a higher amount than for any other farming type in California. Irrigated vegetable farms aim to maximize output by multiple cropping and through heavy investment in machinery and labour. The average investment per farm in the early 1970s was half-a-million dollars.[38] And it is to this type of farming that the term 'agribusiness' is most applicable, for an increasing number are owned by large food corporations, who have incorporated processing and packaging into the farm enterprise.

The recent changes in agriculture which have had such a direct effect on the landscape and structure of farm settlement are likely to alter the traditional economic relationships of farmers with the local community. Increases in capital intensity have for some time now virtually eliminated the farm as a source of local employment. The main exception to this is in the use of labour during harvest periods and in fruit and vegetable production in the continuously cropped areas such as the southwest of the United States. But in these situations labour is rarely local for it is the migrant farm worker who makes up the bulk of the rural population. It should be pointed out that, despite the use of relatively large amounts of labour, the vegetable farms of southern California remain capital intensive, for labour is poorly paid in comparison with capital investment costs.

The economic links of many agricultural enterprises, therefore, are now likely to be predominantly outside the local rural community. This is partly because of the reduction in demand for and availability of local labour but much more because of the industrialized nature of modern agriculture. High levels of capital investment in factory-produced buildings, machinery, fertilizers, prepared feeds, pesticides and fuel force farmers into the general industrial economy. Specialization of production, too, requires linkages with a vertically-integrated food industry and an urban marketplace. There are those who see dangers in the breakdown of traditional agricultural relationships. The 'manufactured paradise' is, for Wendell Berry, a system of agriculture which is inherently exploitative, viewing land as merely another input to be used for the maximization of profit.[39] 'That one American farmer can now feed himself and fifty-six other people,' writes Berry, 'may be . . . a triumph of economics and technology; by no stretch of reason can it be considered a triumph of agriculture or of culture.'[40]

What Berry is suggesting is that increasing commercialization and industrialization in agriculture leads to an exploitative view of the soil and therefore a breakdown of the interdependent relationship of settlement and land. Furthermore, as agriculture becomes more commercialized, its traditional rural ties are weakened and it becomes simply another sector of an urban-dominated economy. In the case of commercialized agriculture in most underdeveloped regions, it becomes a sector of a world market economy, for most commercial development emphasizes export production. Thus any increase in farm income will therefore stimulate the economy as a whole, rather than the local rural economy in particular.

Notes

1. Polly Hill, *Rural Capitalism in West Africa* (Cambridge: Cambridge University Press, 1970); W.B. Morgan, 'Peasant Agriculture in Tropical Africa', in M.F. Thomas and G.W. Whittington (eds.), *Environmental and Land Use in Africa* (London: Methuen, 1969), pp. 241-72.

2. Ibid., p. 246.

3. Allan R. Beals, 'Namahalli, 1953-66, Urban Influence and Change in Southern Mysore', in K. Ishwaran (ed.), *Change and Continuity in India's Villages* (New York: Columbia University Press, 1970), pp. 57-72.

4. Elizabeth Colson and T. Scudder, 'New Economic Relationships Between the Givembe Valley and the Line of Rail', in David Parkin (ed.), *Town and Country in Central and Eastern Africa* (London: Oxford University Press, 1975).

5. S.N. Eisenstadt, *Modernization: Protest and Change* (Englewood Cliffs, NJ: Prentice-Hall, 1966).

6. N. Long, *An Introduction to the Sociology of Rural Development* (London: Tavistock Publications, 1977), pp. 10-11.

7. Hill, *Rural Capitalism*, pp. 21-9.

8. A.L. Mabogunje, 'The Evolution of Rural Settlement in Egba Division, Nigeria', *Journal of Tropical Geography*, Vol. 13 (1959), pp. 65-80; R.K. Udo, 'Disintegration of Nucleated Settlement in Eastern Nigeria', *Geographical Review*, Vol. 55 (1965), pp. 53-67.

9. Edmundo Flores, 'Rural Development in Mexico', in Raanan Weitz, *Rural Development in a Changing World* (Cambridge, Mass.: MIT Press, 1971), pp. 515-31.

10. V.P. Pande, *Village Community Projects in India* (New York: Asia Publishing House, 1967), pp. 171-7.

11. Ibid., p. 182.

12. Keith Buchanan, *The Transformation of the Chinese Earth* (London: G. Bell & Sons, 1970), pp. 114-42.

13. G.G. Burmantov, 'The Formation of Functional Types of Settlements in the Southern Taiga', *Soviet Geography*, Review and Translation, Vol. 9, 1968, pp. 112-19.

14. S.A. Kovalev, 'Transformation of Rural Settlements in the Soviet Union', *Geoforum*, Vol. 9-12 (1972), pp. 33-45.

15. C. Davis Fogg, 'Smallholder agriculture in Eastern Nigeria', in George Dalton (ed.), *Economic Development and Social Change* (New York: Natural History Press, 1971), pp. 575-96.

16. J.D. MacArthur, 'Agricultural Settlement in Kenya', in G.K. Helleiner (ed.), *Agricultural Planning in East Africa* (Nairobi: East African Publishing House, 1968), pp. 117-35.

17. D.R.F. Taylor, 'Agricultural Change in Kikuyuland', in Thomas and Whittington, *Africa*, pp. 463-93.

18. D.J. Siddle, 'Rural Development Schemes', in D. Hywel Davies (ed.),

Zambia in Maps (London: University of London Press, 1971), p. 70.

19. M. Hirst, 'Recent Villagization in Tanzania', *Geography*, Vol. 63 (1978), pp. 122-5.

20. A. Mayhew, 'Structural Reform and the Future of West German Agriculture', *Geographical Review*, Vol. 60 (1970), pp. 54-68.

21. Idem, 'Agrarian Reform in West Germany: an assessment of the integrated development project Moorriem', *Transactions*, Institute of British Geographers, No. 52 (1971), pp. 61-76.

22. Earl O. Heady *et al.*, *Roots of the Farm Problem* (Ames, Iowa: Iowa State University Press, 1965).

23. US Dept. of Agriculture Economic Research Service, *Corporations With Farming Operations*, AER–209 (Washington, 1971).

24. Wayne E. Kiefer, 'An Agricultural Settlement Complex in Indiana', *Annals*, Association of American Geographers, Vol. 62 (1972), pp. 487-506. Kiefer's study of modern additions to this farmstead were discussed also in Chapter 3 of this book.

25. John Weller, *Modern Agriculture and Rural Planning* (London: Architectural Press, 1967).

26. Kiefer, 'Agricultural Settlement', p. 490.

27. Countryside Commission, *New Agricultural Landscapes* (Cheltenham, 1977).

28. Robert Diller, *Farm Ownership, Tenancy and Land Use in a Nebraska Community* (Chicago: University of Chicago Press, 1941), p. 178.

29. Walter M. Kollmorgen and George F. Jenks, 'Suitcase Farming in Sully Country, South Dakota', *Annals*, Association of American Geographers, Vol. 48 (1958), pp. 27-40; and idem, 'Sidewalk Farming in Toole County, Montana, and Trail County, North Dakota', *Annals*, Association of American Geographers, Vol. 48 (1958), pp. 209-31.

30. Everett G. Smith, Jr., 'Fragmented Farms in the United States', *Annals*, Association of American Geographers, Vol. 65 (1975), pp. 58-70.

31. H.F. Gregor, *An Agricultural Typology of California* (Budapest: Akadémiai Kiado, 1974), p. 26.

32. G.J. Fielding, 'The Los Angeles Milkshed', *Geographical Review*, Vol. 54 (1964), pp. 1-12; H.F. Gregor, 'Industrialized Drylot Dairying: An Overview', *Economic Geography*, Vol. 39 (1963), pp. 299-318.

33. Ross B. Talbot, *The Chicken War* (Ames, Iowa: Iowa State University Press, 1978), pp. 3-12.

34. J.F. Hart and E.L. Chestang, 'Rural Revolution in East Carolina', *Geographical Review*, Vol. 68 (1978), pp. 435-58.

35. Ibid., p. 447.

36. H.F. Gregor, 'The Large, Industrialized American Crop Farm', *Geographical Review*, Vol. 69 (1970), pp. 151-75.

37. Gregor, *California*, p. 55.

38. Ibid., pp. 91-2.

39. Wendell Berry, *The Unsettling of America, Culture and Agriculture* (New York: Aaron Books, 1977).

40. Ibid., p. 33.

7 RESIDENTIAL AND RECREATIONAL DEVELOPMENT

The spread of commerce and industry into agriculture is one facet of a fundamental change in rural-urban relationships. Another is the transformation of many rural areas in advanced, industrialized countries into predominantly residential and recreational hinterlands of metropolitan regions. This is primarily a function of increased mobility, affluence and leisure time in certain sectors of modern society, as well as a reorientation of economic activity. The effect has been to produce important changes in rural land use, in the structure of rural settlement, and in the nature of rural society.

The Residential Hinterland

Rural settlements are traditionally residential. However, in recent decades, as with agriculture, the conventional relationships between the home and the local community have experienced a radical alteration in some rural areas. Essentially this has involved the growing use of rural settlements as primarily residential places. The aspect of this which has received most research attention is the movement of urban dwellers into those rural areas which are within daily commuting distance of urban jobs and regular access to other urban services. Some of this group have developed certain functional relationships with rural land by becoming hobby farmers, but most have purely residential objectives. In addition, a significant proportion of rural residential growth has involved retired people. However, this outward movement of urbanites into rural areas is not the only factor in the trend towards residential specialization, for its origins can be traced also to the increase in commuting to urban jobs on the part of the rural population. This includes the established rural non-farm population and growing numbers of farm residents and farmers who engage in off-farm work. There is, therefore, a two-way movement of urban workers seeking rural residence and rural residents seeking urban work. Furthermore, recent trends in certain areas suggest that an expansion of manufacturing and other non-farm jobs in nonmetropolitan and rural areas has provided new opportunities for rural residents beyond the immediate urban hinterland.

There is some evidence for these developments in the rural population trends of the past few years. While many rural regions and communities continue to experience out-migration and depopulation, in some industrialized countries the direction of population flow has actually been reversed. Vining and Kontuly have examined population dispersal in ten industrial nations and have shown that Japan, Sweden, Italy, Norway, France and West Germany have experienced a recent decline in the rate of migration from peripheral regions to metropolitan areas.[1] This began in the 1960s but has gathered its real momentum during the 1970s decade so that the first four of these countries now show a reversal of the traditional rural to urban population flow. The logical interpretation of this is that population has spread into the non-metropolitan areas adjacent to cities. This is certainly the case in Japan and France, for example, where the Paris and Tokyo-Osaka conurbations have grown through the spread of population into the urban fringe, while the urban core has experienced a decline in net in-migration. However Vining and Kontuly have described a somewhat different situation in Sweden, Norway and West Germany, where population dispersal has included migration to areas which are not contiguous with metropolitan regions. Recent population growth in northern Sweden is one example of such a trend, although Vining and Kontuly suggest that 'people, in moving back to peripheral regions have tended to concentrate in a limited number of small and medium-sized cities there'.[2]

Perhaps the most remarkable turnaround in non-metropolitan population growth has occurred in the United States. Beale's studies have shown that non-metropolitan counties increased their populations by 5.6 per cent between 1970 and 1974, compared with 3.4 per cent in metropolitan counties.[3] Yet this growth was not confined to areas adjacent to metropolitan counties. These certainly continue to show the highest non-metropolitan increases as they did in the fifties and sixties, but in the early seventies concern over increasing congestion in cities paradoxically was accompanied by an upswing of population growth in areas beyond the metropolitan fringe. Between 1970 and 1974, non-metropolitan counties not adjacent to SMSAs (Standard Metropolitan Statistical Areas) grew more rapidly than did metropolitan areas. Nor was this growth restricted to counties with large centres, for completely rural counties (those with no town of 2,500) not adjacent to an SMSA experienced a higher rate of immigration than any metro-politan category. This was a lower rate than for adjacent rural counties but it does indicate the reversal of rural population decline in both fringe and peripheral areas.[4]

These general trends do not mean that all of rural America is now on the road to permanent demographic revival. The changes have been identified over only a relatively short time period, while even sub-regional aggregations obscure continued migration from the poorer, more isolated communities. Furthermore, non-metropolitan population growth remains highest in counties adjacent to metropolitan areas. Finally, the designation 'non-metropolitan' should not be regarded as being synonymous with 'rural'. In fact Beale's own studies of county level changes show that the presence of State colleges, military establishments and, above all, industrial development is a major factor in stimulating population growth, while predominantly agricultural counties tend to continue to lose population.[5]

The Urban Fringe: a Problem of Concept

Despite the apparent resurgence of population growth in some rural areas beyond the fringes of metropolitan areas, most post-World War II growth in rural areas occurred in the so-called urban fringe. Gottmann's study of the metropolitan-dominated regions of the northeastern United States showed that as early as 1930 the proportion of the population officially classed as urban began to decrease in some states, included Massachusetts, Rhode Island, Connecticut and New York. He showed, too, that during the 1940s and 1950s the rural non-farm population as a proportion of the rural farm population was, for almost all the region, 12 per cent above the national average.[6] Pahl, with somewhat more precise figures, has described similar trends in what he terms the Outer Metropolitan Region of London, which experienced a 65 per cent increase in population between 1951 and 1961.[7] And in the very recent trends analyzed by Beale, the highest rates of non-metropolitan growth between 1960 and 1974 were in counties adjacent to metropolitan areas.[8]

This concentration of rural population growth in areas close to cities has led to a proliferation of research interest in the urban fringe. Yet as a concept it suffers from a confusion of meanings. The terms used to describe it are various: the rural-urban fringe (which is probably the most common), urbs in rure, commuting zone, dispersed city. The essence of all these terms is that the changes in land use, economy and society in fringe areas have created a special regional category which is part-way between urban and rural, but which is dynamically dominated by the urban centre. Wehrwein, in one of the earliest studies of such regions, saw the fringe as a zone of complexity and dynamic variation.[9] Above all, it was, for Wehrwein and others who have followed his model, a zone of transition which satisfied the concept of a rural-urban continuum. This is particularly well expressed by Russwurm who says, 'In a conceptual and spatial sense it includes the zone which will handle most of the building additions to existing cities for the imaginable future.'[10]

This notion sees the rural part of the fringe as the area into which urban development will expand, in which land-use relationships are in flux and which will eventually be gobbled up by the continuously built-up metropolitan area. In this view, rural settlement ceases to exist, as does any distinction between urban and rural. There is, however, another interpretation of the fringe which is more acceptable and comes closer to the principle of rural distinctiveness which this book espouses. This alternative view sees the fringe as the explicit 'symbiosis (rather than fusion) of urban and rural,' in which 'urban people and activities have taken on more rural aspects, and traditionally rural pursuits have acquired urban characteristics.'[11] This concept of a new kind of rurality was taken further by Spectorsky who coined the term 'exurbia' to describe the areas outside cities as distinctive zones in which urban people have taken up residence in the countryside.[12] The emphasis here is on adaptation, not absorption, and Spectorsky's interpretation has been followed by a number of studies which see the fringe as a peculiarly modern rural landscape and society. It is that area which has experienced a change from 'rural homogeneity to rural heterogeneity'.[13]

There is one final problem with the concept of the rural-urban fringe which must be considered; that is the view that residential expansion declines linearly with distance from the city. In the most general of senses this is true, yet three recent trends have seriously complicated this model. Firstly, the dispersal of industrial activities into smaller cities and towns in the United States has stimulated exurban development away from metropolitan regions. Secondly, increases in commuting distance and changes in work habits have permitted exurban development well beyond the boundaries of the traditional fringe. Finally, intensification of planning legislation has distorted the relationships between the urban and rural areas.

Residential Development by Exurbanites

In this section, the main concern is with the nature and impact of exurbanite residential development on rural settlements whether or not that occurs within a clearly defined urban fringe. For our purposes, exurbanites include those who leave urban areas to take up permanent residence in rural areas while retaining regular employment and other links with the city, as well as those who move to rural areas to retire.

Who are these exurbanites? A considerable amount of primarily sociological research has been carried out on the socio-economic and cultural make-up of this group. Most of this research agrees that exurbanites are upwardly mobile and are predominantly from the professional, executive and managerial middle-class groups. The classic study which shows this is Dobriner's. His examination of Huntington, Long Island, revealed that 60 per cent of those who moved to this village in the 1950s were 'upper white collar workers,' nearly one half of whom worked in New York City.[14] Pahl's analysis of commuter villages in Hertfordshire emphasized the significance of the middle-class professional in recent residential development.[15] There is an historical precedent for the more affluent members of urban society to move out to country residences. Exurban development of this kind, albeit on a more grandiose level, spawned the country estate in parts of Europe and especially in New England in the later nineteenth and early twentieth centuries. However, we should be cautious of deterministically assuming that those who become exurbanites today are a modern version of the social élite. At least two studies have indicated that urban to rural migrants in recent years consist mainly of white-collar workers who aspire to no more than a three-bedroom home in a residential sub-division.[16]

Why do urbanites move to rural areas? As with any migration decision it is extremely difficult to answer this, for reasons invariably personal and often regionally specific. Studies which have questioned urban to rural migrants on their motives tend to stress the importance of rural landscape, lifestyle, the escape from urban problems, the chance for privacy and better property. Spectorsky has proposed that exurbia represents the 'Limited Dream' of the harassed urban executive.[17] Unable to achieve the 'Unlimited Dream' of going to the South Seas, a two-acre country estate or a country village becomes the limited retreat from the city. This vision of the rural hinterland as a retreat for urban man is a recurring theme in Western culture, as Williams has shown.[18]

Insofar as it represents the desires of the potential exurbanite, modern advertising of even the most mundane of rural properties provides a vivid illustration of the symbolic value of rural life and landscape. Real estate agents appear to be keenly aware of a strong sentiment within certain sections of urban society for the various virtues of country living. So the inconveniences of commuting, of poorly serviced villages and of some degree of isolation are obscured by extolling the spiritual and physical pleasures of a rural setting. In a survey of real estate advertisements in a Toronto newspaper, seven attributes of rural living were recognized in advertisements for rural and exurban properties: proximity to nature, recreation, rural landscape, atmosphere, community, rural designs and agricultural environment. These were expressed in ways which capture the essence of change in attitude to rural land with exurbanite residential development (Table 7.1).

What is the impact of exurban residential development on rural settlements? Clearly one would expect there to be profound changes in society, land use and landscape, and research into the subject largely supports this expectation. Much of this research, however, has examined only the sociological implications. The main reason for this is the strong emphasis on the class distinctiveness of exurbanites and the effect this is likely to have on rural communities. Dobriner's Huntington was two communities: the high income, well educated, cosmopolitan newcomers, and the comfortable, locally-oriented old-timers.[19] The exclusivity of exurban groups in rural communities in New England is a well-known phenomenon, which has been described recently by Duncan in his study of Bedford Village, 35 miles north of New York City. 'Bedford is the image of affluence and cultural homogeneity,' in which, 'the majority of residents are upper-middle and upper-class, white, Anglo-Saxon Protestants.' Few of the houses are valued at less than $40,000, while the average value is around $80,000.[20]

The existence of class segregation in exurban communities is supported by a number of British studies where sociological interest in class structure is highly developed. Pahl's work has been the model for subsequent studies, for his detailed analysis of the northern urban fringe of London showed significant differences between the lifestyles of middle-class newcomers and working-class rural people.[21] The primary cause of segregation in Pahl's communities was the relative affluence of the newcomers. But class and affluence as factors are not easily separated from the important geographical factors which distinguish exurban development. Two of these appear to be equally likely to contribute to the creation of two communities. Firstly, whether middle-class and affluent or not, exurbanites are newcomers and commuters. Hence exurbanized rural settlements are often called commuter settlements and have even been seen as part of the 'cocktail belt', the places to which the tired urban executive returns in time for a martini or two before dinner. Newcomers traditionally are slow to be absorbed into rural communities, particularly if they arrive in large numbers and, more importantly, if they do not work in the community.

The second segregative factor has to do with the territorial patterns

Table 7.1: Attributes of Rural Living Mentioned in Rural Real Estate Advertising

			Attribute Categories			
Nature	Landscape	Recreation	Atmosphere	Design	Agriculture	Community
Birds	Countryside	Boating	Escape	Country comfort	Farmer's market	Country village atmosphere
Clean air	Parkland	Camping	Rural 'feel'	Old-time stateliness	Fresh picked vegetables	Neighbourly attitude
Flowers	Pastoral setting	Fishing	Rustic charm	Rural architectural theme		
Nature trails	Rolling hills	Horseriding	Seclusion			
Nature unspoiled	Space	Parkland	Small-town			
Sunshine	Wooded Knolls	Walking	Tranquillity			
Trees	Views					
Water						
Woodland						

Source: Advertisements in *Toronto Star*, October 1978.

which develop with exurbanization. A recent study by Walker suggests that the divisions between new and old populations in an Ontario village are strongly influenced by the fact that the two groups occupy different spaces within the village. The old-timers live in the traditional village area while the newcomers occupy a suburban-like subdivision on the edge of the village. This has created a sense of separate territories, while the suburban style of the subdivision reinforces the tendency for social contacts on a localized rather than a community scale.[22]

However, Walker warns against assuming complete segregation in Bond Head, for there is evidence of relative homogeneity in the larger community.[23] Indeed there is good cause to question the general assumption that exurban development in rural areas will always create two communities. The first reason for this is that in recent years there has been an increase in migration from urban areas of people from a wide range of social and economic backgrounds. Secondly, rural people themselves, even farmers, as we have already seen, are coming more under the influence of the same universal values as exurbanites. This point is made by Ambrose in his study of a commuter village in Sussex, England. While important inequalities of wealth, property ownership and power exist in this village, these reflect national inequalities and furthermore cannot any longer be understood in simple class terms in a complex society.[24]

While the social impact of exurban residential development is somewhat obscure, the changes that have occurred in the physical structure of rural settlement are readily apparent. Furthermore, if the movement of exurbanites into rural areas may not necessarily result in obvious symptoms of social segregation, it does bring with it new settlement elements and quite radical transformations of existing settlement structure. Three main types of residential development can be identified: rural estates, subdivisions, and conversions of existing buildings.

Rural Estates. The desire for open space, privacy, pleasant landscape and property has resulted in the strong preference for rural residences set on large lots and dispersed in open countryside. It is this kind of exurban development which tends to involve the more affluent members of society, for pressure on rural land, where it has occurred on a large scale, has forced an escalation of property prices. Most rural estate properties in exurbia have been severed from existing farmland, an attractive prospect for farmers who can make money by selling off portions of their land. The pattern of such lots and their spatial relationship with

surrounding farmland is clearly an incursive one which, as we shall see
in more detail later, tends to break up rural areas into larger numbers of
small land parcels. Low-density residential development by its very
nature can occupy large areas. In the most popular areas country
estates can produce a well-packed residential landscape, such as the
one in southeast Connecticut shown in Figure 7.1.

Figure 7.1: Residential Sprawl in Exurban Connecticut

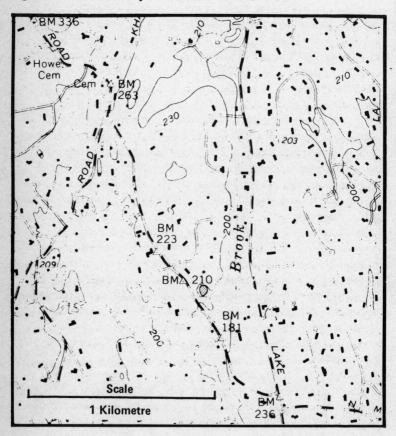

Source: US Geological Survey, Topographic Series.

The obvious impact of the pattern of rural settlement in which the
space along roads between farmsteads and other traditional elements
has been filled in, is matched by the remarkable change in the visual

landscape. This has led at least one observer to see the English country-side as a 'landscape in distress' being rapidly overwhelmed by the 'subtopia' of urban sprawl.[25] Yet there are few good studies of the landscape of rural estates. One exception is that by Punter on the residential landscapes of the Toronto exurban region.[26] The study shows that rural estates may be occupied by houses built in a wide range of individualistic designs as well as fairly conventional urban-style residences. The siting of the house in relation to natural features such as slopes, streams, ponds and woodland is an important illustration of the desire for an appropriately rural landscape. But artificial landscaping has perhaps the greatest impact on the appearance of rural settlement. White rail fences, ornamental shrubs and trees, curving driveways, particularly where they are accompanied by the demolition of old agricultural buildings, bring about at least the beginnings of a transform-ation in the rural landscape.

There is a sense in which the appearance of residential estates is a reflection of certain preconceived notions of a genteel and elegant rural landscape. This is readily seen in parts of New England and has been discussed by Duncan.[27] In Bedford Village the older established residential estates emphasize the importance of a rural, natural atmosphere. Many of the larger properties have an English garden atmosphere of meadowland and trees which is consistent with the desire for an elegant, pastoral landscape, so different from a functional, agricultural one.

The intrusion of residential estates into agricultural areas has had an important effect on agricultural land use. It is not intended here to discuss agriculture in the rural-urban fringe in general for this is a large topic in its own right. However, it is important to show how the kind of residential development described above tends to stimulate changes in the patterns of agricultural landholding and the types of agricultural enterprise. The patterns of landholding are most directly influenced by the fragmentation of farm property which results from residential sprawl. Frequently, farmers who have sold off portions of their land for residential use are left with an agricultural parcel which is too small to farm efficiently. In this situation some farmers will sell or rent their remaining land while others will enlarge their operations through fragmented ownership and rental. In fact, given the large amount of land assembly by property developers and speculators in exurbia, the renting of scattered land parcels by farmers is a common phenomenon.

This trend is not entirely unassociated with the general pressure on land prices caused by residential sprawl. This makes farmland rental the only way of maintaining adequate acreage. Alternatively it leads to radical changes in the nature of agricultural enterprises which themselves contribute to the transformation of rural settlement. One change involves a reduction in investment in agricultural land which is a function of urban anticipation: the situation in which farmers are reluctant to farm efficiently when land speculation is more lucrative. Yet exurban agriculture can also mean a shift to more specialized, high-intensity land use. Market gardening, including pick-your-own farming, is the most commonly cited type of agriculture, but horse farms, sod farms, nursery gardens and intensive livestock operations are also typical elements of exurban settlement.

Residential Subdivisions. The other major residential addition to rural settlement is the subdivision or housing estate. As a form of exurban development this has grown in popularity and quantity as pressure on rural land and planning restrictions have reduced the opportunities for dispersed properties. Subdivisions are located both in open countryside and in or adjacent to existing rural settlements. Some of the earlier exurban subdivisions in the United States were the result of the assembly of parcels of farmland by developers who constructed completely new settlements. A few of these were, like Herbert Gans' Levittown, fairly large residential new towns planned and promoted by big development companies.[28] However, most of the sprouting-up of subdivisions in the midst of tracts of farmland has been on a smaller scale. There is considerable variation in the size of lots and the style of development. Some subdivisions consist of properties which approximate the image of the rural estate. Such prestige developments were popular in the early exurban development of southern New England, particularly in areas of woodland and rolling topography. The large lots result in the occupance of sizeable chunks of open space while the generally grandiose design of the houses creates a prominent addition to the rural landscape.

Scattered subdivisions, however, consist also of modest suburban-style homes on conventional, suburban-sized lots. This kind of development, in fact, has been going on in rural areas since well before World War II. It was a common way of responding to housing demand in Britain in the 1920s and 1930s and usually involved the severance of a farmland parcel on which a single cul-de-sac street was constructed with rows of houses or bungalows on either side. Planning restrictions designed to eliminate ribbon development put a stop to this in Britain after the last war, but similar types of small subdivisions have continued to appear around North American cities. As purely residential settlements they are designed for complete dependence on the automobile, while the opportunist and scattered nature of their development often means that they are not fully serviced. Indeed, their proliferation in recent years has posed problems for municipalities and led to the introduction of more restrictive legislation.

Because of the soaring price of land, the increased cost of living in isolated locations, and the growth of planning restrictions, scattered residential development in rural areas, both in Europe and North America, has in recent years tended to diminish. Instead, some new housing is now located in or adjacent to existing hamlets, villages and small towns. Where local planning is well developed, land is strictly zoned and designated for particular kinds of subdivision. The recent trend is towards relatively small-scale, suburban-style subdivisions which are constructed either on open space within the existing village or through the expansion of the built-up area. It is easy to see the effect of this kind of development on the spatial structure of villages. The area occupied by housing tends to be greatly increased, while the suburban-style layout with its orderly, neat arrangement of curving roads, cul-de-sacs and boulevards, transforms village morphology (Figure 7.2). Village population may double in a matter of months, while the tendency for young families to occupy the new housing alters the demographic structure of the community.

We have already noted the research emphasis which has been placed on the changing social structure which results from an influx of urbanites into rural communities. However, new subdivisions in villages are no longer the preserve of the affluent, 'prestige' home-owner. In North America, a wider range of residential types is coming on to the market in these developments, including town houses, semi-detached, and smaller detached homes. In some western European countries, in particular Britain, Holland and Scandinavia, substantial amounts of public housing have been built in villages. In any village undergoing exurban residential development, therefore, there may be several types of subdivisions and associated social groups. For this reason, Walker's interpretation of the importance of the territorial separation of new and old areas of the village may well be a better explanation of the community impact of newcomers.[29] However, it is likely that the effect of spatial differentiation is intensified by the obvious contrast between the landscape and atmosphere of the new suburban style area and that of the old village core. Nor is this merely a contrast between old and new, but rather evidence of the temporal and functional discontinuity created by exurban residential development in rural settlements.

Figure 7.2: Contrasting Morphologies of Old Village Core and New Subdivisions, Tottenham, Ontario

Infilling and Conversion. The influx of urbanites into rural areas does not always create the kind of new elements and the discontinuity which has been described above. In many instances it has involved a more subtle process of residential addition and change. Thus new homes are added to villages and small towns through the occupation of individual vacant lots, and existing buildings are converted to exurban residential use.

The addition of new homes to villages has often been made possible by the relatively large lot size of existing village properties, the owners of which perceive the financial attraction of a demand for building land. Then, too, there are the vacant lots which are common in those small towns and villages which, through earlier depopulation or failure to achieve expected growth, have not reached maximum residential density. Such places are characteristic of those regions of North America, such as the Middle West and Ontario, where villages and small towns were laid out and subdivided by private speculators and public authorities. In many cases, the plan for settlement included far more lots than could be occupied in an agricultural economy. However, where exurban demand for residential land exists, vacant village lots have provided a relatively easy way of satisfying that demand. The availability of this type of land within the serviced area of the village and in areas usually designated for residential use has been an important attraction for urbanites seeking a rural residence. Many villages, therefore, have grown in residential density not through the addition of new subdivisions, but with the infilling of open spaces both within and on the edge of the settlement.

The conversion of existing buildings to exurban residential use represents the most subtle change in the fabric of rural settlement. It is a process which has been made possible by the abandonment of traditional rural buildings in so many rural areas through depopulation or agricultural change. This has created a stock of relatively low-cost housing, a phenomenon which Lewis has identified in Vermont, New Hampshire and Maine.[30] It has also provided various types of originally non-residential buildings such as barns, school houses, windmills and even churches which have been converted to residential use.

Not all changes in use and ownership from traditional rural to modern exurbanite involve the physical conversion of buildings. Yet the modernization, refurbishing and conversion process is an increasingly important aspect of urbanite incursion into rural settlement. It is probably at its most sophisticated in some of the villages and country towns of Europe. In English villages, for example, there is a well-established tradition of converting cottages, stables and barns into residential properties. Planning controls have a strong influence over the design of such conversions, and the desire of many urbanites for a property which matches their image of a picturesque and traditional rural residence reinforces design concerns (Figure 7.3).

To some extent the apparent desire to re-create a romanticized image of old-style country living has stimulated a surge of refurbishing of old property in rural North America. The reproduction of the 'original' colonial look has been an important feature of exurban conversions in many small towns. The regional location of this is a function both of the level of exurban pressure and the relative longevity of settlement. So nostalgia for a rural past is expressed in the conversion of cottages and farmhouses by people whose relationship with the community is far from traditional. However, much of the conversion of buildings to residential use has a more practical objective for it is a convenient way of obtaining a rural residence without constructing a

Figure 7.3: Modernized Cottages in an English Village; Burwash, Sussex

completely new building. This advantage is true particularly of the use of rural housing stock and is one reason for the increasing conversion of farmhouses and even whole farmsteads to purely residential use.

Locally-generated Rural Residential Development

An implicit assumption of much of the research on exurban development, commuter settlements and new residential trends in rural areas is that it is caused exclusively by the movement of urbanites. Yet it would be erroneous to assume that the residential growth which has been described in the preceding pages does, in fact, involve only urbanite newcomers. Some of the increasing residential character of many rural settlements is internally generated. Of course there is nothing new in the additions of housing made on farms and in villages to accommodate family members and retired people. In Upsala village in Minnesota, for example, at least 30 per cent of residents in the village were retired farmers.[31]

However, the new mobility of this century has been available to rural as well as to urban society. Thus while many rural people have emigrated permanently from rural areas when employment opportunities and community attractiveness declined, there is a growing tendency for those within reach of urban employment to commute to this from their rural homes. In addition, the revival of population in the urban fringe has created new economic opportunities for rural residents. Improved employment opportunities have extended into rural areas beyond the fringe, with resultant increases in non-farm population and the stimulation of local residential development.

Part-time Farming

One group of rural inhabitants who are increasingly becoming involved in urban employment are farmers and their families. Part-time farming is a complex phenomenon, but one aspect of it involves the desire on the part of farm families to place less reliance on agriculture as a source of income. The commuting of farmers to nearby industrial employment is a well-established and well-documented phenomenon in Europe. Franklin has provided evidence that 'worker-peasants' are a traditional element in rural society.[32] However, the significant increase in farmer-factory workers came with post-war industrial developments. Clout has summarized this in Europe, describing the general increase in part-time farming around major industrial centres in Poland, France, Germany and Yugoslavia.[33] The consensus of research opinion is that the worker-peasant lifestyle, particularly where regular and well-paid factory work is available, leads to a reduction in investment on the farm, to under-use of machinery, to the growing of less demanding crops and to the abandonment of fields to scrub and weed.[34]

While part-time farming has become a widespread phenomenon in North America, the evidence of reduced commitment to agriculture with increased off-farm work is somewhat less conclusive. Bishop and Fliegel, in their studies of part-time farmers in the United States, have noted a positive relationship between low-income farming and the incidence of part-time farmers.[35] This suggests the desire on the part of less successful farmers to obtain alternative and regular sources of income while maintaining their rural residence and property. However, in terms of commitment to farming, there appear to be three main types of part-time farmer: the persistent part-time farmer, those leaving farming and those entering farming through the part-time method.[36] Fuguitt has shown that in Wisconsin, the combination of off-farm work with farming is used both to enter full-time farming and to leave farming altogether.[37] Indeed it is possible that non-farm income can be used to improve the efficiency of the farm enterprise.

However, the more usual impact of full-time urban employment of farmers and members of their families is, as in Europe, a reduction in farming activity. There is evidence for severe underutilization of land where persistent part-time farmers have reduced their allocation of days worked on the farm.[38] Furthermore, farmers who are engaged in substantial amounts of off-farm work continue to retain farm units in their original size but farm at well below maximum productivity and with substantial reductions in gross farm sales.[39] At least one detailed study has indicated that 'farmers' engaged in full-time factory employment earn between 80 and 100 per cent of their total income from this source.[40] The farm, therefore, ceases to be a significant enterprise and takes on a residential status reminiscent of the rural estate which was described above. This is evident where the farmholding has been reduced in size through the selling or renting of parcels of land to nearby full-time farmers or to non-farm users. It can also be apparent in changes in the physical appearance of the farmstead, with the modernization of the farmhouse, and the addition of the same kinds of non-functional decorations which were recognized with the occupation of farmsteads by exurbanites.

The shift to a more residential use of rural areas by some farm families is part of a larger trend within the established rural population of a number of regions. One of the persistent problems of rural areas has been unemployment and poverty among a growing non-farm population and also among farm family members who are surplus to labour needs on the farm. This problem continues in many regions of the world, but in certain rural areas, the possibility of combining rural residence with urban employment has been extended to the rural workforce. This new mobility among the established rural non-farm population has not been widely studied. Yet it is undoubtedly as important a feature of commuter settlements as the worker-peasant phenomenon, for rural non-farm people are equally able to take advantage of the mobility created by the automobile. It has even been recognized in a south Indian village where 20 miles from the industrial city of Bangalore, villagers have been able to transform their lifestyle by travelling daily to work in factory jobs.[41]

Industrial Development in Rural Areas

Recent studies in the United States indicate that the traditional pattern of rural people having to commute to urban jobs is undergoing significant changes. The main reason for this is the decentralization of manufacturing and associated activities into non-metropolitan and rural areas. Lonsdale suggests that this is an international process.[42] Yet while government programmes exist to encourage industrial dispersal, there is little evidence that, outside of the United States, it has occurred in other than the urban fringe and smaller cities. One problem in Europe is that of distinguishing between urban- and rural-based employment, for in many regions rural inhabitants are never far from an urban centre. Furthermore, planning controls tend to prevent industrial development in rural settlements and open countryside.

Such restrictions are not significant in the United States which differs also in the greater distances which separate rural inhabitants from urban centres and in the deterioration of many large cities. Thus industrial decentralization has probably had more impact on rural America than anywhere else in the world. The process has been examined in detail by a number of recent studies. These indicate that industrial expansion into small towns and rural areas is one of the major trends in industrial development in the United States. To quote Lonsdale, 'It represents a dramatic departure from the classic pattern of industrial concentration in or near metropolitan centres.'[43]

Between 1962 and 1978, 56 per cent of the increase in US manufacturing jobs occurred in non-metropolitan and rural areas. This represents a gain of 1.8 million jobs in non-metropolitan areas as against 1.4 million in metropolitan areas.[44] Much of this growth occurred during the sixties, with more than half the gain occurring by 1967 and all of the remainder before March 1974.[45] In fact, between 1960 and 1970, manufacturing employment in metropolitan areas grew by 4 per cent while non-metropolitan areas experienced a 22 per cent growth.[46] In the past few years there has been a slight downturn in this trend and at least one study suggests that 'a great many rural-oriented industries and subindustries have lost employment or barely held their own'.[47] The future trends, therefore, are somewhat unclear, particularly with the recent recession in the US economy. Furthermore, there is considerable regional variation in non-metropolitan manufacturing growth. Fifty per cent of all non-metropolitan manufacturing expansion between 1962 and 1978 occurred in the south and 30 per cent in the north central region. By contrast, manufacturing growth in the north east and the west was predominantly metropolitan in location.[48]

However, there is little doubt that the rapid expansion of non-metropolitan manufacturing in the sixties had the potential for making a significant contribution to the revival of rural employment opportunities and therefore to the reversal of rural out-migration. Heaton and Fuguitt have shown that, at least during the peak of dispersal during the sixties, the level of manufacturing had a greater impact on migration in rural areas compared with non-metropolitan areas in the proximity of urban centres.[49] This is supported by Kuehn in his study of the Ozarks region. An area of persistent depression throughout much of this century, the Ozarks Economic Development Region attracted 2,617 new manufacturing plants between 1967 and 1974. Sixty per cent were located in non-metropolitan areas, with 40 per cent in counties with no cities over 25,000 and not adjacent to metropolitan areas. There was also considerable diversity in this industrial development.[50]

Kuehn suggests that the expansion of non-metropolitan job opportunities has enabled many people to satisfy a growing national preference for living in small towns and rural areas, even where this may involve lower incomes.[51] The amenities of small towns, proximity to recreational open space and the better working conditions of a small factory are important reasons for the increased retention rate of existing residents and the growth of immigration into Ozark non-metropolitan counties. Of over 14,000 non-metropolitan employees surveyed in 1975, 19 per cent were local residents who had worked in the area for at least ten years, 21 per cent were new immigrants, 6 per cent were returnees (those who had left the area for work in the previous ten years and had since returned), and the remainder were new entrants or workers with no known work location in 1965. More new immigrants and returnees were employed in rural than in urbanized and fringe counties, with returnees being particularly attracted to small towns and open country areas. Kuehn has concluded that non-metropolitan industrialization does provide job opportunities for new and returning immigrants and that current immigration into areas like the Ozarks redresses the effects of earlier out-migration of younger people, and therefore 'rebuilds the human resource base within rural areas'.[52]

The impact on local economies, however, is difficult to predict, for much depends upon the type of industrial development that occurs and where it is located. Heaton and Fuguitt have shown that the rate of manufacturing growth in rural and non-adjacent counties is greatest in low-wage industries.[53] Indeed, one of the attractions for plants to move to rural areas, particularly in the south, is lower labour costs. Yet the muliplier benefits of low-wage industries are limited, so that while personal incomes may improve sufficiently to stabilize and even attract population, they may not increase enough to stimulate sustained growth.

Another problem is that much non-metropolitan manufacturing growth consists of branch plants of urban-based companies. There is, therefore, a strong tendency for multipliers to be more external than internal and for the future of local factories to be dependent on the policies of large corporations. The location of such plants, too, is indicative of the importance of links with the metropolitan economy, for they tend to follow closely the pattern of the Interstate Highway System.[54]

The location of non-metropolitan manufacturing plants is critical to local development patterns. Some are located in small towns and therefore contribute directly to the local economy; others are situated in open countryside, frequently at highway interchanges, where local business linkages are more tenuous. Either way, new factories can have an influence over employment patterns over a wide area. In the south, the effect of the dramatic increase in non-metropolitan manufacturing has been to shift agricultural workers to industrial employment with a concomitant proliferation of commuting and residential development in rural areas. Lonsdale's study of plant development in a small North Carolina city indicated that workers were attracted from a wide geographical area.[55] Many of these, and those who commuted the greatest distance, came from rural areas with low agricultural wages and high unemployment.[56] More recent evidence is of new factory development in all sizes of rural and non-metropolitan settlement in parts of the south. Hart describes the coincidence of this 'boom in manufacturing employment' and the mechanization of tobacco farming in eastern North Carolina. 'Many factory workers, black and white alike, prefer to remain in the country instead of moving into town.'[57]

Thus while the question of how much non-metropolitan manufacturing development will contribute to a sustained revival of rural economies remains in doubt, there is evidence that the upsurge in the availability of nearby factory jobs has persuaded many people to stay in rural areas as well as attracting both returnees and newcomers. Resultant increases in personal income, combined with property prices which are substantially lower than most urban areas, has led to a residential boom amongst a newly affluent non-farm population. Small towns have been extended by new subdivisions and apartments, but, more significantly for rural areas in the United States, new dwellings are springing up in large numbers along country roads.

A distinctive manifestation of this phenomenon is the proliferation of mobile homes in the rural areas of North America. To some extent the occupance of mobile homes has been an exurban trend, but in both Canada and the United States it has become important beyond the urban fringe amongst low and middle-income rural residents. The attractions of mobile homes for this group are obvious. They are cheaper than conventional housing, easier and quicker to assemble, and much easier to move from site to site. Between 1970 and 1975,

approximately 32 per cent of new homes in non-metropolitan areas of
the United States were mobile homes.[58] In Canada in 1974, 21 per
cent of all single detached houses constructed were mobile homes.[59]
Considerable attention has been paid by planners and local municipalities
to the problems of mobile home parks, for much of this development
occurs in subdivisions. Recent opposition by local residents to what
they consider the unsightly character of these subdivisions has led to
increasing zoning restrictions by a number of town administrations in
the United States. In Canada, too, most of the larger urban areas have
adopted the National Building Code which does not permit the
installation of any mobile homes.

For these reasons, recent mobile home construction has tended to
occur on individual land parcels beyond town boundaries. This trend
also reflects the demand for rural property on which a mobile home can
provide immediate accommodation until a conventional house can be
constructed. In British Columbia, for example, which has been termed
the 'mobile home heartland of Canada,' 40 per cent of mobile homes are
not located in parks.[60] Instead, as in much of the rural United States,
they are dotted along rural roads and highways. Many, despite their
theoretically mobile character, have become permanent features of the
rural landscape, with concrete basements, personalized additions and
landscaped grounds.

Rural Residential Development: An Overview

The residential transformation of some rural areas has produced
important structural changes in settlement and society. Clearly, a major
source of these changes continues to be an adventitious, urban, affluent
middle-class population. It is this group which creates distinctly new
residential elements in the landscape and introduces new social and
economic groups into rural communities. In certain situations the conventional notion of élitist and segregative elements in landscape and
society continues to hold true.

Yet residential development is no longer restricted to the fringes of
metropolitan areas, for it is now occurring in rural areas within commuting distance of even small employment centres. Thus the process has
become more complex for it includes the established rural population
which also participates in the new mobility. Thus the relationship of
urban newcomers with rural settlements is strengthened, while the
links of rural people with land and the local workplace are weakened.
This suggests a convergence of lifestyles rather than the segregation of
urban and rural, old and new settlements, middle and working

class, which is so often assumed.

With increasingly residential use of rural settlements coming from various sectors of both urban and rural society, the local rural area is seen as the milieu for satisfying the same types of needs which are common to all residential areas: schools, churches, grocery, drug and variety stores, pubs, clubs and restaurants. Of course these are functions of traditional rural communities. The difference with the new residential trends is that they are no longer part of a diversified local economy but exist as a convenience for an urbane and mobile population.

The Recreational Invasion of Rural Settlements

The growth of leisure as a major time-consuming activity is one of the most important facets of modern industrial society. It has led to a substantial increase in demand for a wide range of recreational opportunities outside the home. With the greater, if selective, affluence and mobility of recent years this has been manifested by a growing desire for open-air recreation outside urban areas. The result has been an invasion of rural and wilderness areas by an urban and an urbanized rural society which sees these areas as recreational hinterlands.

In the recreational use of rural areas great stress is placed on the importance of open-air activities. Clearly this is mainly a reflection of a desire to escape from the indoor life so typical of modern society, so that the 'beneficial nature of exercise, unpolluted air and quietness are thought to be a good antitheses to urban living'.[61] Whether rural areas, therefore, are seen as offering an escape from the city is debatable, for much open-air recreation also takes place within urban confines. However, as with exurbanite residential development, rural recreation is certainly a manifestation of a desire for regular doses of unpolluted air, nature, fine scenery and tranquillity. This is readily apparent in the emphasis on the more dramatic environmental elements of mountains, forests, lakes, beaches and sea, but also in the apparent attraction of the settled countryside.

The rural environment, therefore, is a playground for urban society in the industrialized world. And it is a playground which accommodates a wide range of recreational activities. Actual levels of participation in rural recreation are extremely difficult to estimate and many of the figures available are out of date. Twenty per cent of the Swedish population reported in a 1963 survey that rural recreation was their most important leisure-time activity, while 74 per cent of Danish urban dwellers have expressed a desire to be in open country.[62] However, these figures can only suggest the general level of demand for rural recreation and all that can really be claimed is that most European countries experience strong recreational pressures on their rural areas. The figures in Table 7.2 indicate a more precise measurement of participation rates in North America. What is more interesting in this table, however, are the types of recreational activities. The most important of these appear to involve unorganized recreation of a spontaneous nature. Looking at scenery, driving for pleasure, swimming, walking, fishing and simply 'getting away from it all' are the most popular pursuits in rural areas.

Table 7.2: Participation in Selected Recreation Activities, Canada, 1976 (persons 18 years and over)

Activity	Percent
Driving for pleasure	67
Picknicking	57
Walking or hiking	54
Sightseeing from vehicle	49
Visiting historic sites	49
Swimming (non-pool)	42
Visiting national parks	29
Tent camping	19
Wilderness tripping	17
Canoeing	14
Trailer camping	12
Cross-country skiing	10

Source: Statistics Canada, *Travel, Tourism and Outdoor Recreation, A Statistical Digest, 1975 and 1976* (Ottawa, 1978), Cat. 66-202, Table 10.6, p. 186.

An important inference to be made from these surveys is that simply 'touring around' in rural areas is one of the more popular activities. With the growth in automobile ownership and highways to match, long-distance touring has become common. Yet the automobile is probably used more frequently by many urban dwellers for weekend jaunts and afternoon drives in the country. This casual use of the rural hinterland has added a further dimension to the settlement structure of these areas, with the introduction of elements designed for the tourist.

Most studies of rural hinterland recreation emphasize two main kinds of impact: firstly the pressure at peak periods of large numbers of automobiles on rural roads and settlements, and secondly the demand for parkland and rural open space within easy reach of the city. Research on these, in the main, has concentrated on traffic flows, car parking provisions and the problems of land use conflict. Yet the physical and economic structure of rural settlement is also affected in more direct ways. The most obvious is the introduction of various types of parks. These may be created out of existing agricultural land, but in most cases involve the conversion of areas of special landscape attraction into controlled parkland. This generally has two aims: to provide for the open space needs and to control the activities of the recreational population, and to conserve the rural and natural environment. Private parkland, with its commercial objectives, emphasizes the first of these aims, and therefore tends to be a more intrusive addition to rural settlement than public parks.

Public parkland in rural areas has expanded rapidly since World War II. Much attention has been paid to the development of large national and state parks in wilderness areas. Yet the integration of parkland into the existing framework of rural settlement closer to urban areas has also been the focus of much government activity in most industrialized countries. The main objective has been to set aside areas which can be used for various kinds of recreational activity, including casual viewing of scenery. The British approach, in the main, has been to establish a number of national and local parks in which recreational land use is integrated with existing land uses and settlement and the whole area is protected by strict planning controls. By contrast the North American approach has tended to favour the acquisition of land and the development of parks which are separate from other rural land uses. Under the management of various levels of government these have proliferated in the immediate rural hinterlands of the major urban centres.

Day and weekend excursions into rural areas, however, are not exclusively oriented to park usage, for an equally popular activity is the casual touring of scenic areas, villages and farmscapes. The main effect of this has been on the commercial structure, and through this, the visual appearance of nucleated and dispersed rural settlements. Remarkably little research attention has been paid to this phenomenon. Yet in the rural areas surrounding more affluent metropolitan regions it has had a significant impact. First there has been the inevitable expansion of services for the motorist, which has led to the proliferation of roadside service stations, restaurants and snack bars.

However, in addition there has been a growth in commercial

enterprises which are designed to satisfy the urbanite sense of rural
nostalgia. This is a sentiment which appears to have peculiarly English
origins, with the result that it is characteristic of the rural hinterland
of Britain, and regions such as New England and Ontario. The new
enterprises are dominated by pottery studios, craft and antique shops,
sales barns, tea-rooms, country restaurants and village inns. These
transform the economic structure of rural communities by adding a new
entrepreneurial element, which is often composed of people who have
moved out of the city to establish rural business. It is, therefore, part
of the general exurbanite influx into the rural hinterland and one which
changes the economic base of rural communities from functional to
luxury consumerism. This change is readily apparent in the physical
appearance of affected rural settlements. Conversions of village buildings,
barns, even farmhouses, and the construction of new buildings are
usually designed to express the nostalgia for a former rural architecture.
Sand-blasted brick, natural wood, thatched roofs, colonial-style store-
fronts, red barns, are all part of the commercial image of 'olde worlde'
rurality (Figure 7.4).

The Vacation Resort

The advent of annual paid vacations around the turn of the century
saw the development of vacation resorts for a much wider spectrum of
the population than before. Previously, resorts had been for the idle
rich and even the rapid expansion of cheaper rail travel did little to
permit the movement of the average urbanite out of the city for more
than a day trip. However, through the 1920s and 1930s the annual
family vacation became a reality for many Europeans and North
Americans and sparked the influx of resorts into certain kinds of rural
areas and settlements. The dramatic rise in tourism and its expansion to
an international scale in recent decades has seen the development of
huge resort cities, particularly along the sunny coastlines of the Mediterranean, Caribbean and Pacific. However, the attraction of smaller rural
resorts remains for those seeking to avoid an urban atmosphere.

　　It is in mountainous and coastal regions that the main influx of
resort development into rural settlement has occurred. In some instances
the physical additions are made through the integration of accommodation
and services in single resort enterprises separated from existing settlements.
Such resorts are common in areas like the Catskills in New York State,
the lakelands of the Canadian shield in Ontario and along the coastlines
of Atlantic Europe. They include the large, custom-built holiday villages
and camps of Europe which specialize in the provision of complete

Figure 7.4: Country Sales Barn, Manchester, Vermont

family vacations. Their North American counterpart is the family resort,
usually within easy reach of the city and located on a lake or coastal
shoreline. Both types of resort consist of cabins, central entertainment
facilities and are set in private grounds often with strong security
against intruders. A third type of specialized resort is quite different,
for this is the genteel, country house establishment, which caters to
more affluent families but, in some cases, is designed for adults without
children, providing luxury accommodation and activities such as tennis
and horse riding. Finally, of course, there is the ski resort, which has
grown in popularity in recent years in the European Alps, the mountains
of New England, the Canadian Shield and the Rockies.

Because they are concentrated in mountains and coastal areas, the
resorts described above tend not to cause disruptions of existing rural
settlement patterns. Many have led to an extension of settlement into
previously unsettled or sparsely populated areas. The main impact on
the physical structure of rural settlement has been with resort development in and around existing villages and settled areas. The transformation

of villages into predominantly resort settlements is probably the most important change to have occurred in certain coastal and mountain regions. Few villages and hamlets in the Alps have not been affected by some degree of resort development. The same is true of some of the coastal settlements of Europe and North America, particularly along Atlantic shorelines.

The changes that occur in the physical structure of such settlements depend on the nature of vacation demand. In general, it is the pressure for various types of accommodation which has the greatest impact. However, there is now a wide range of types of accommodation, including cottages, overnight cabins, chalets, tourist homes, trailer-parks and hotels. Some of the more exclusive resort villages have restricted tourist accommodation to hotels. This is apparent in a few Atlantic seaboard villages in North America. However, it is in the Alps that so many villages are dominated by hotel accommodation. This, presumably, is a function of the special demands of the skiing tourist but also the relative affluence of vacationers in these areas. By contrast, most coastal villages in areas such as New England, Nova Scotia, southwest England and northwest France, contain the whole range of tourist accommodation, which usually involves both new construction and conversion of existing properties. If the provision of large amounts of accommodation aids in transformation of the physical appearance of settlements, so too does the addition of a range of tourist attractions. Restaurants and snack bars are probably the most numerous, followed by gift shops, amusement arcades, antique stores, and craft shops. More conventional services such as service stations and grocery stores tend to increase in number to satisfy increased demand.

These developments are the visible expression of the considerable change that rural settlements experience when they become resorts. The social and economic impact of tourism is somewhat more difficult to ascertain. Clearly it leads to a diversification in the structure of local employment by providing jobs in the service sector. There is no doubt that this has been the salvation of some settlements which otherwise would have continued to experience the effects of remoteness and a weak local economy. Fishermen and farmers are able to supplement their income with a variety of activities, while their families find employment in stores, hotels and restaurants. Alexander has indicated how tourism transformed the local economy of Cape Cod in Massachusetts, permitting farmers to leave agriculture altogether for the more lucrative opportunities of the tourist industry.[63]

However, the extent to which the local economy is stimulated is likely to depend on the amount and type of tourist activity. The main problem is its seasonality and the predominantly service nature of employment. This tends to change unemployment to underemployment, while entrepreneurial income is substantial only in the more affluent resorts. A further complication is the tendency for enterprises to be operated by urbanites who have moved into rural areas to take advantage of the tourist economy. In these circumstances, the bulk of the rural population is employed seasonally at relatively low wages. Nevertheless, the addition of resort activities has had the effect of diversifying the economic base of rural areas and maintaining many settlements which might otherwise have been seriously reduced in size or even have disappeared altogether.

Second Homes

The remarkable increase in recent years in second homes in rural areas has received considerable research attention. What was for so long the exclusive preserve of an extremely small minority, has now become an accepted symbol of urban, middle-class success. The ownership of a cottage, cabin, beach-house, farmhouse or villa for use at weekends and for vacations is consistent with the increases in exurban residential development described earlier in this chapter. Thus the second home is seen as a means of regularly escaping the city and weekly routine, as an important investment opportunity, as a status symbol, and as a foothold in an attractive environment.

The spread of second homes into rural areas began on a large scale during the 1950s, although certain types of 'places in the country' and less prestigious properties such as beach cabins were common before the war. In the United States the rate of recent development has been phenomenal, particularly during the 1960s when it was estimated that second homes increased at the rate of 55,000 per annum to reach a total of 1.55 million by 1967.[64] Since then the growth rate has increased, with one estimate putting it at 100,000 to 200,000 annually.[65] Accurate figures are difficult to arrive at as estimates do vary. In part this is because they are based upon different methods of measurement. The 1967 estimate of total numbers of second homes, for example, is at variance with a 1970 estimate of the number of families owning second homes which put the figure at 3 million, which is about five per cent of the total number of families in the United States.[66] As Ragatz points out, this figure does not include the occupation of rental units, mobile homes, houseboats and old farmhouses which could substantially increase the total occupancy of vacation homes.

On a *per capita* basis, at least two European countries have a greater incidence of second homes than the United States. France has a relatively long history of country property ownership and rental by the urban middle class. Indeed it was quite common early in this century amongst fairly modest Parisian shopkeepers and merchants who acquired cottages and gardens on the outskirts of the city, for the purposes of growing fruit and vegetables.[67] Thus by 1938 there were 320,000 newly built second homes in France. However, post-war increases have been considerable so that by 1970 the figure stood at 1.5 million.[68] This means that France has roughly three times the number of second homes *per capita* than the United States. The other European country which has a large number of second homes per family is Sweden, which in 1970 had 490,000 second homes, which represented one for approximately every fifth household.[69] Other European countries have a shorter tradition of second home ownership than France and Sweden, although Norway, Denmark and Switzerland have experienced an increase in recent years. Britain lags behind France and the Scandinavian countries for it is estimated that only one per cent of households possessed second homes in 1967, although Clout suggests that this proportion is growing rapidly.[70]

The general trend of the past 20 to 30 years, therefore, has been of a noticeable influx of second home ownership and usage into rural areas. There is considerable variation in the locations which are preferred for second home properties. However, in general, two factors appear to be most important: distance from principal residence and the desire for an attractive area and site. With the growth of second home demand in rural areas, three further factors have also increased in significance: the relative availability of land, the existing settlement pattern, and planning policy.

The proximity of the second home to the principal residence has long been an important locational factor, largely because of the pattern of second home usage. The main attraction of owning a recreational property in a rural area is to be able to use it as frequently as possible. Two patterns of use predominate; firstly, weekend visits and secondly, longer vacations in which working members of the family travel to the second home on weekends. This frequency in movement between principal and second residence has led to the concentration of second homes in rural areas which are within an easy drive of the city. This has been recognized particularly in Europe, where urban dwellers appear to be less willing than their American counterparts to drive long distances for weekend trips. Hence in Sweden, the main concentration of second homes are within 20 kilometres of urban areas of more than 25,000 people, with the greatest densities in the Stockholm area.[71] In France, the Paris region contains a large proportion of second homes, and in the country as a whole, 40 per cent of all second homes are within 40 kilometres of principal residences.[72]

In North America, permanent residential and industrial pressure on the exurban fringe, combined with a willingness to drive greater distances, has in recent years tended to push second homes further away from urban centres. Tombaugh's study indicates that 65 per cent of American second homes are within 320 kilometres of the principal residence, although there are considerable differences between the more densely settled northern and eastern regions and those farther west. In Wisconsin, for example, 35 per cent of second home owners were willing to travel more than 320 kilometres.[73] However, in the northeast, the main concentrations are between 160 and 240 kilometres of principal residences with a strong pattern of concentricity around major cities.[74] This is reflected in the concentration of American second homes in the northeastern and northcentral regions.

Distances from principal residence, however, cannot be viewed separately from the desirability of an attractive recreational environment and the availability of suitable property. Thus the short distances which separate second homes from principal residences in Stockholm are partly due to the attractiveness of the coastline in the Stockholm region. The northern and northeastern states of the United States, too, contain a fortunate combination of a large urban population with a variety of attractive vacation home areas on its doorstep. Ragatz has suggested that, 'If two areas have comparable attractions most families will probably choose the one nearer to the place of residence'.[75] However, it is not quite as simple as this in reality. For one thing, the nearer location will be more expensive, for another the strong preference for certain types of natural and rural environments tends to predetermine the distances between principal and second homes. Proximity and access to water is particularly important. In Michigan, for example, of second homes purchased after 1952, 55 per cent were on an inland lake, 24 per cent on one of the Great Lakes and 10 per cent on a river or stream.[76] In the cottage-land of Muskoka and Haliburton in Ontario the desirable locations are all lakeshore ones. In Europe, lakes are less important than coastlines, for in Britain, Scandinavia and France second homes with access to a beach are considered among the most desirable properties. The attraction of waterside locations is, of course, a function of summertime demand, and this type of seasonal use of second homes predominates. In the United States, 70 per cent of all seasonal occupation comes during the summer months.[77]

The use of second homes, however, is not entirely restricted to the summer, for there is evidence of a growing trend both to winter and year-round use. In New England, second homes dot the shorelines of Lakes Champlain and Winnepesaukee, as well as that of the Atlantic in Maine and Massachusetts, but the attractions of the wooded hill lands of the Catskills, the Poconos and the Adirondacks are year-round. In addition the surge in popularity of winter sports has led to an increase in winterized cottages which can be used for skiing weekends. Finally, the continuing attraction of the villages and farmsteads of the settled landscape should not be forgotten, for, mainly in Europe, these satisfy the twin demands for easy access and a pleasant rural environment.

Demand for particular kinds of recreational environment also has a strong influence on the various types of second homes in rural areas. Essentially, development has occurred in three quite different ways. Firstly, the conversion of existing rural buildings to second home use continues to be popular. This is far more frequent in Europe than in North America, although Lewis has mentioned the purchase of abandoned houses in northern New England by vacation-home buyers.[78] In Europe the conversion method is widespread. In France, it is estimated that almost two-thirds of new second home units each year consist of conversions of old buildings.[79] The buying up of old properties in the villages of the Paris Basin and their expensive conversion for weekend use by affluent Parisians is a well-established trend. Yet elsewhere, the pressure on urban fringe villages for permanent residence has pushed second home conversion into remoter rural settlements. Here the availability of abandoned or rundown housing stock provides cheaper property, and a ready-made supply of housing. This method of obtaining a weekend and vacation cottage has spread second home ownership into the villages and hill farms of the remoter areas of Britain which have their own attractions for recreational activities. In Sweden, the simple huts formerly used on the summer grazing lands have become a popular target for second home conversion. In some cases, second homes from existing building stock have been acquired through inheritance. This is likely to become more important in all kinds of rural areas, with the resultant paradox of offspring who have moved away from their home village, returning to occupy the ancestral home on a seasonal basis.

The second major type of second home development is the purpose-built cottage set on its own private piece of land. Individual, private development of this kind is more common in North America than in

Europe, where planning restrictions and land shortages have tended to limit it to a few coastlines. However, Simmons describes the importance of the summerhouse along the coasts of Denmark which have proliferated to such an extent that they form long strips of uninterrupted settlement.[80] While the pace of second home construction in some areas of North America has led to similar concentrations, the main objective of the cottage and beach house owner on this continent has been to acquire a property which provides separation and privacy. In addition, second home properties are seen as an investment and as a material acquisition in their own right. Thus development has, until recently, occurred mainly through the acquisition of a parcel of land and the subsequent placement on it of some kind of structure. The term structure is appropriate, for 'cottages' come in a variety of styles, including tar-paper shacks, trailers, log cabins and, most commonly, prefabricated buildings. The latter are available in a range of popular styles which emphasize ease of construction, the use of wood and picture windows.

The rapid growth in demand for second homes during the 1960s stimulated the expansion of the third of our major types of second home development: the recreational version of the exurban subdivision. These second home estates represent the arrival of development companies into the recreation home market. Large-scale developments of this kind are common in the sun-belt areas of Florida and southern California and are virtually indistinguishable from urban sprawl. However, the commercialized second home subdivision has appeared also in the recreational regions further north. Their layout is predictable: suburban-style road patterns, sometimes with artificial waterways and lagoons, equal-sized lots, and integrated facilities such as boat marinas, golf courses and parks (Figure 7.5). One example of a second home subdivision is the Boise Cascade project in Puget Sound in the state of Washington. Here 6,478 dwelling units were built on 15,737 hectares, in what was described by the developers as a rural, living environment. Projected population is 20,000.[81]

Socially and economically second homes bring about important changes to rural communities. The introduction of a part-time residential element tends to create two communities, for weekenders and vacationers tend not to be involved in local community affairs. Where the influx of second homes is on a large scale, the year-round community tends to be overwhelmed and obscured at weekends and during vacation seasons. The result is the development of temporally distinct communities. The economic base of rural areas is certainly affected by

Figure 7.5: 'Lagoon City', a Recreational Subdivision at Brechin, Ontario

second home development, although detailed studies of this are rare. Positive impacts on the local economy would seem to be more likely than negative ones, for extra properties generate increased tax income, and even part-time residents demand certain commercial services. Furthermore, because of their pattern of occupancy, second home owners tend not to place pressure on municipal facilities such as schools and medical services. One study of the impact of 8,700 vacation cottages in Wales estimated that they generated $9 million per year and 1,500 rural jobs.[82] To which sectors of the local population this money accrued is difficult to assess, for like recreational activity in general, employment is predominantly seasonal and low-income. However, second home development does create important entrepreneurial opportunities in the construction industry and in maintenance services for second home owners. In addition, the increasing popularity for the year round use of second homes is likely to reduce the seasonal character of settlements and therefore create a more permanent stimulus to the local economy.

Summary

The growing use of some rural areas in the industrialized world for residential and recreational purposes is indicative of a radical alteration in rural-urban relationships. The traditional dependency of urban population on rural communities for the supply of food and raw materials has been supplemented by an urban dependency on rural land for living and leisure space. Furthermore, increased mobility amongst rural people has changed their work patterns and relationships with the local economy. These changes are manifest in the greater diversity of land use and landscape, in the substantial increases in movement within and in and out of rural areas, in a more heterogeneous rural society, and in a broader economic base which contains a large service sector.

Notes

1. Daniel R. Vining, Jr., and Thomas Kontuly, *Population Dispersal from Major Metropolitan Regions: An International Comparison*, Discussion Paper Series No. 100 (Philadelphia: Regional Science Research Institute, 1977).

2. Ibid., pp. 21 and 78.

3. Calvin L. Beale and Glenn V. Fuguitt, *The New Pattern of Nonmetropolitan Population Change*, Centre for Demography and Ecology Working Paper 75-22 (Madison: University of Wisconsin, 1976), p. 4.

4. Ibid., pp. 6-7.

5. Ibid., pp. 12-17.

6. Jean Gottmann, *Megalopolis, The Urbanized Northeastern Seaboard of the United States* (New York: The Twentieth Century Fund, 1961), pp. 219-20.

7. R.E. Pahl, *Urbs in Rure* (London School of Economics: Geographical Paper, No. 2, 1965), p. 9.

8. Beale and Fuguitt, *Population Change*, p. 4.

9. G.S. Wehrwein, 'Rural-Urban Fringe', *Economic Geography*, Vol. 18 (1942), pp. 217-28.

10. Lorne H. Russwurm, *The Urban Fringe in Canada: Problems, Policy Implications, Research Needs*, Report Submitted to the Research Branch, Ministry of State, Urban Affairs, Ottawa (Waterloo, Ontario: Department of Geography, 1973), p. 1.

11. Gottmann, *Megalopolis*, p. 217.

12. A.C. Spectorsky, *The Exurbanites* (Philadelphia: Lippincott, 1955).

13. Pahl, *Urbs in Rure*, p. 76.

14. W.M. Dobriner, *The Impact of Metropolitan Decentralization on a Village Social Structure*, Unpublished Ph.D. Thesis (New York: Columbia University, 1956), quoted in Pahl, *Urbs in Rure*, p. 76.

15. Pahl, *Urbs in Rure*, pp. 41-62.

16. P.J. Ambrose, *The Quiet Revolution, Social Change in a Sussex Village, 1871-1971* (London: Chatto and Windus, 1974); R. Drewett and W. Heidemann, 'Migration and Social Polarization: a Study in Five Areas of the Megalopolis', in P. Hall *et al.* (eds.), *The Containment of Urban England*, Vol. 1 (London: Allen and Unwin, 1973).

17. Spectorsky, *Exurbanites*, pp. 253-78.

18. Raymond Williams, *The Country and the City* (New York: Oxford University Press, 1973).

19. Dobriner, *Village Social Structure*.

20. James S. Duncan, Jr., 'Landscape Taste as a Symbol of Group Identity, A Westchester Country Village', *Geographical Review*, Vol. 63 (1973), p. 336.

21. Pahl, *Urbs in Rure*, pp. 27-71.

22. Gerald Walker, 'Social Networks and Territory in a Commuter Village, Bond Head, Ontario', *Canadian Geographer*, Vol. 21 (1977), pp. 329-50.

23. Ibid., p. 344.

24. Ambrose, *Quiet Revolution*, pp. 206-7.

25. L. Brett, *Landscape in Distress* (London: Architectural Press, 1965).

26. John V. Punter, *Urbanites in the Countryside*, Unpublished Ph.D. Thesis (University of Toronto, 1973).

27. Duncan, 'Landscape Taste', p. 343.

28. H.J. Gans, *The Levittowners: Ways of Life and Politics in a New Suburban Community* (New York: Random House, 1969).

29. Walker, 'Social Networks', pp. 345-9.

30. George K. Lewis, 'Population Change in Northern New England', *Annals*, Association of American Geographers, Vol. 62 (1972), p. 318.

31. R.H. Brown, 'The Upsala Community: a case study in rural dynamics', *Annals*, Association of American Geographers, Vol. 57 (1967), pp. 267-300.

32. S.H. Franklin, *The European Peasantry: the Final Phase* (London: Metheun, 1969).

33. Hugh D. Clout, *Rural Geography* (New York: Pergamon, 1972), pp. 54-60.

34. Ibid., p. 57.

35. E.C. Bishop, 'Part-time Farming and the Low-Income Farm Problem', *American Journal of Agricultural Economics*, Vol. 41 (1961), pp. 1215-6; F.C. Fliegel, 'Aspirations of Low-Income Farmers and their Performance and Potential for Change', *Rural Sociology*, Vol. 24 (1959), pp. 204-14.

36. A.M. Fuller, 'The Problems of Part-Time Farming Conceptualized', in A.M. Fuller and J.A. Mage (eds.), *Part-Time Farming, Problem or Resource in Rural Development* (Guelph, Ontario: Geo Abstracts, 1976), pp. 38-56.

37. G.V. Fuguitt, 'Urban Influence and the Extent of Part-Time Farming', *Rural Sociology*, Vol. 23 (1958), pp. 392-7.

38. Fuller, 'Part-Time Farming', p. 51.

39. J.A. Mage, 'A Comparative Analysis of Part-Time Farming and Full-Time Farming in Ontario — Some Selected Aspects', in Fuller and Mage, *Part-Time Farming*, pp. 170-93.

40. M.F. Bunce, 'The Contribution of the Part-Time Farmer to the Rural Economy', in Fuller and Mage, *Part-Time Farming*, pp. 249-57.

41. Allan R. Beals, 'Namahalli, 1953-56, Urban Influences and Change in Southern Mysore', in K. Ishwaran (ed.), *Change and Continuity in India's Villages* (Columbia University Press: New York, 1970), p. 68.

42. Richard E. Lonsdale, 'Background and Issues', in Richard E. Lonsdale and H.L. Seyler, *Nonmetropolitan Industrialization* (Winston: Washington, 1979), p. 5.

43. Ibid., p. 3.

44. Claude C. Haren and Ronald W. Holling, 'Industrial Development in Non-metropolitan America', in Lonsdale and Seyler, *Nonmetropolitan Industrialization*, pp. 13-45.

45. Ibid., p. 13.

46. Gene F. Summers *et al.*, *Industrial Invasion of Nonmetropolitan American* (New York: Praeger, 1976), p. 1.

47. Haren and Holling, 'Industrial Development', p. 44.

48. Ibid., p. 26.

49. Tim Heaton and Glenn Fuguitt, 'Nonmetropolitan Industrial Growth and Net Migration', in Lonsdale and Seyler, *Nonmetropolitan Industrialization*, pp. 119-36.

50. John A. Kuehn, 'Nonmetropolitan Industrialization and Migration: An Overview with Special Emphasis on the Ozarks Region', in Lonsdale and Seyler, *Nonmetropolitan Industrialization*, pp. 137-48.

51. Ibid., pp. 142-4.

52. Ibid., p. 146.

53. Heaton and Fuguitt, 'Growth and Migration', p. 127.

54. Rodney A. Erickson and Thomas R. Leinbach, 'Characteristics of Branch Plants Attracted to Nonmetropolitan Areas', in Lonsdale and Seyler, *Nonmetropolitan Industrialization*, pp. 57-78.

55. Richard E. Lonsdale, 'Two North Carolina Commuting Patterns', *Economic Geography*, Vol. 42 (1966), pp. 114-38.

56. Richard E. Lonsdale and C.E. Browning, 'Rural-Urban Locational References of Southern Manufacturers', *Annals*, Association of American Geographers, Vol. 61 (1971), pp. 255-68.

57. J. Fraser Hart and E.L. Chestang, 'Rural Revolution in East Carolina', *Geographical Review*, Vol. 68 (1978), pp. 435-58.

58. US Department of Housing and Urban Development, *Development Needs of Small Cities* (Washington, DC, 1979), p. 69.

59. Michael J. Audain, *Mobile Homes: Problems and Prospects* (Vancouver: Government of British Columbia, 1975), p. 8.

60. Ibid., pp. 8-10.

61. I.G. Simmons, *Rural Recreation in the Industrial World* (London: Arnold, 1975), p. 5.

62. Ibid., pp. 29-30.

63. L.M. Alexander, 'The impact of tourism on the economy of Cape Cod', *Economic Geography*, Vol. 29 (1953), pp. 320-26.

64. United States Department of Commerce, Bureau of the Census, *Second Homes in the United States*, Current Housing Reports, Ser. H. 21, No. 10.

65. R.L. Ragatz, 'Vacation Homes in the Northeastern United States: Seasonality in Population Distribution', *Annals*, Association of American Geographers, Vol. 60 (1970), pp. 447-55.

66. This was derived from an unpublished nationwide survey the American Telephone and Telegraph Company, reported in Ibid., p. 449.

67. Hugh Clout, *Second Homes in France*, paper presented to Second-Homes Symposium, Annual Conference of the Institute of British Geographers (Norwich, England, 1973), p. 2.

68. Ibid., p. 2.

69. B. Bielckus, *Second Homes in Scandinavia*, Paper presented to Second-Homes Symposium, Annual Conference of the Institute of British Geographers (Norwich, England, 1973), p. iv.

70. Clout, *Second Homes*, p. 73.

71. Bielckus, *Second Homes*, p. iv.

72. Clout, *Second Homes*, p. 3.

73. Larry W. Tombough, 'Factors Influencing Vacation Home Locations', *Journal of Leisure Research*, Vol. 2 (1970), pp. 54-63.

74. Ragatz, 'Vacation Homes', p. 453.

75. Ibid., p. 452.

76. Tombough, 'Vacation Home Locations', p. 56.

77. H.D. Clout, 'Second Homes in the United States', *Tijdschrift voor Economische en Sociale Geografie*, Vol. 63 (1972), p. 63.

78. Lewis, 'New England', p. 318.

79. Clout, *Vacation Homes*, p. 3.

80. Simmons, *Rural Recreation*, pp. 161-2.

81. H.L. Boschken, 'The Second Home Subdivision: Market Suitability for Recreational and Pastoral Use', *Journal of Leisure Research*, Vol. 7 (1975), pp. 63-72.

82. P. Downing and M. Dower, *Second Homes in England and Wales*, Countryside Commission Report (London, 1973), quoted in Simmons, *Rural Recreation*, p. 167.

8 PUBLIC POLICY AND THE FUTURE OF RURAL SETTLEMENT

The widespread and radical changes which are discussed in the foregoing chapters inevitably raise serious questions about the future of rural settlement. No longer is it possible to see rural society as a haven of stability and tradition, for it has been drawn into the unstable conditions of a rapidly urbanizing world. Rural settlements clearly will continue to be affected by the general social and economic evolution of contemporary civilization. However, the future patterns of society appear likely to come under the growing influence of various forms of government interference. And this is particularly true for rural settlements because in these the forces of change tend to be more disruptive than in other sectors.

As a conclusion to this book, therefore, this chapter presents a brief discussion of the future prospects for rural settlement in the context of the main influences of public policy. Clearly, general government policy on economic and social matters will be influential. Yet there are aspects of public policy which are directed specifically towards rural areas, and where these are operative they appear likely to play a significant role in the future of rural settlement. Paradoxically, rural policies are dominated by two essentially divergent approaches. One incorporates programmes and policies for rural development which aim to solve problems of stagnation, decline and rural poverty. The other involves the protection and conservation of rural areas and settlements through controls on new development.

Rural Development Policies and Programmes

Virtually all governments have some form of policy to deal specifically with the economic and social problems of rural areas. Policies and programmes fall into two main categories: those which concentrate on providing support for and stimulating development in the agricultural sector, and those which aim at comprehensive rural development. The type of policy is influenced by a number of factors: political and economic ideology, the level of national affluence, the degree of government concern for rural and depressed regions, the need for agricultural

189

development and the nature of rural problems. Ideological constraints are important, for they determine the degree of compulsion and social reorganization in development programmes. They determine, too, how the benefits of development are distributed and who bears the costs. Yet government concern for rural areas varies considerably, so that some programmes are merely token gestures of rural support while others are a major element of national policy.

Agricultural Support and Development

Few sectors have experienced as much government involvement and received as many public funds as modern agriculture. The primary reason for this is that farming is regarded as an essential industry to any nation. As a result, agricultural settlement in recent years has been influenced increasingly by agricultural support and development policies. The extent of this influence varies according to the degree to which policies aim to interfere in the rural economy. There are essentially three levels of intervention: support and extension, development and modernization, and structural reform.

Support and Extension Policies. General support for agriculture through extension and education services, subsidies, grants, marketing boards and trade controls is now viewed as an essential and unavoidable aspect of most agricultural economies. In a sense, such programmes are not aimed at rural development but rather the maintenance of a viable agricultural sector and the stabilization of the farm population. Yet they have had, and will continue to have, an increasingly important influence on rural settlement. Even general financial and legislative support for agriculture can determine the number, size and distribution of farms, the economic health of an agricultural community, and, indeed, the whole character of the rural landscape.

Among the most sophisticated and extensive set of agricultural support and extension programmes in the world are those operated by the United States Department of Agriculture. Extension services operated by the Department, like those of most other countries, offer technical, managerial and financial advice, organize education programmes and generally encourage farmers to keep pace with modern developments in the agricultural industry. Clearly one of the most significant effects of this in the United States will be the increasing industrialization of farming and the enlargement of agricultural enterprises.

The Department of Agriculture, however, also spends large amounts on direct intervention in the United States agricultural economy. Between 1956 and 1970 federal budget outlays for farm price support programmes and direct payments to farmers averaged $3.1 billion per year, and $5 billion between 1968 and 1970.[1] Price support programmes originated in the 1930s but expanded during the 1950s and particularly during the years of the Kennedy administration. The main reason for them was the depression in prices of a wide range of farm commodities caused mainly by improvements in productivity. Direct payments are used as a means of buying output restrictions from farmers, while subsidies guarantee farmers a particular price even when market prices are lower.

Farm subsidies are a common feature of the support programmes of other western nations. With its great need to improve domestic output, Britain has maintained subsidies at adjustable levels for major cereal crops and, at various times, for certain livestock products. Canada, too, has a long history of price support policies, the best known of which is the national Wheat Board which dominates the agricultural economies of the grain producing provinces. The Wheat Board, however, is also an excellent example of another aspect of government involvement in agriculture which is becoming important in many countries. This is the control of marketing procedures through various forms of marketing boards and structures. The Canadian Wheat Board has complete control over the way in which wheat is marketed as well as being responsible for providing support for stabilizing the price of wheat. Not all marketing boards are as powerful, yet there are other examples of boards which have had a profound effect on the location and extent of particular types of farming. For example, dairy farming in Britain has been strongly influenced by the establishment of a marketing board which has centralized transportation and processing, and established quotas on milk production.[2]

Intervention in the pricing and marketing of agricultural commodities represents considerable government control over the agricultural economy. In theory, such policy stabilizes farm settlement. Certainly in parts of the United States and Canada this has occurred in practice, for the large number of family farm enterprises has persisted primarily as a result of government support schemes. Yet rationalization has also occurred, partly because large producers tend to benefit more from subsidies than small ones, but also because marketing boards control production levels. Thus, as Schultze says of American programmes, 'The bulk of subsidies accrue to that small group of farmers with net incomes averaging $20,000.'[3] And the policies of the Milk Marketing Board in

England and Wales have intentionally eliminated small producers in favour of those with herd sizes which are most appropriate to milk quotas and regional demand.

Because most support and extension programmes are assigned primarily to ensure the continued wellbeing of national agricultural economies, their impact on the settlement structure of particular areas will always be difficult to predict. In contrast, some programmes are directed at special agricultural problems. Thus Britain's hill pasture subsidies are designed to help marginal farmers in upland areas by offering incentives to improve pasture quality and thereby increase productivity and income. A common characteristic of marginal farm problems is that enterprises are too small to be economically viable, and therefore a number of governments have introduced programmes to assist small farmers. The United States' Department of Agriculture's small farm extension programmes offer the opportunity for the improvement of agricultural efficiency, but they tend to involve only small numbers of farmers and only those who choose to take advantage of the schemes.

An alternative strategy for small, marginal farms is to recognize that many can never be viable. This is the approach of Ontario's Agricultural Rehabilitation Development Act (ARDA for short), which operates Farm Consolidation and Enlargement Programmes.[4] This has a two-fold objective: to assist marginal farmers to leave the land and to help other operators to enlarge their farms. The first of these objectives is achieved through the purchase of land up to a specified value per acre and the operation of rehabilitation programmes to retrain farmers in alternative skills. Land acquired in this manner may be used for forestry schemes, or leased with an option for later purchase to farmers who wish and are considered able to improve the viability of their operation. As participation is voluntary, the programme does not reach all marginal farms, yet with 3,059 farms involved by 1978 it has clearly had some impact on the numbers and sizes of farms, particularly in the poorer regions of eastern and northern Ontario.

Development and Modernization. Agricultural support programmes in advanced, industrialized nations may improve national and regional agricultural economies as well as minimize the decline of agriculture in marginal areas and on smaller farms. Yet it cannot generate significant amounts of local income, for only a small proportion of the rural population can depend on farming for a livelihood. By contrast, development and modernization programmes can play a significant role in influencing rural settlement in those areas of the world where the bulk of the rural population is engaged in agriculture.

Agricultural development policies in most developing countries are founded on the recognition of inherent productive weaknesses in peasant farming. These include low productivity *per capita*, low technology, small farms, high labour intensity, inefficient marketing systems, low levels of specialization and severe shortages of capital. The main objective of public policy in many areas is to achieve greater commercialization in agriculture. Most programmes therefore stress the need to improve both overall productivity and the income of individual enterprises and labourers.

This approach to agricultural development has been termed the 'improvement strategy' by Long, for rather than requiring the complete reform of agrarian structure, the aim is to modernize existing systems.[5] There is little doubt that various forms of foreign aid have had considerable influence in the adoption of modernization approaches. This is mainly because most western development theorists have seen technological improvement as the prerequisite to increased productivity. Yet it is also because foreign aid is most readily supplied through financial and technical assistance.

The emphasis upon programmes for the use of new crop types and production systems is evidence of the desire to transform traditional agriculture through changes in technology. One example of this is the so-called 'Green Revolution'. This began as a programme funded by the Ford and Rockefeller Foundations to develop new, high-yielding varieties of rice and wheat for use in tropical regions.[6] The adoption of the new seed varieties has been in most countries encouraged by government programmes and accompanied by substantial amounts of foreign, in particular American, aid. Multinational corporations, too, have established a strong presence in many rural areas in order to promote the fertilizers, pesticides and machinery which are necessary for the maximization of yields from the new strains. In India, the adoption of high-yielding varieties has been taking place through a government-initiated mass-action programme.[7] Under the High Yielding Varieties Program, participants in selected areas are provided with the necessary credit through co-operatives and supplied with seeds, fertilizers and technical assistance. Irrigation is also improved through the tube-well programme.

One of the major problems with such programmes is that they require substantial increases in the purchase of inputs. Thus financial assistance from government is a necessity. The extent of adoption and, with it, the

degree of change in rural settlements therefore depends on the level
of financial assistance available as well as upon the technical success of
the new systems. Sen has shown that adoption of the new seed
varieties in India has been uniform right across the spectrum of farm
sizes.[8] However, the acquisition of the necessary credit is always a
problem for small, low-income farmers. This is why the Indian government has encouraged the expansion of the Cooperative Credit System.[9]
The need to improve credit availability for small and medium-sized
farms has, in fact, led to credit financing taking up the lion's share of
agricultural development funding in many countries.

Most agricultural development policies do not concentrate on a single
programme but make some attempt to be comprehensive. A fairly
typical example is that of Trinidad and Tobago whose policy is aimed
at switching from an essentially dualistic to a more broadly-based
agricultural economy.[10] There are five major components to the
programme: the Agricultural Credit Bank; the provision of marketing
facilities and access roads to farms, which includes the establishment of
a central marketing agency; the development of forestry and fishing;
the initiation of dairy and beef farming; the provision of fertilizer
subsidies, the extension of agricultural land and research into soil
conservation and agricultural technology. It is hoped that this policy
will establish a productive small and medium farm economy producing
larger quantities of livestock and poultry products, vegetables and root
crops for the local market.[11]

However, apart from rare examples such as Mexico and Taiwan,
there is no clear evidence that the modernization approach has led to
significant improvements in rural economies in general.[12] At best,
specific projects have improved the living conditions of participating
farmers while the dubious benefits of modernizing influences have
undoubtedly extended to the remotest rural communities. Yet, as Lele
has pointed out in the context of African rural development,
'Agricultural development programmes on the whole have not been
successful in making the process of development of the low-income
sector self-sustaining.'[13] He cites limited funds, knowledge and
objectives, as well as the lack of trained manpower and a poor knowledge
of the local cultural environment as the primary reasons for this.

Structural Reform in Agriculture. The apparent difficulties of achieving
agricultural development simply through the provision of financial
support, capital projects, information and education has been a major
factor in the growing emphasis on structural reform in agriculture as a

prerequisite for rural development. This approach recognizes the problems of inefficient and inequitable distributions of land and capital, particularly in peasant society. The policy response ranges from minor tinkering with landholdings to radical land tenure reform.

The need to rationalize the distribution of land parcels in order to improve agricultural efficiency is an important feature of some European agricultural development policies. Structural reform in West German agriculture emphasizes consolidation of fragmented holdings and the enlargement of farms.[14] In France the establishment of the regional *Sociêtês d'Amênagement Foncier et d'Établissement Rural* (SAFERS) is aimed at acquiring farmland which comes up for sale, and redistributing it to create larger, more consolidated holdings.[15] However, these programmes tend not to involve compulsory acquisition of land and so may not have a widespread effect on land tenure structure.

This is an inevitable dilemma for democratic political systems, and is repeated in other areas where the inequitable rather than the merely inefficient distribution of land tenure is an obstacle to development. India remains the largest underdeveloped country in the world still operating more or less under a democratic system. As a consequence its land reform programmes have not always had the desired level of success. Nevertheless certain legal changes in land ownership and tenancy have had the effect of loosening traditional structures even if they have not led to major reforms. Two aspects of land reform are particularly important: the abolition of the intermediary landlords and the placement of size ceilings on private holdings of land. The difficulties of universal implementation and supervision of these reforms has led the Indian government to switch to a programme of co-operative and community development on the assumption that economic progress at the village level will yield its own structural reforms.[16]

It is in Latin America that land tenure reform has been the most important issue in agricultural development policies. However, that is about the only generalization that can be made, for land reform in Latin America is a bewildering and fluctuating confusion of socialist, liberal and conservative ideologies. Most Latin American countries have at some time or another adopted agrarian reform policies, a universal element of which has been some attempt to redistribute land in a more equitable fashion. In some cases the main objective of reform has been to create larger, more efficient peasant holdings; in others the principles of social justice have been uppermost. Aside from the recent socialist reforms in Cuba and, abortively, in Chile, the most influential combinations of economic stimulation and land tenure reform have been in Mexico, Bolivia and Peru. In all three countries, redistribution has, at least to some degree, broken down the traditional latifundia-minifundia structure. In Mexico, land reform has long been the basis of rural development policy for the establishment of *ejidos* (communal village lands) begun in 1917. These were created from land expropriated from the large estates, a process which has continued until the present day.[17] Yet it appears that recent Mexican development efforts have by-passed the *ejidos* and concentrated on the creation of medium and large-size commercial farms which can boost the country's export earnings.[18]

Bolivian land tenure reform began in 1952 with a revolution followed by a spontaneous peasant takeover of estate lands. In fact land reform in Bolivia has never been formalized into a comprehensive agricultural development programmes as in Mexico and half the peasants still have not received titles for their land.[19] Bolivia is a good example of the limited economic benefits of simple expropriation and redistribution programmes. This was the basis of Peruvian reforms begun in 1968, but more recently the Peruvian government has concentrated on structural reforms which promote the reorganization of peasant communities aimed at transforming them into modern production or multi-purpose co-operatives. The 1970 Statute for Peasant Communities set out to encourage the modernization and commercialization of agriculture, stimulate the development of co-operatives and, significantly, control the excessive fragmentation of holdings characteristic of areas where redistribution of estate lands had occurred.[20]

The consolidation of fragmented holdings, the imposition of ceilings on the size of personal holdings, the establishment of co-operatives and even the creation of new agricultural settlements are seen by some observers as, at best, partial reforms. As Frank, among others, has suggested, they do not change the fundamental problem of structural dependency in which peasant society is exploited by metropolitan and colonial domination.[21] This is an essentially Marxist view which has found expression in the socialist and communist land reforms of the Soviet Union, China and Cuba, and now of a few parts of Africa and southeast Asia. The essence of these reforms is agricultural development through the centrally-planned control of a completely reorganized system of land tenure and use. This has generally involved the national-ization of land according to state socialist principles. Thus Cuban land reform, which began in 1959 by redistributing estate lands and setting

limits on the size of holdings, rapidly moved to collectivization of small
farms and, by 1963, state ownership of all holdings over 11 hectares
(three-quarters of all agricultural land).[22] This pattern has been repeated
elsewhere, the most recent example being in Nigeria where early in
1978 all land was officially nationalized to 'be held in trust for the use
and common benefit of all Nigerians'.[23] The aim is to abolish individual
or family ownership, a move which, if successful, would radically alter
the structure of Nigerian rural society.

Rural Development

In areas where it is the livelihood of the bulk of the rural population,
agriculture continues to be the major focus for rural development
policies. Yet the growth potential of a labour-intensive agricultural
sector is generally very limited, while modernization of farming itself
tends to make rural economies even more dependent on the metropolitan
core. Consequently, some governments have become aware of the need
for more comprehensive rural development. This is particularly apparent
in advanced, industrialized nations, but the need to deal with all sectors
of rural society has also been recognized in certain developing economies.
General rural development policies can be grouped into three main
categories: those that are subsumed under policies for depressed, marginal
and remote areas, those aimed at the development of the rural sector
per se, and those that are based upon the radical reform of rural
society.

Marginal Area Policies. Given the conditions under which rural stagnation
and decline occurs, it is hardly surprising that many regional development
policies are directed at regions which are predominantly rural in nature.
In western Europe and North America policies for depressed and remote
regions tend to emphasize the importance of overall economic development and incorporate programmes for the creation of alternative
employment opportunities and the improvement of regional infrastructure.
The most common method of achieving the latter is through public
works programmes in which national funds are used to provide roads,
industrial sites, water and power supply, hospitals and so on.
Alternative employment is created through public works, subsidies and
grants to existing industries and incentives to attract new industry.

In Britain, for example, remoter regions, which are predominantly
rural, qualify as special development areas. The Highlands and Islands
Development Board was set up in 1965 to initiate industrial
development projects, and to invest in projects to create employment

in agriculture, tourism, fishing and social facilities. Parallels to this type of development programme have been established in other European countries, in particular France and Italy. In the United States, the Area Redevelopment Act, 1961, provided funds for loans, grants, technical assistance, retraining programmes and planning for use in areas characterized by persistent unemployment and underdevelopment. Most of the responsibility for depressed areas now lies with six Regional Commissions set up in 1966, for Appalachia, the Ozarks, New England, the Four Corners (of Utah, Colorado, Arizona and New Mexico), the Coastal Plains and the Upper Great Lakes. The Commissions were authorized to give financial aid for the construction and equipment of public facilities, land acquisition and education.

A common principle for much regional development planning which has important implications for rural settlement is that of concentrating investment in strategic growth centres. The logic of this is that if growth occurs at a number of centres, the surrounding rural areas will benefit through a ripple effect. Growth centre policy has been applied to the economic development of the lagging regions of France. In fact French regional economic development policy as set out by the Fifth Plan emphasizes the importance of industrialization in the predominantly rural regions of the west, Central Massif and the southwest. Regional objectives are set within a national plan for an hierarchy of centres in which local growth poles are to relay the influence of larger cities to the countryside. This is to be achieved largely through the activities of Regional Economic Development Commissions, with financial aid to private firms, public overhead capital investment and the decentralization of government activities.[24] For the west, an objective of a 35 to 40 per cent increase in national industrial employment has been planned. In the tradition of French economic development theory, this development is centred on growth poles, such as Rennes. Moseley has analysed the impact of development at Rennes on the surrounding rural areas and shown that growth centre policy has the effect of drawing the immediate hinterland into the urban sphere while leaving remoter areas virtually untouched by development impulses.[25]

Rural Area Policies. The distinction between policies for marginal areas and those for the rural sector is not always clear-cut, for rural problems are frequently synonymous with marginality. However, some governments have policies which recognize the distinctiveness of the problems of rural areas.

One of the main problems is employment and service provision in small settlements. A number of governments have attempted to tackle this by rationalizing the location of economic activities and institutional services. One example of such a policy is the designation of key settlements by some British local planning authorities. The usual approach is to classify villages according to the various levels and types of development which will be permitted by planning controls. Cloke has summarized the various objectives of key settlement policies as follows:[26]

1. The promotion of growth in remote rural areas.
2. The reduction or reversal of rural depopulation through the creation of locations of intervening opportunity.
3. The achievement of the most efficient pattern of rural services.
4. The concentration of resources in centres of greatest need.

Where development controls are used to maintain settlement designations, the settlement pattern and the socio-economic structure of individual settlements is fundamentally controlled by public policy. This control reached its peak in County Durham in northeastern England where some small mining settlements have been designated as non-viable and eliminated from the settlement pattern. An equally controversial degree of government interference in the pattern of rural settlement characterized the Newfoundland resettlement scheme. Because of the serious difficulty of providing even minimal services to small, outlying fishing villages, and of serious rural unemployment problems, the Centralization Programme was introduced in 1954. This was superseded in 1965 by the Federal-Provincial Newfoundland Fisheries Household Resettlement Programmes, which provided strong financial incentives to families to relocate in larger centres. In general, however, relocation assistance was granted only to those living in designated settlements; those in which at least 80 per cent of the population applied to move. This was intended to ensure the complete evacuation of settlements so that savings in the provision of services could be made.[27] Opinion as to the economic benefits of the resettlement programmes has been sharply divided, and, in fact, it is no longer in operation. Yet it certainly hastened the depopulation of smaller communities, and reduced some to merely a collection of mostly abandoned houses.

Perhaps the most significant shift towards an explicit and extensive policy for development in rural areas has occurred in the past few years in the United States. 'There are growing indications,' writes Orville Bentley, 'that the rural development concept is reaching a "take-off point," that we may be moving into a new stage of development for rural America.'[28] The main evidence for this is the 1972 Rural Development Act which marks the culmination of a decade of increasing concern for the future of non-metropolitan and rural areas. This reflected a growing awareness of the extent of rural poverty in the United States as well as a recognition of the need to seek alternatives to the congestion and unrest of the cities.

The Rural Development Act's overriding objective is revitalization and development of rural areas. In many ways it is the national culmination of previous regional development programmes for its emphasis is upon economic growth. Thus, in addition to expanding resource development assistance for agriculture and rural communities, the Department of Agriculture is now responsible for rural development. This is to be achieved, not simply through agricultural improvement, water resource programmes and other public works, but mainly through massive government support for industrial development. Guaranteed loans for rural industrialization in open countryside, or in towns and cities with populations of up to 50,000, community facilities loans, rural enterprise real estate loans, and rural enterprise operating loans are the central features of the funding programme. The switch in the philosophy of rural development is most apparent in the initiation of co-ordinated, nationwide, rural development programmes with goals for employment, income, population, housing and the quality of community services in rural areas.[29]

Reform of Rural Society. The Rural Development Act is one example of policies which are common in democratic societies, for they rely on enabling legislation and financial incentive to bring about change. Yet this type of policy is concerned primarily with the improvement of the economic status of rural areas *within* the existing social framework.

This approach must be viewed in sharp contrast to rural development policy which aims to reform rural society. A few attempts have been made to do this within democratic political structures. A good example of this is India's Community Development Programme. This was established soon after independence with the objective of improving village levels of living through cultural change which would transform village life. The basis of this idea was that, given the incentives to improve their own social and economic conditions, village communities would soon adopt progressive strategies in agriculture and other activities. In successive Five Year Plans development programmes initiated agricultural, social, educational, rural health and public works within new administrative frameworks designed to supersede traditional village authority.[30]

However, the Community Development Programme has done little to alter the traditionally unequal allocation of resources within village society, for it wrongly assumes that social change will be the natural consequence of economic improvement. It is the recognition of this which has led to more radical change in certain rural societies. In contrast to India, the Chinese revolution saw rural development in terms of the complete destruction of existing social and economic structures and their replacement by collective forms of activity. The change in structure was seen as an essential prerequisite to the initiation of economic development. Furthermore, under communist governments, the economic and social life of rural communities is entirely directed by public policy.

This overall control is readily apparent in the Chinese agricultural communes which are the basic political, administrative, social and economic units of rural China. One recently studied example of such a unit is that of Ping Chow Commune in the south of the country.[31] The commune is an amalgamation of villages and therefore has a large population (69,100 in 1975). The People's Committee manages the commune, setting all work and production targets and ensuring the observance of central government objectives. The primary objective of commune organization, however, is to encourage local self-sufficiency in the provision of necessary services for a rural community. Thus the commune runs processing and manufacturing activities related to agriculture, local workshops, the irrigation schemes, as well as institutional facilities. In short, it controls every facet of rural life.

The recent increase in Marxist administrations has meant that various forms of centralized planning and control of rural society are now to be found in a number of regions. Planned rural systems are universal in China, the Soviet Union, Cuba and Albania. They dominate rural life in eastern Europe, Vietnam, and Iraq. Finally, Africa is now the world focus of revolutionary activity, and five countries—Angola, Ethiopia, Mozambique, Nigeria and Tanzania—are approaching rural development through socialist principles. The *ujamaa* policy in Tanzania, for example, aims to establish a fully collective system with communal control of land and other resources. The early idealism of autonomous communities has given way to increasing central government involvement which has turned the *ujamaa* programme effectively into one of compulsory villagization.[32]

Rural Protection and Conservation

The central paradox of public policies towards rural settlement is that
they also embrace planning for protection and conservation from new
development. This is not as globally significant as development policy,
for it is a recent trend in regions where urban and industrial expansion
have placed pressure upon rural land use and settlement. Rural planning
of this kind has reached its most advanced stage in a number of
European countries where population pressure on land is great and
where concern for rural landscape is culturally entrenched. Yet, in
certain ways, conservational approaches to rural planning are becoming
increasingly apparent in parts of North America.

There is a strong ideological basis to policies which aim to control
and limit development in rural areas. 'We are bewildered and disturbed,'
writes Bonham Carter, 'by the radical changes that seem rapidly to be
destroying our countryside.'[33] This is a recurring theme on both sides
of the Atlantic: the rape of rural by urban. The conservational pressure
that stems from it has three main concerns: the preservation of
agricultural land, the protection of the rural landscape and natural
environments, and the maintenance of the character of rural communities
and settlements.

Agricultural Land Preservation

Concern over the loss of agricultural land has a long history. William
Cobbett lamented the problem in England over 150 years ago, but its
real momentum has been gained in the past 30 or so years. In Britain,
which has probably the most sophisticated of land use planning systems,
one of the basic principles of town and country planning legislation is
that development of rural land should not occur at the expense of good
farm land. Hence the importance of urban containment, largely through
green-belt legislation, in British planning. More recently, national
policy discouraging building in open countryside for other than
agricultural purposes has led to development controls which seriously
restrict the non-farm development of agricultural land.

The ideology behind farmland preservation, at first sight, may appear
straightforward; that is the economic necessity of maintaining the
agricultural economy. This is certainly an issue in the more densely
populated regions of North America where urban pressures on
agricultural land values and productivity have led to some attempts to
develop farm land protection policies. In general these have involved the
granting of powers to local municipalities to control urban sprawl in

areas of good agricultural land by means of zoning and subdivision by-laws. These designate agricultural zones in which farmland owners are restricted from severing parcels for non-agricultural development. In Canada, British Columbia and Ontario have established protection of high-quality farmland as provincial policy. British Columbia's Land Commission oversees legislation preventing the sale of agricultural land for non-agricultural uses, while Ontario's Food Land Guidelines are clearly intended to persuade municipalities to control development on prime farmland.

In the United States, recent concern over the development of prime agricultural land has been translated into a growing number of state land use policies. Most of these are in their infancy and yet to be legally tested. However, the trend towards state controls over particular types of rural land is manifested in Hawaii's Land Use Law which originated in the potential threat of residential and commercial development to valuable sugar and pineapple lands. Hawaii is unique in the United States in having comprehensive land use controls at the state rather than the local level. Thus agricultural land is protected through the designation of agricultural districts by the Land Use Commission and the virtual prevention of new developments in these districts.[34]

Inevitably, restrictions placed by official plans on the sale and use of designated land has caused objections on the grounds that it removes development rights from landowners. One alternative to restrictive zoning is to encourage the continuance of farming through incentive schemes such as New York State's Agricultural District Programme. Another solution is that used, for example, by Suffolk County, New York, where development rights are purchased in return for the prohibition of the use of agricultural lands for any purpose other than agricultural production.[35]

To some extent, concern for the loss of farmland reflects a well-mellowed piece of North American philosophy. The Jeffersonian glorification of the agricultural way of life is a precise physiocratic philosophy which stresses the morality of agricultural communities and their centrality to the American way of life. Modern attitudes are more confused, but as urbanization has intensified so has the sense that our ultimate security lies with the soil.

Protection of Rural Landscape and Natural Environments

The Jeffersonian ideal, however, is more relevant to modern attitudes towards agricultural land when it speaks of the pastoral, harmonious landscape and society that agriculture is supposed to create. This is the landscape which is cherished by exurbanites in their rural retreats, and, paradoxically, planning policies for the conservation of these landscapes are concerned as much with exurban residential sprawl as with other types of development.

Concern for the appearance of the countryside is probably more firmly rooted in British landscape traditions than it is elsewhere. Attractive countryside, rather than wilderness, is valued for its harmonious blend of farmland, hedgerows, woods, farm buildings and villages. This is a landscape, too, which is composed of many historical layers. Planning controls, which attempt to preserve this heritage as well as conserve visual amenities in rural areas, have increased substantially over the past 30 years.[36] Thus a considerable proportion of England and Wales is occupied by areas which are specially designated because they are particularly attractive areas of countryside. One of the main pressures for such conservation is recreation.

Planning controls in specially designated areas extend to the smallest details of building design and siting as well as to the protection of natural elements. Planning in the National Parks is governed by the National Parks Act which requires each park authority to have an official plan. The primary aim of the Exmoor National Park Plan, for example, is the conservation of 'natural, man-made and historic elements'. Development controls are enforced by requiring planning permission for every addition or conversion, while in special conservation areas, 'planning permission will only be granted in exceptional circumstances'.[37]

Most English counties have followed the requirements of the Countryside Act to designate Areas of Outstanding Natural Beauty. In these the aim of planning is to control development in such a way that their visual character is preserved or if necessary restored. Yet even outside these specially controlled areas, British planning authorities are placing increasing emphasis on countryside conservation and therefore are having considerable influence over the extent and nature of rural development. Structure plans (the official plans of planning areas) now include policy statements which discourage building in open countryside. For example the Kent County Structure Plan states explicitly that its aim is to 'conserve, and where possible enhance, the landscape quality and identity of the Kent countryside whilst accepting changes necessary for efficient agricultural practice . . .'[38] Such a policy is achieved through development controls which not only influence the type of development but also regulate the design of buildings. As an official policy of the Staffordshire County Council states, 'the building should

not be intrusive in the landscape, either in its siting or design'.[39]
Planning approval depends, therefore, upon what the planning committee
considers to be consistent with an attractive rural landscape.

The emphasis of such a policy is on the tranquillity and order of the
countryside which offer an escape for our urban senses; a recreational
haven, as well as a visual heritage to be preserved. In the United States
this view has surfaced in some New England states such as Massachusetts
and Vermont where both state and county policies contain development
controls to protect attractive rural landscapes. Yet the main concern
in these areas is not so much with the settled, agricultural landscape
(the countryside) as with the natural scenery.

What constitutes natural scenery is not always clear, but for most
planning policies, it is determined by the pressures for recreation among
the symbols of nature and for the conservation of natural environments.
The idea that rural and wilderness areas are one big parkland has led to
legislation which attempts to ensure that agricultural activities and urban
development are controlled in such a way that they do not interfere
with enjoyment of the natural elements of rural areas. American parkland policy has in the past tended to be based on the separation of
recreational and wildlife areas from other land uses. However, recent
developments in environmental planning suggest that legislation to
protect natural environments in the United States will become more
comprehensive and emphasize state rather than local control.

Most states which have introduced environmental controls have
directed these at special types of environment. Thus Wisconsin has
enacted a Shoreline Protection Programme, Massachusetts has its
Wetlands Protection Programme and New England its River Basins
Commission.[40] Vermont, however, has gone a good deal further by
introducing an Environmental Control Law which sets out to control
the rapid expansion of recreational and residential land use into
attractive landscape and environmentally sensitive areas.[41] It does so
by requiring permits for any development regardless of acreage or
number of units involved, for commercial, industrial or residential
use above the elevation of 2,500 feet. This is designed to preserve the
ecosystems of mountain areas. However, to control the general spread
of second homes the legislation requires permits for the sale and construction of any subdivision, including the sale of unimproved lots on
subdivisions. This is a significant departure from traditional local
government zoning practices, but it may represent the first of many
state policies to protect rural landscape and environment.

Planning Controls for Existing Settlements

In addition to the increase in institutional controls over developments which affect rural landscapes and environments, planning policies in a number of countries recognize also the importance of controlling development in and around existing rural settlements and communities. There appear to be two main reasons for this. Firstly local governments responsible for providing services are often forced to limit development in smaller communities according to the level of services which can be financed. Secondly, and more important, many small town and village communities retain a strong sense of identity with that vague quality of the 'character' of their settlement. In some areas, for example the United States, it is the communities themselves which restrict certain kinds of development for this reason. In others, such as Britain, France and Holland, national policies require local planning authorities to exercise considerable control over the nature of change in village structure.

One way in which the expansion of existing settlements is controlled on both sides of the Atlantic is through the restriction of building on prime agricultural land and in attractive areas of countryside. Yet these same restrictions tend to force development into existing settlements and thereby increase the need for planning controls within their boundaries. One of the main concerns of British planning policies is to keep villages and small towns to a size which is appropriate for a rural settlement. This is achieved by drawing a clear boundary which separates settlement from the surrounding countryside and prohibiting development beyond the boundary. This 'envelope' consolidates the rural settlement pattern, prevents communities from losing the sense of identity which comes with smallness, and reduces the tendency for ribbon development along roads which connect different settlements.[42]

Not all rural settlements are controlled in this way, for where population pressure is great, villages have been permitted to grow into large, suburban-style settlements to accommodate overspill population from nearby cities. By contrast, another concern of British planning policy is to preserve and enhance the character of attractive villages and towns. The historical and architectural heritage, as well as the visual attractiveness of such settlements, is widely recognized. Thus the tendency is to designate as Conservation Areas parts of, and even whole, villages. Under such a designation new development and the appearance of existing structures are subject to strict design controls.

This degree of control, and the existence of national policies to ensure that local authorities exercise it, in the main has not extended to

North America. Certainly in the United States, the Hoover Act has, since the 1930s, permitted local municipalities to plan their development through the zoning of land use. However, the central ideology of American land use controls is to permit local governments to determine the nature of development in their own communities. As Delafors has said, 'The scope of planning in America today, therefore, is no wider than the local community's interests.'[43] Thus the Standard Zoning Enabling Act (Hoover Act) was directed at delegating land use control to the local level, where it is up to each community to decide to what extent and in what ways their settlements should evolve.[44]

Controls, therefore, remain in most states the sole responsibility of individual local governments. Furthermore, beyond the boundaries of incorporated towns and villages, development in rural areas is largely uncontrolled by any zoning or subdivision legislation. It is this phenomenon, as well as the patchwork character of community planning policy, which has prompted increased pressure for state land use policies. This has resulted in what Bosselman and Callies have called 'the quiet revolution' in land use control, for a number of states, including Hawaii, Vermont, New York, Wisconsin and Massachusetts, have now adopted land regulatory systems which attempt to integrate local planning objectives with those of the state. Thus in Vermont, in addition to the controls aimed to protect landscape and environment, recent legislation for a land capability plan includes provisions for state policies on population growth and optimum settlement patterns.[45]

The Future of Rural Settlements

The relative importance of rural settlements in demographic economic and political terms clearly will be influenced considerably by the nature and extent of rural development policies. Where the emphasis is on agricultural development, improvements in farm incomes and in local and national food production may occur. Yet in advanced, industrial areas, this will affect only a small proportion of the rural population and push agriculture further into the urban-industrial sector. In under-developed areas an improvement approach to agricultural development may succeed in increasing the significance of rural people to the national economy. However, only with substantial structural reform in agriculture is a significant improvement in peasant livelihood a possibility.

General rural development policy recognizes the integrated and distinct nature of rural problems and therefore is likely to have a greater impact on rural settlements than policies which are simply agriculturally oriented. There is some evidence that programmes for rural improvement and for the development of depressed areas do stimulate local employment and income and therefore arrest the process of decline. The Highland and Islands Development Board in Scotland is estimated to have created 10,700 jobs between 1965 and 1974.[46] Yet there is a danger in overestimating the impact of such programmes for, relative to general economic growth, even the creation of new jobs may not result in a significant reduction in rural-urban disparity. Furthermore, development may occur which is not directly attributable to programmed investments. In the United States, for example, Area Development programmes and the Rural Development Act have been credited with establishing the momentum for industrial development in rural areas. Yet as Seyler has pointed out, most programmes are oriented to the most depressed areas and therefore cannot have influenced industrial growth in areas and communities which fail to qualify for assistance. Indeed, Seyler goes further and suggests that, 'if there had been no developmental programmes emphasizing industrial growth, there is every reason to assume the redistribution of industry would have taken a form much as it has.'[47]

So even with large amounts of funding, the extent to which rural development policies actually bring about change and improvement is extremely variable. One of the main problems is that the provision of capital and expertise to depressed areas has to be in large amounts and be allocated to all relevant sectors simultaneously for satisfactory levels of development to occur. In addition economic orientation cannot always yield significant change in social and economic stratification to permit a major redistribution of wealth within rural society. This may mean the perpetuation of the already serious problem of lower-income groups in the marginal and remote rural areas of America. In underdeveloped countries it tends to encourage the channelling of development funds to the more affluent and influential members of rural society. It also introduces new production and marketing structures which transform peasant agriculture but, because of increased costs and the vagaries of the export economy, do not necessarily improve levels of living. In other words, both within existing settlements and with new settlement schemes transformation of traditional rural society is likely but the old problems of rural poverty will probably continue.

There is no question that the structural reforms in rural society brought about by socialist and communist revolution make public policy the single most important factor in the future of rural settlement. The crucial questions, however, are how durable are these policies and for how long will they continue to emphasize the importance of rural settlements^ Certainly there has been a recent shift in China towards a policy of industrialization which may reduce the importance of rural communes. And in the Soviet Union, the rationalization of rural settlement has proceeded to the point that it is now an integral part of a controlled urban hierarchy. Yet the most interesting prospects are in those areas which are now being influenced by revolutionary processes. The future of much of rural Africa appears likely to be determined by some form of socialist ideology. The possibilities for this exist, as they have for decades, in parts of Latin America and the Caribbean, and also in the more unstable countries of southeast Asia.

While development policies appear likely to initiate a variety of changes in rural areas, the growing importance of planning controls in the industrialized countries of the western world promises to bring greater restrictions to the urban development of rural land. In some European countries, land use, landscape and settlement planning at all government levels is now so sophisticated that the future of all aspects of rural settlement will be affected more by public than by private decisions. A further prospect is that professional planners will determine the physical, economic and social structure of rural settlements. The role of this type of planning in North America is somewhat more difficult to predict for, by comparison with Europe, it is in its infancy. Yet there are signs of a change in attitudes towards land from one which sees it as a commodity to one which regards it as a basic resource requiring public protection. Add to this the growing public interest in heritage conservation and the demand for greater participation in the planning process it appears as though the future development of American rural land and settlement will come increasingly under the direct influence of public policy. The main question that remains is the extent to which policy is actually implemented. The latest developments in state land use control legislation, such as that enacted in Vermont, face a long and complex test in the courts before it is apparent how enforceable the new laws are. Even where the legal validity of policy is secure as in Britain, local planning authorities are not always consistent in the implementation of policy when decisions over particular developments are taken.

Nevertheless, in certain European countries total planning control over land development is already a reality. Local variations in the methods and extent of implementing policy do exist, yet rural settlement and landscape appear likely to be increasingly protected from urbanization and large-scale development. Some would suggest that the more attractive and historic landscapes and settlements will be fossilized by development controls. If that is so, then the physical continuity of some rural settlements is assured, although their economic future would appear more doubtful.

Whether this situation will extend to North America is open to question, for, while there are signs of a growing official concern for the protection of agricultural land, rural landscapes and small settlements, the traditional independence of the property owner remains constitutionally entrenched. Furthermore, together with much of the developing world, American and Canadian governments have been more concerned with stimulating the development of rural regions than with protecting them from development. This holds out the theoretical possibility of the continued and improved viability of rural society as a distinct entity in areas where programmes take effect. In reality it results either in the irreversible alteration of rural society without any significant improvement in living standards, or a degree of modernization and economic improvement which draws rural communities into an urban-dominated commercialized world. Either way, not even the remotest community can remain untouched by bureaucratic influences.

Notes

1. Charles L. Schultze, *The Distribution of Farm Subsidies: Who Gets the Benefits?* (Brookings Institute: Washington 1971), p. 1.

2. W.B. Morgan and R.J.C. Munton, *Agricultural Geography* (London: Methuen 1971), pp. 96-7.

3. Schultze, *Farm Subsidies*, p. 3.

4. M.F. Bunce, 'Farm Consolidation and Enlargement in Ontario and its Relevance to Rural Development', *AREA* Vol. 5 (1973), pp. 13-16.

5. N. Long, *An Introduction to the Sociology of Rural Development* (Tavistock Publications: London, 1977).

6. Lester Brown, *The Seeds of Change* (New York: Praeger, 1970).

7. B. Sen, *The Green Revolution in India* (New Delhi: Wiley Eastern Private Ltd., 1974).

8. Ibid., pp. 43-54.

9. P.V. Shenoi, *Agricultural Development in India* (Delhi: Vikas Publishing House, 1975), pp. 285-94.

10. B.W. Hodder, *Economic Development in the Tropics* (London: Methuen, 1973), p. 142.

11. Ibid., pp. 141-5.

12. Both Mexico and Taiwan have had extensive agricultural development programmes for many years, but these have not been exclusively 'improvement'

in approach for they have incorporated a significant emphasis upon land reform. See E.L. Venezian and W.K. Gamble, *The Agricultural Development of Mexico* (New York: Praefer, 1969); and S.P. Ho, *Economic Development of Taiwan* (New Haven: Yale University Press, 1978).

13. Uma Lele, 'Designing Rural Development Programs: Lessons from Past Experience in Africa', *Economic Development and Cultural Change*, Vol. 24 (1975-6), p. 291.

14. A. Mayhew, 'Structural Reform and the Future of West German Agriculture', *Geographical Review*, Vol. 60 (1970), pp. 54-60.

15. H.D. Clout, 'Planned and Unplanned Changes in French Farm Structures', *Geography*, Vol. 53 (1968), pp. 311-15.

16. G. Myrdal, *Asian Drama* Vol. II (New York: Partheon, 1968), p. 1339.

17. Folke Dovring, 'Land Reform and Productivity in Mexico', *Land Economics*, Vol. 49 (1970), pp. 264-74.

18. S. Barraclough, 'Alternate Land Tenure Systems Resulting from Agrarian Reform in Latin America', *Land Economics*, Vol. 46 (1970), pp. 215-28.

19. F.M. Foland, 'Agrarian Reform in Latin America', *Foreign Affairs*, Vol. 48 (1969), pp. 97-112.

20. Norman Long and David Winder, 'From Peasant Community to Production Co-operative: An Analysis of Recent Government Policy in Peru', *Journal of Development Studies*, Vol. 12 (1975), pp. 75-94.

21. A.G. Frank, *Capitalism and Under-development in Latin America* (New York: Monthly Review Press), 1969.

22. Lowry Nelson, *Cuba, The Measure of a Revolution* (Minneapolis: University of Minnesota Press, 1972), pp. 72-98.

23. B. Floyd and R.A. Olu Sule, 'The Nigerian Land Use Decree', *Geography*, Vol. 64 (1) (1979), pp. 125-8.

24. Niles M. Hansen, *French Regional Planning* (Bloomington: Indiana University Press, 1968), pp. 219-25 and 247-61.

25. M.J. Moseley, 'The Impact of Growth Centres in Rural Regions – I', *Regional Studies*, Vol. 7 (1973), pp. 57-75.

26. Paul Cloke, 'In Defence of Key Settlement Policies', *The Village*, Vol. 32 (1977), pp. 7-11.

27. Parzival Copes, *The Resettlement of Fishing Communities in Newfoundland* (Ottawa: Canadian Council on Rural Development), 1972.

28. Orville G. Bentley, 'National Outlook and Perspective', in North Central Regional Center for Rural Development, *Rural Development: Research Priorities* (Ames: Iowa State University Press), 1973, p. 3.

29. James G. Maddox, *Toward a Rural Development Policy* (Washington: National Planning Association), 1973.

30. Long, *Rural Development*, pp. 148-58.

31. Reported by P. Corrigan, 'Ping Chow: A Chinese Commune', *Geography*, Vol. 62 (1977), pp. 125-8.

32. S.G. Williams, 'Taking the Part of Peasants: Rural Development in Nigeria and Tanzania', in P.C.W. Gutkind and I. Wallerstein, *The Political Economy of Contemporary Africa* (Beverly Hills: Sage Publication), 1976, pp. 131-54. This is referred to also in Long, *Introduction to Sociology of Rural Development*, p. 169, as part of a useful review of transformation approaches to development policy.

33. V. Bonham-Carter, *The Survival of the English Countryside* (London: Hodder and Stoughton), 1971, p. 3.

34. Fred P. Bosselman and David Callies, *The Quiet Revolution in Land Use Control* (Washington, DC: Council on Environmental Quality, 1971), pp. 5-53.

35. W.R. Bryant and H.E. Conklin, 'New Farmland Preservation Programs in New York', *Journal of American Institute of Planners*, Vol. 41 (1975), pp. 390-6.

36. The importance of countryside and the need for good planning to conserve its attractiveness is discussed in detail in Joan Davidson and Gerald Wibberley, *Planning and the Rural Environment* (New York: Pergamon), 1977, pp. 87-106.

37. Exmoor National Park Committee, *Exmoor National Park Plan* (Dulverton: Somerset), 1977, pp. 11 and 52.

38. County of Kent, *County Structure Plan: Rural Conservation* (Maidstone), 1975, p. 1.

39. County of Staffordshire, Design Guide, *Houses in the Countryside* (Stafford), p. 1.

40. Bosselman and Callies, *Land-Use Control*, pp. 1-4.

41. Ibid., pp. 54-99.

42. Andrew Thorburn, *Planning Villages* (London: London Estates Gazette, 1971).

43. John Delafors, *Land-Use Controls in the United States* (Cambridge, Mass.: MIT Press, 1969), p. 35.

44. Bosselman and Callies, *Land-Use Control*, p. 2.

45. Ibid., pp. 72-3.

46. A.W. Gilg, 'Rural Employment', in Gordon E. Cherry (ed.), *Rural Planning Problems* (London: Leonard Hill, 1976), pp. 160-4.

47. H.L. Seyler, 'Dimensions of Social and Economic Change', in Richard E. Lonsdale and H.L. Seyler (eds.), *Nonmetropolitan Industrialization* (New York: Winston/Wiley, 1979), pp. 95-102.

INDEX